VOL. 39
Shonen Sunday Edition

Story and Art by
RUMIKO TAKAHASHI

English Adaptation by Gerard Jones

Translation/Mari Morimoto
Touch-up Art & Lettering/Bill Schuch
Cover and Interior Graphic Design/Yuki Ameda
Editor/Shaenon K. Garrity

VP, Production/Alvin Lu
VP, Publishing Licensing/Rika Inouye
VP, Sales & Product Marketing/Gonzalo Ferreyra
VP, Creative/Linda Espinosa
Publisher/Hyoe Narita

INUYASHA 39 by Rumiko TAKAHASHI
© 2005 Rumiko TAKAHASHI
All rights reserved. Original Japanese edition
published in 2005 by Shogakukan Inc., Tokyo.
The stories, characters and incidents mentioned in
this publication are entirely fictional.

Printed in the U.S.A.

Published by VIZ Media, LLC
P.O. Box 77010
San Francisco, CA 94107

10 9 8 7 6 5 4 3 2 1
First printing, August 2009

www.viz.com   WWW.SHONENSUNDAY.COM

INUYASHA

VOL. 39 Shonen Sunday Edition

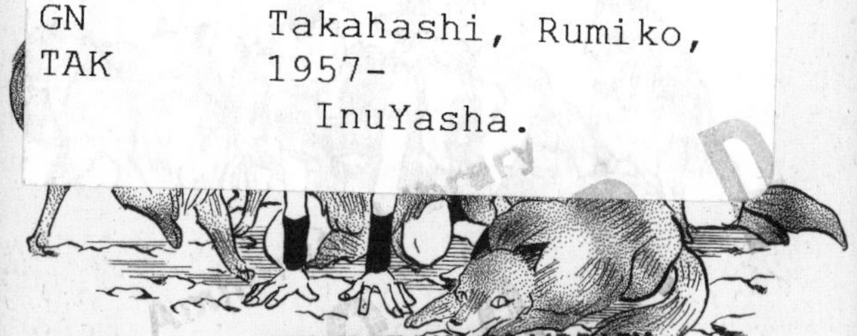

STORY AND ART BY

RUMIKO TAKAHASHI

CONTENTS

THE STORY THUS FAR

Long ago, in the "Warring States" era of Japan's Muromachi period (Sengoku-jidai, approximately 1467-1568 CE), a legendary dog-like half-demon called "Inuyasha" attempted to steal the Shikon Jewel—or "Jewel of Four Souls"—from a village, but was stopped by the enchanted arrow of the village priestess, Kikyo. Inuyasha fell into a deep sleep, pinned to a tree by Kikyo's arrow, while the mortally wounded Kikyo took the Shikon Jewel with her into the fires of her funeral pyre. Years passed.

Fast-forward to the present day. Kagome, a Japanese high school girl, is pulled into a well one day by a mysterious centipede monster and finds herself transported into the past—only to come face to face with the trapped Inuyasha. She frees him, and Inuyasha easily defeats the centipede monster.

The residents of the village, now 50 years older, readily accept Kagome as the reincarnation of their deceased priestess Kikyo, a claim supported by the fact that the Shikon Jewel emerges from a cut on Kagome's body. Unfortunately, the jewel's rediscovery means that the village is soon under attack by a variety of demons in search of this treasure. Then, the jewel is accidentally shattered into many shards, each of which may have the fearsome power of the entire jewel.

Although Inuyasha says he hates Kagome because of her resemblance to Kikyo, the woman who "killed" him, he is forced to team up with her when Kaede, the village leader, binds him to Kagome with a powerful spell. Now the two grudging companions must fight to reclaim and reassemble the shattered shards of the Shikon Jewel before they fall into the wrong hands...

THIS VOLUME The evil Midoriko and Naraku both seek to restore the Shikon Jewel. To do this they must take the final shards from Koga and Kohaku. Then Inuyasha and the gang stumble across a new sword with some intriguing powers that could lead to a victory against both Midoriko and Naraku.

INUYASHA
Half-demon hybrid, son of a human mother and demon father. His necklace is enchanted, allowing Kagome to control him with a word.

KAGOME
Modern-day Japanese schoolgirl who can travel back and forth between the past and present through an enchanted well.

NARAKU
Enigmatic demon-mastermind behind the miseries of nearly everyone in the story.

MIROKU
Lecherous Buddhist priest cursed with a mystical "hellhole" in his hand that's slowly killing him.

KOGA
Leader of the Wolf Clan, Koga is himself a Wolf Demon and, because of several Shikon shards in his legs, possesses super speed. Enamored of Kagome, he quarrels with Inuyasha frequently.

SANGO
"Demon Exterminator" or slayer from the village where the Shikon Jewel was first born.

SCROLL 1

SUDDEN CHANGE

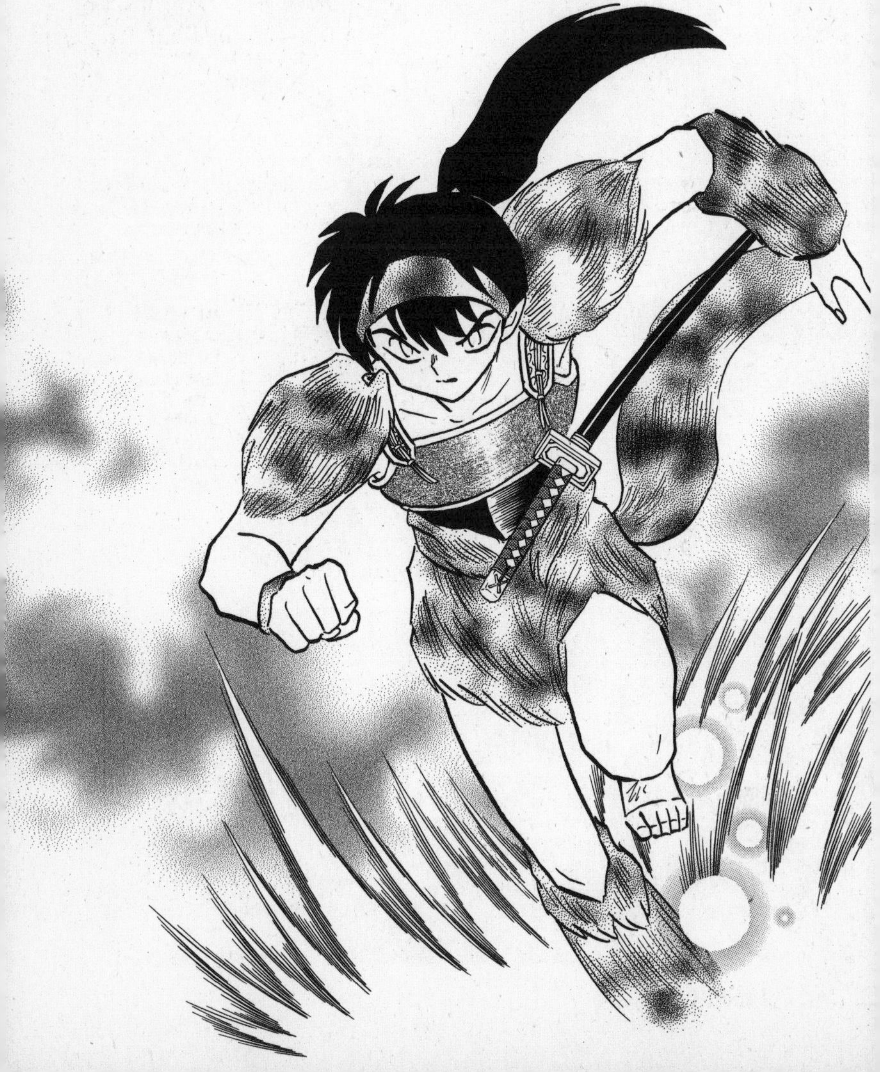

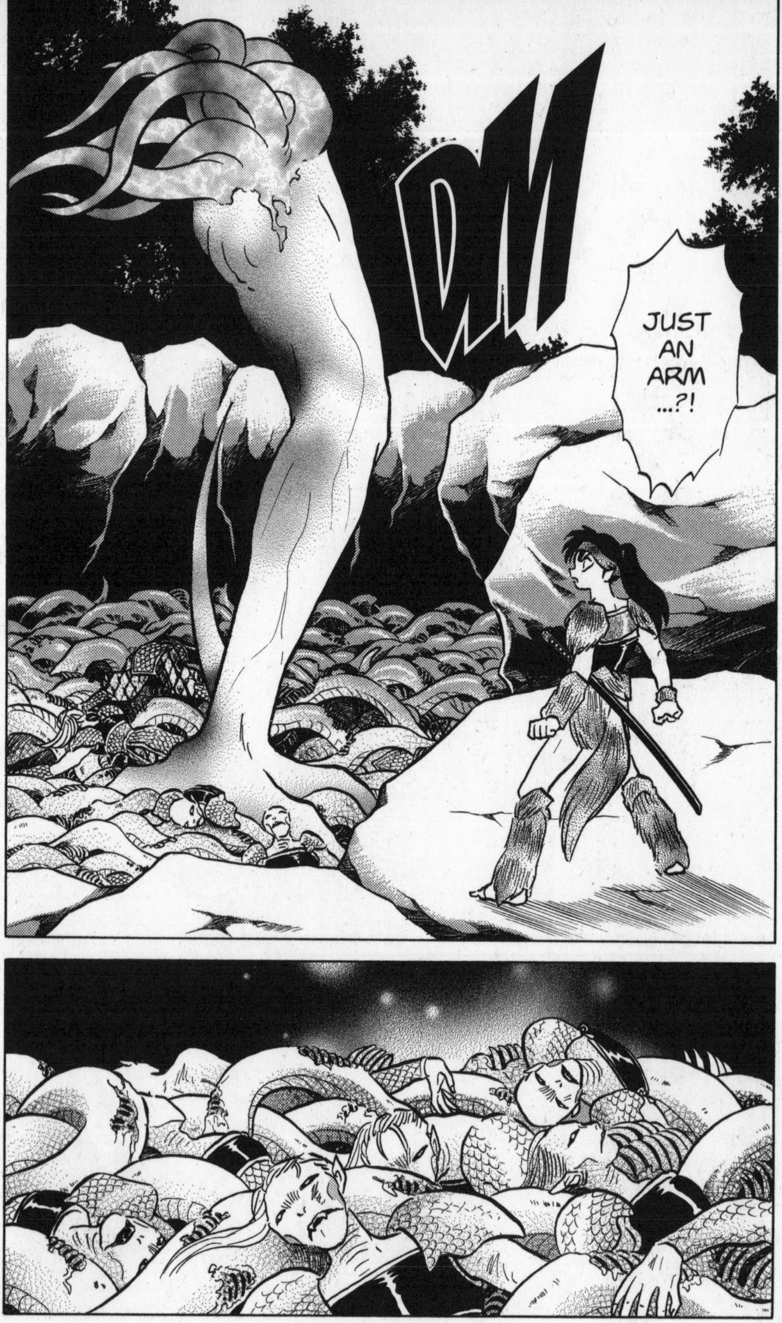
DM
JUST AN ARM ...?!

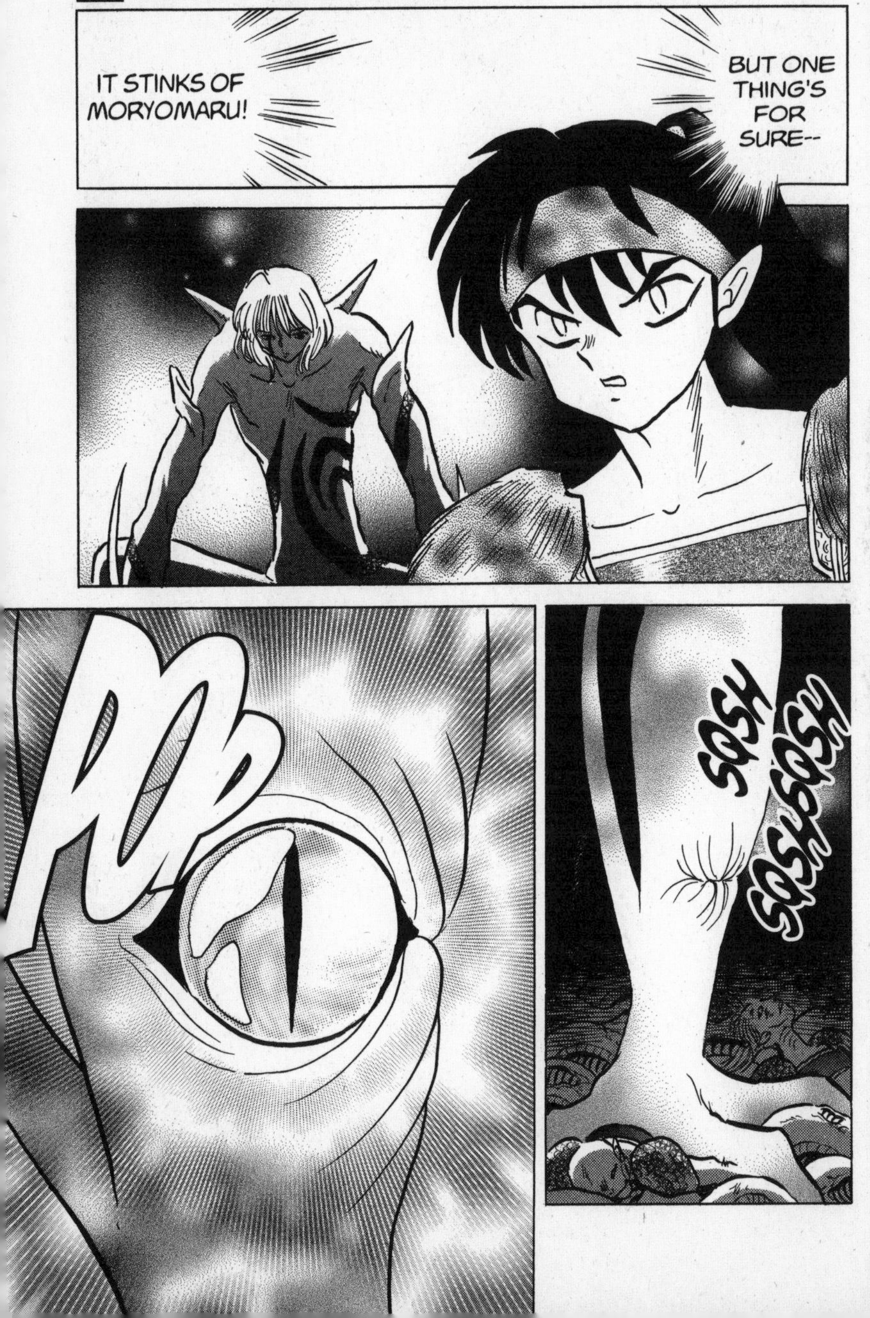
BUT ONE THING'S FOR SURE--
IT STINKS OF MORYOMARU!
SOSH
SOSHSOSH

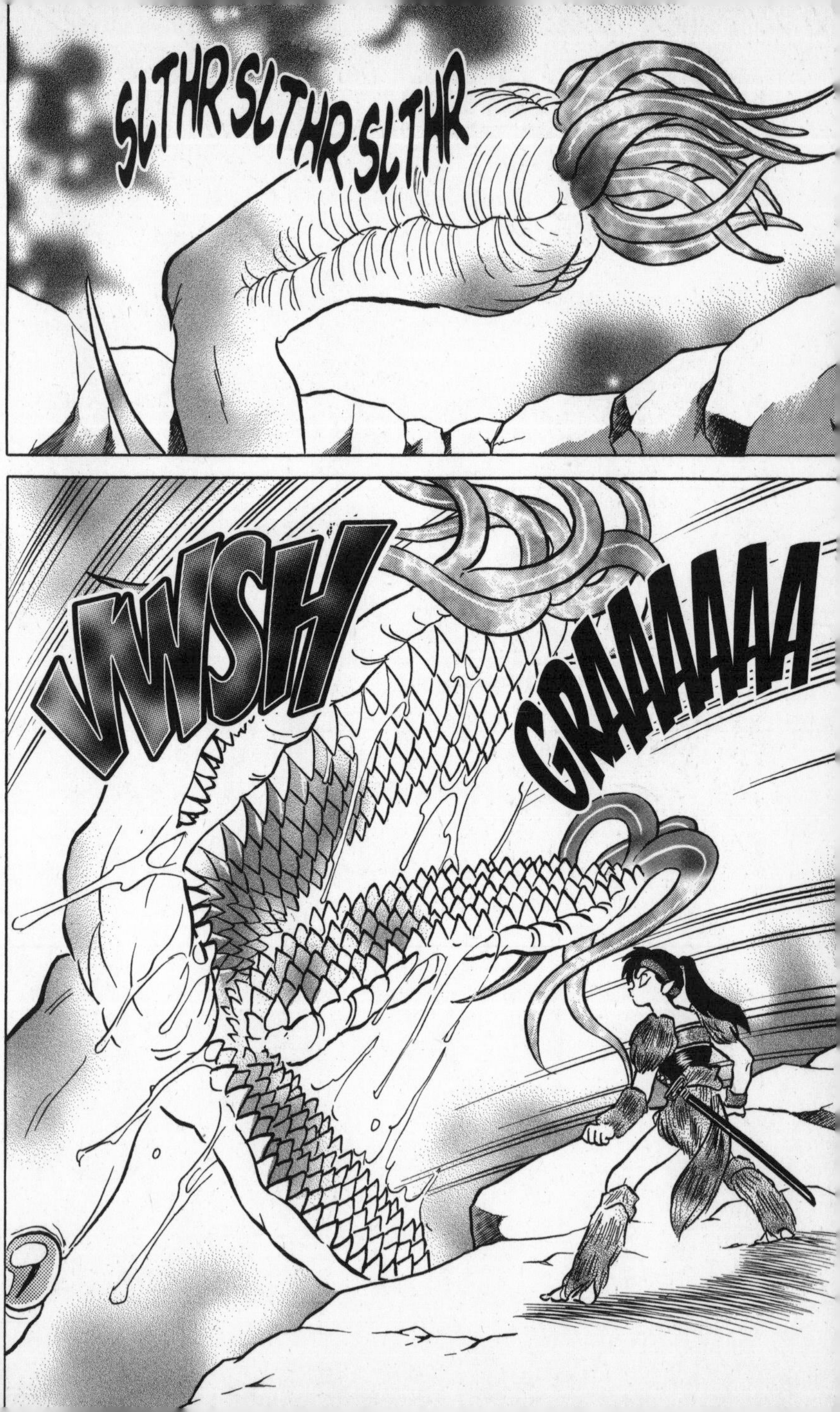
SLTHR SLTHR SLTHR
GRAAAAAA
VWSH

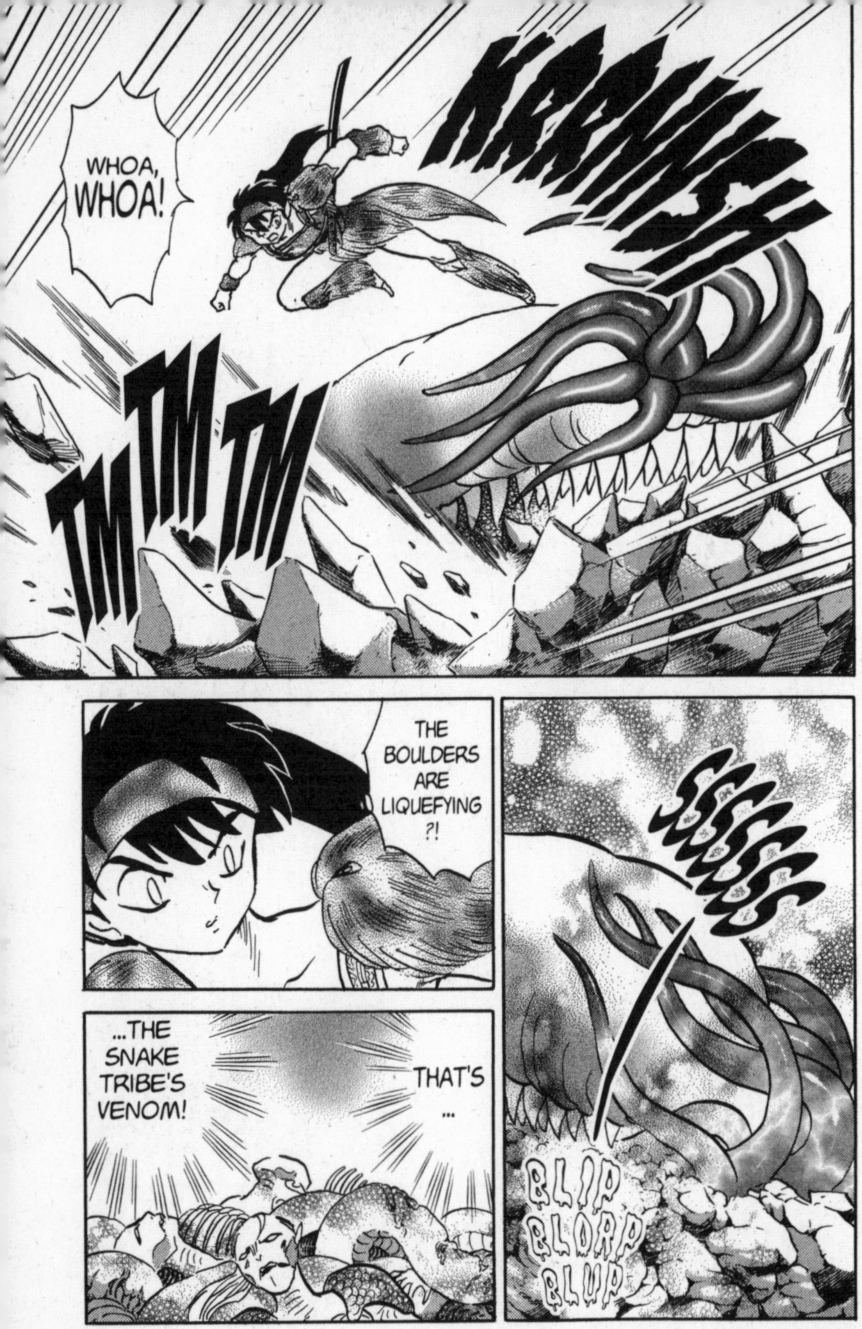
WHOA, WHOA!
TM TM TM
SSSSSS
BLIP BLORP BLUP
THE BOULDERS ARE LIQUEFYING?!
THAT'S...
...THE SNAKE TRIBE'S VENOM!

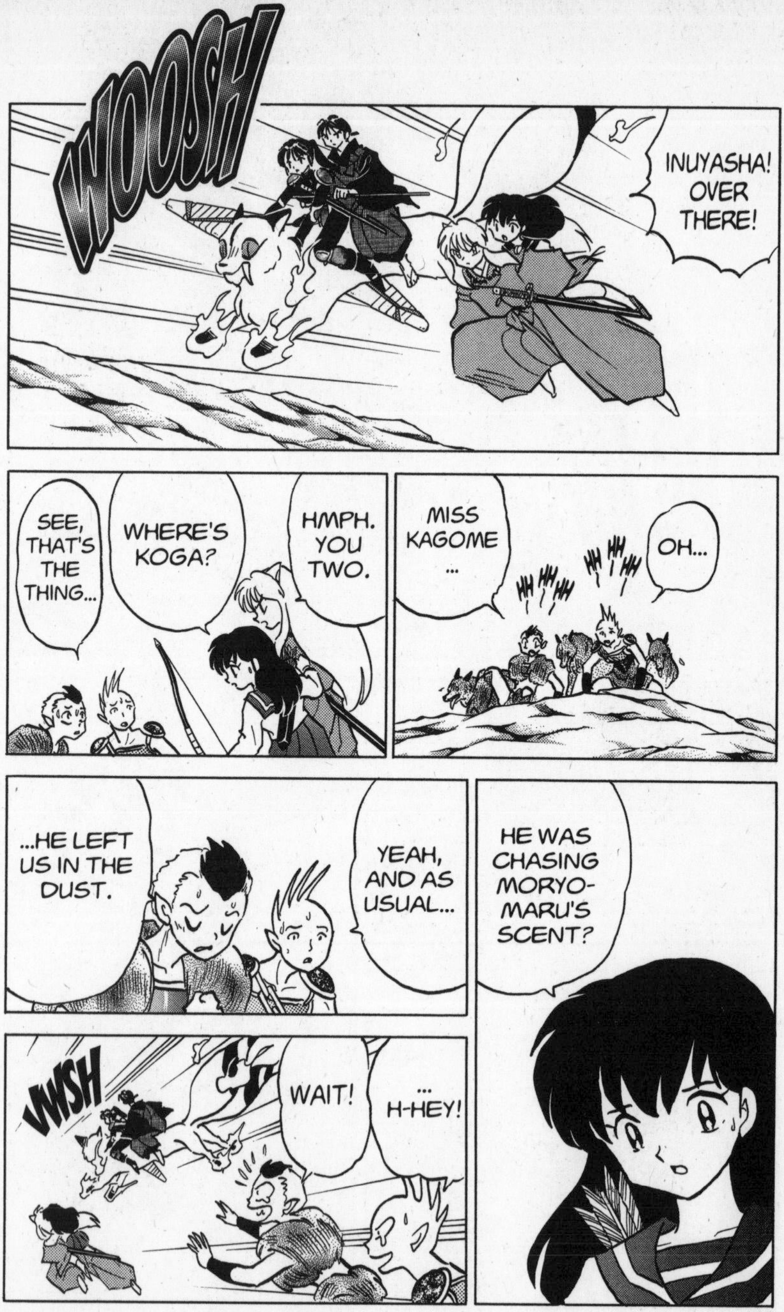
WOOSH
INUYASHA! OVER THERE!
OH...
MISS KAGOME ...
HMPH. YOU TWO.
WHERE'S KOGA?
SEE, THAT'S THE THING...
HE WAS CHASING MORYO-MARU'S SCENT?
YEAH, AND AS USUAL...
...HE LEFT US IN THE DUST.
... H-HEY!
WAIT!
VWSH

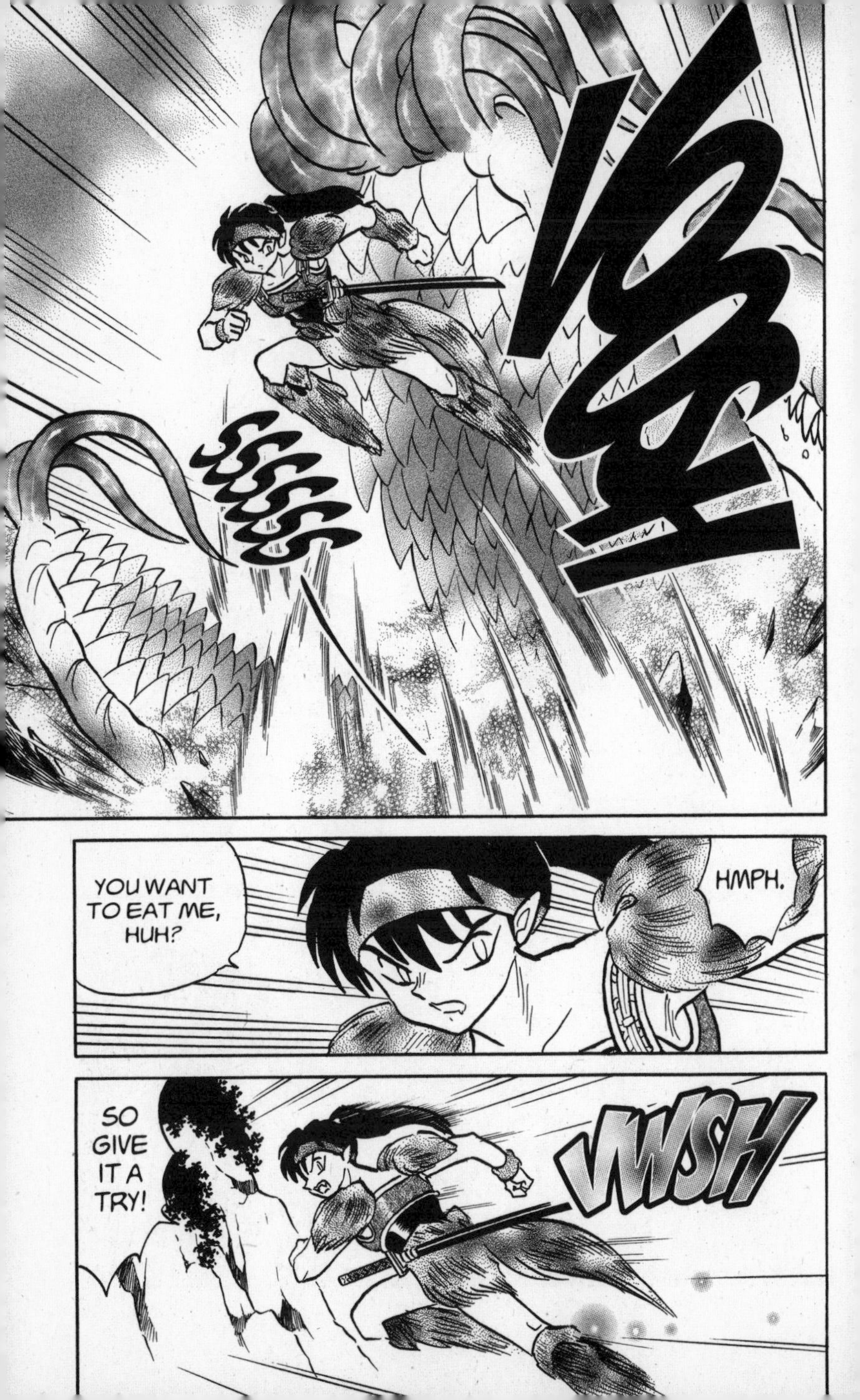
VOOSH!
SSSSSS
HMPH.
YOU WANT TO EAT ME, HUH?
VWSH
SO GIVE IT A TRY!

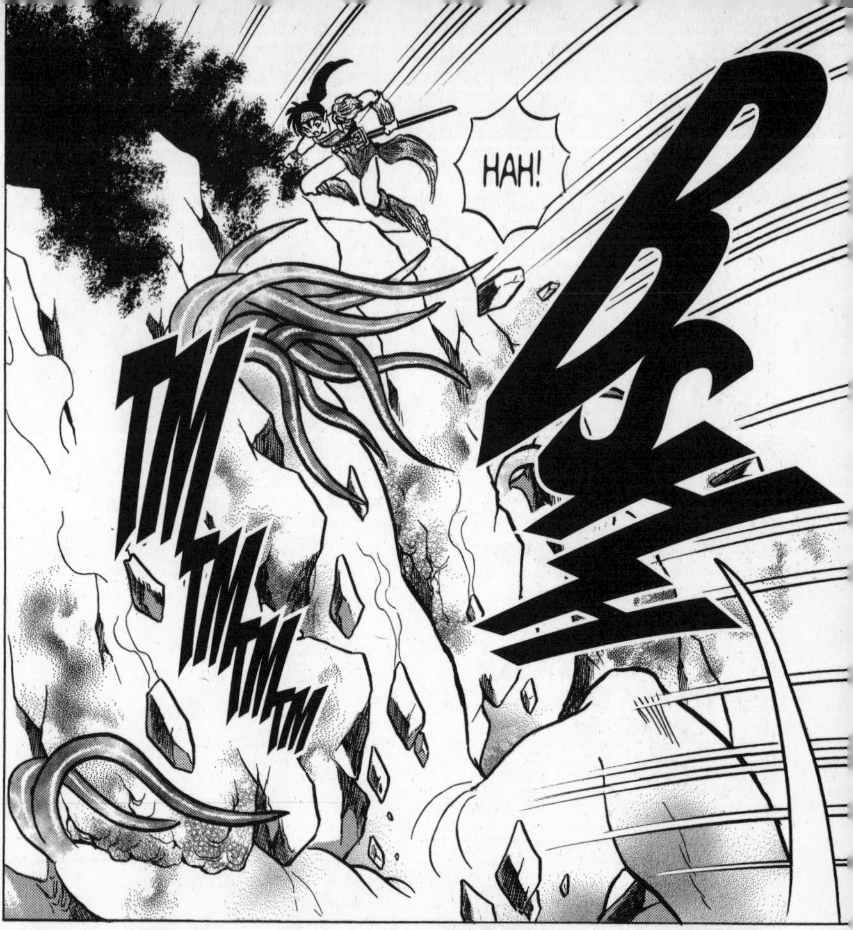
HAH!
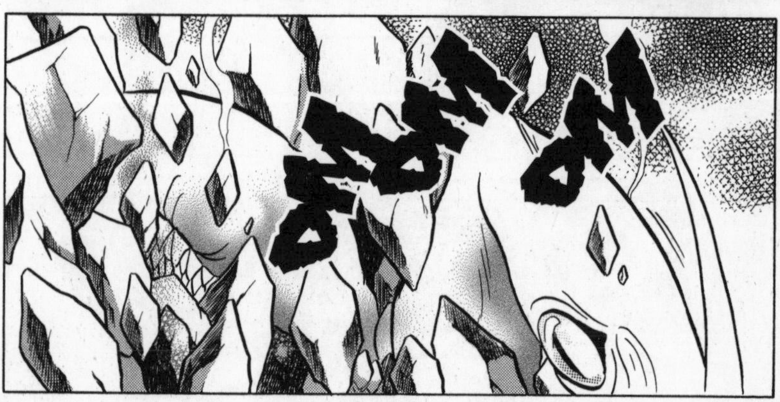

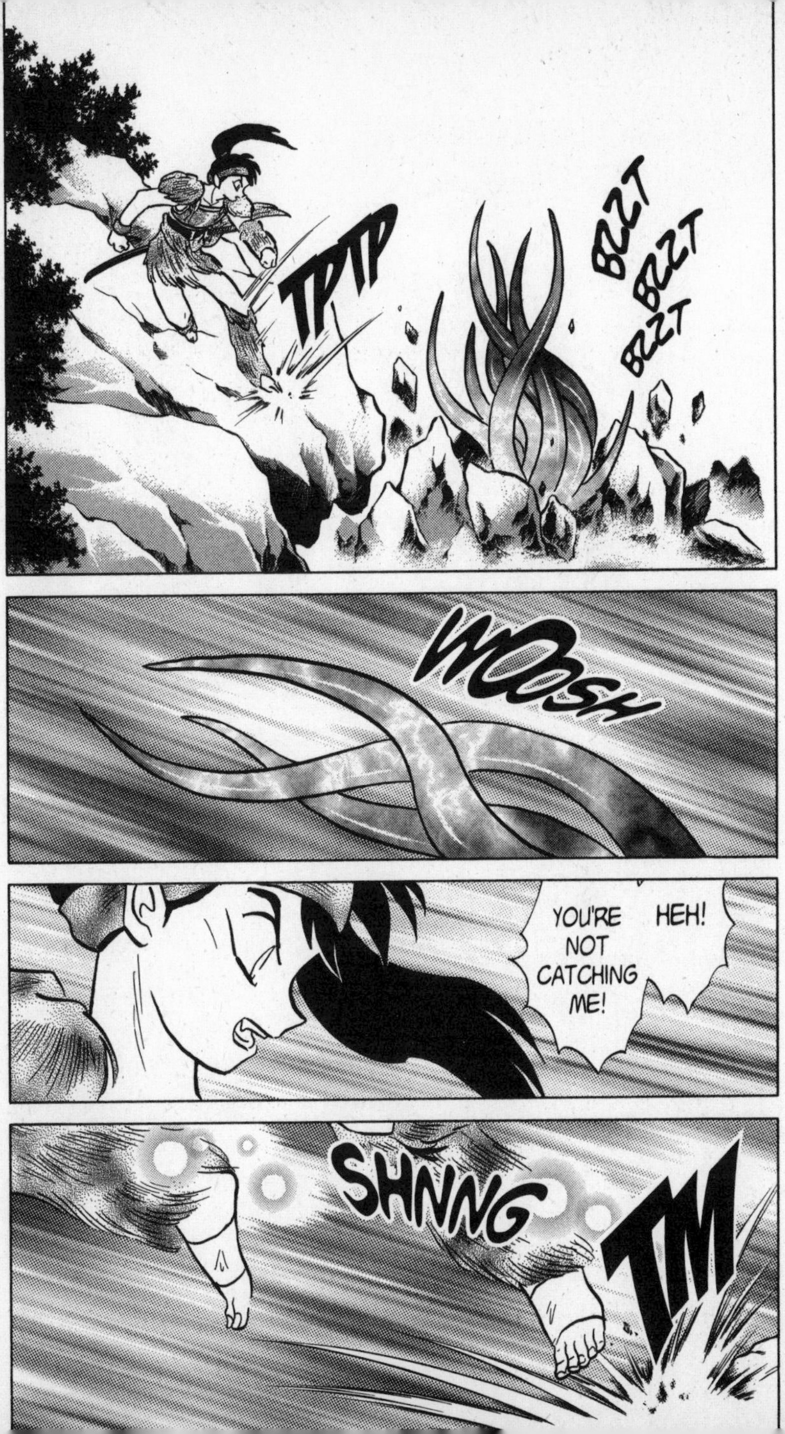
BZZT BZZT BZZT
TPTP
WOOSH
HEH!
YOU'RE NOT CATCHING ME!
TM
SHNNG

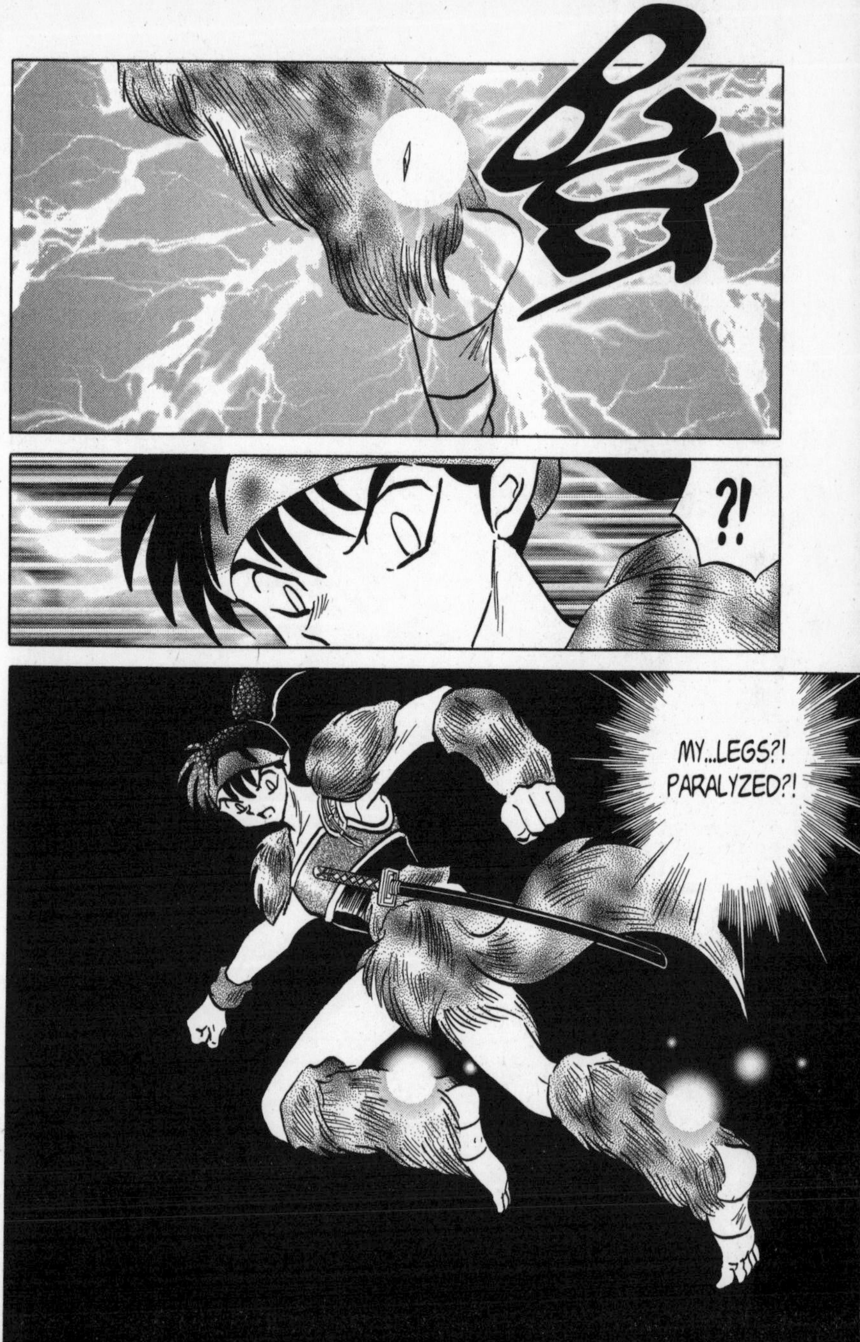

?!
MY...LEGS?! PARALYZED?!

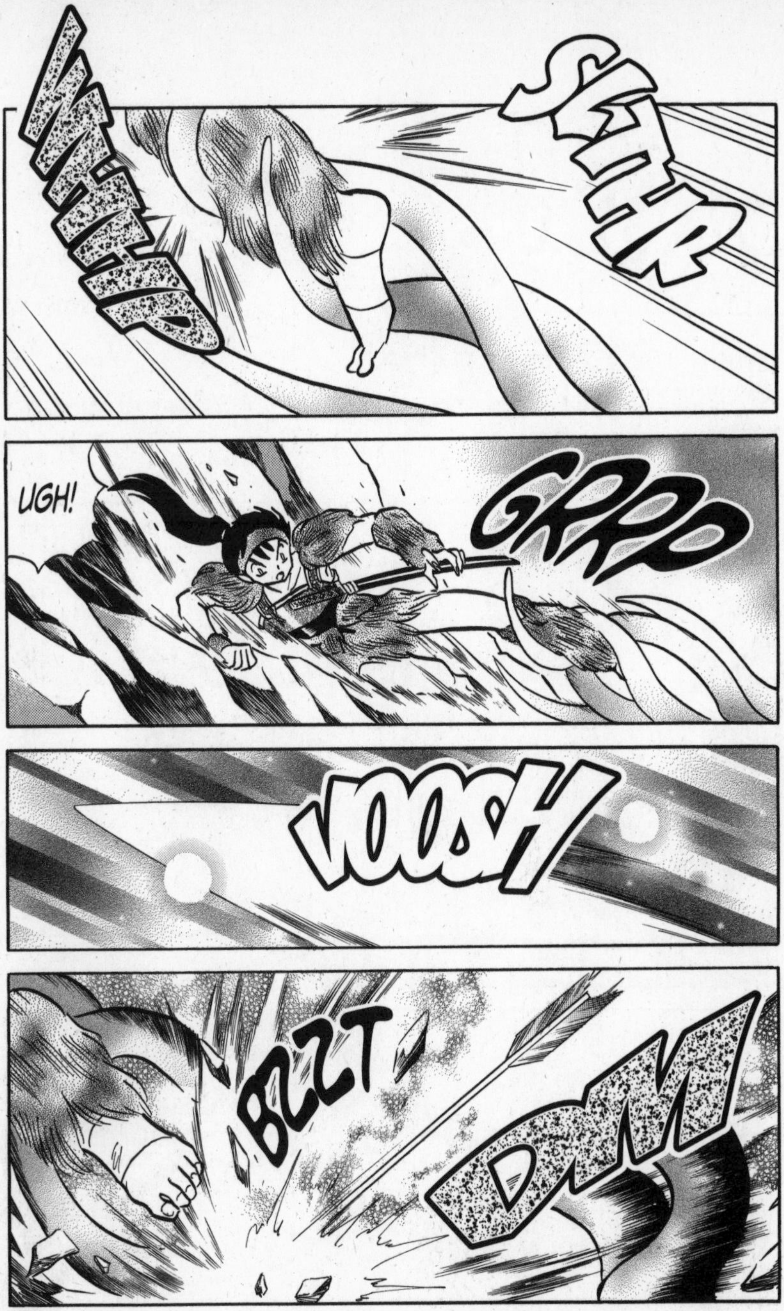
UGH!
VOOSH
DOM
BZZT

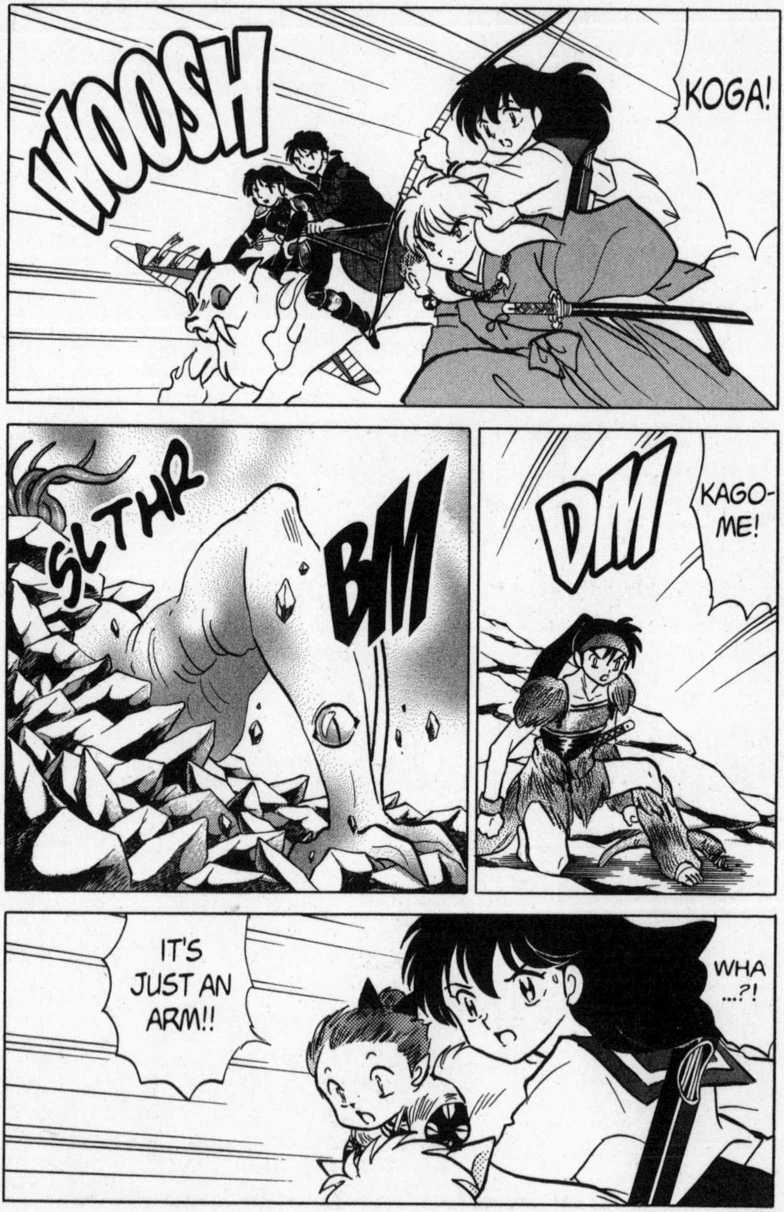
KOGA!
WOOSH
KAGO-ME!
DM
BM
SLTHR
WHA ...?!
IT'S JUST AN ARM!!

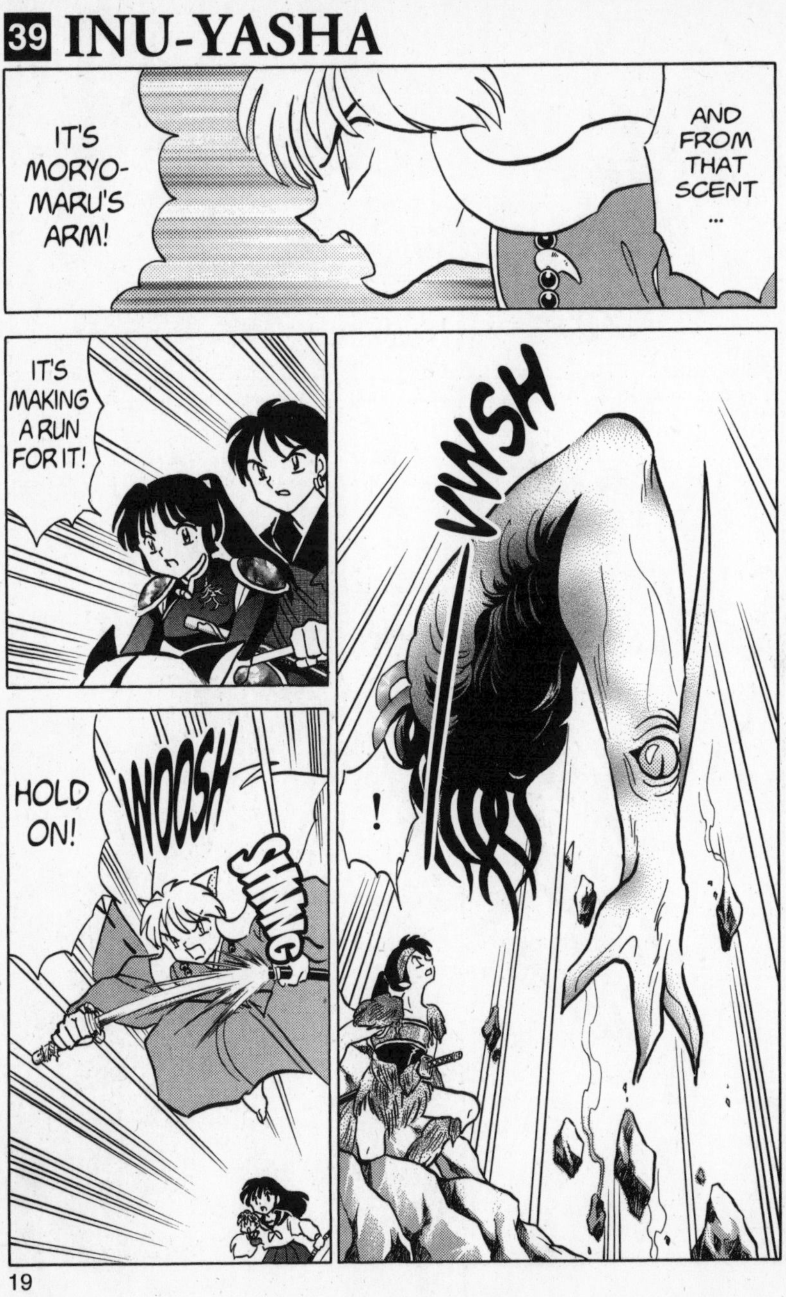
AND FROM THAT SCENT ...
IT'S MORYO-MARU'S ARM!
VWSH
!
IT'S MAKING A RUN FOR IT!
HOLD ON!
WOOSH
SHING

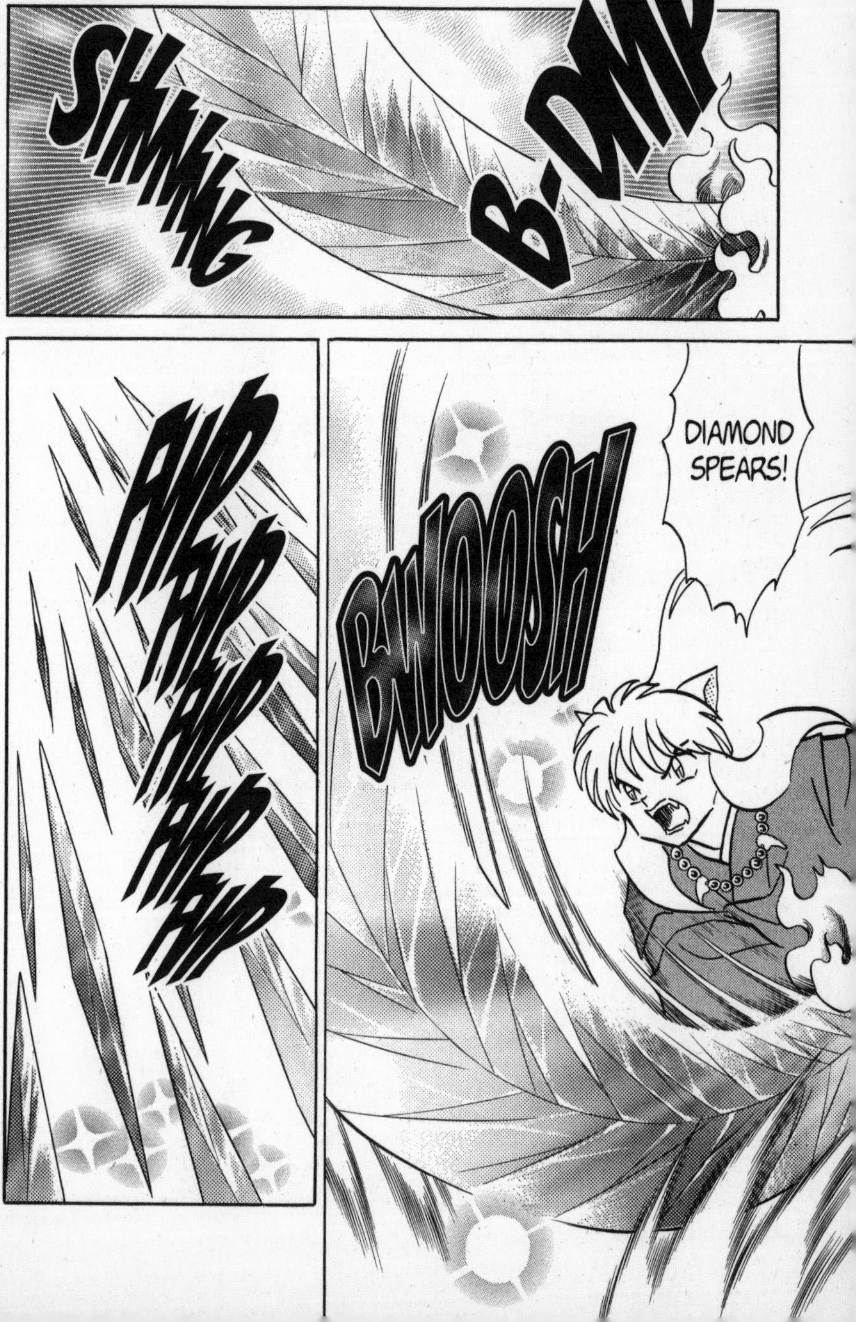
B-DMP
DIAMOND SPEARS!
BWOOSH

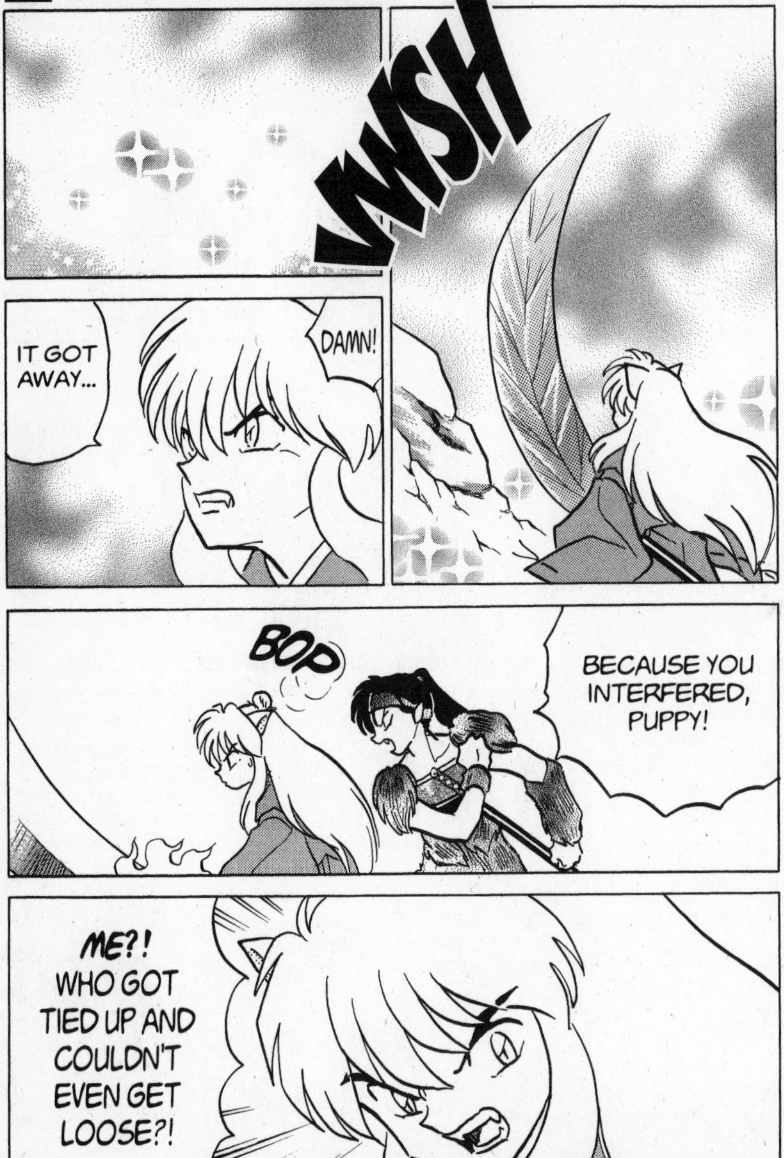
WSH
DAMN!
IT GOT AWAY...
BECAUSE YOU INTERFERED, PUPPY!
BOP
ME?! WHO GOT TIED UP AND COULDN'T EVEN GET LOOSE?!

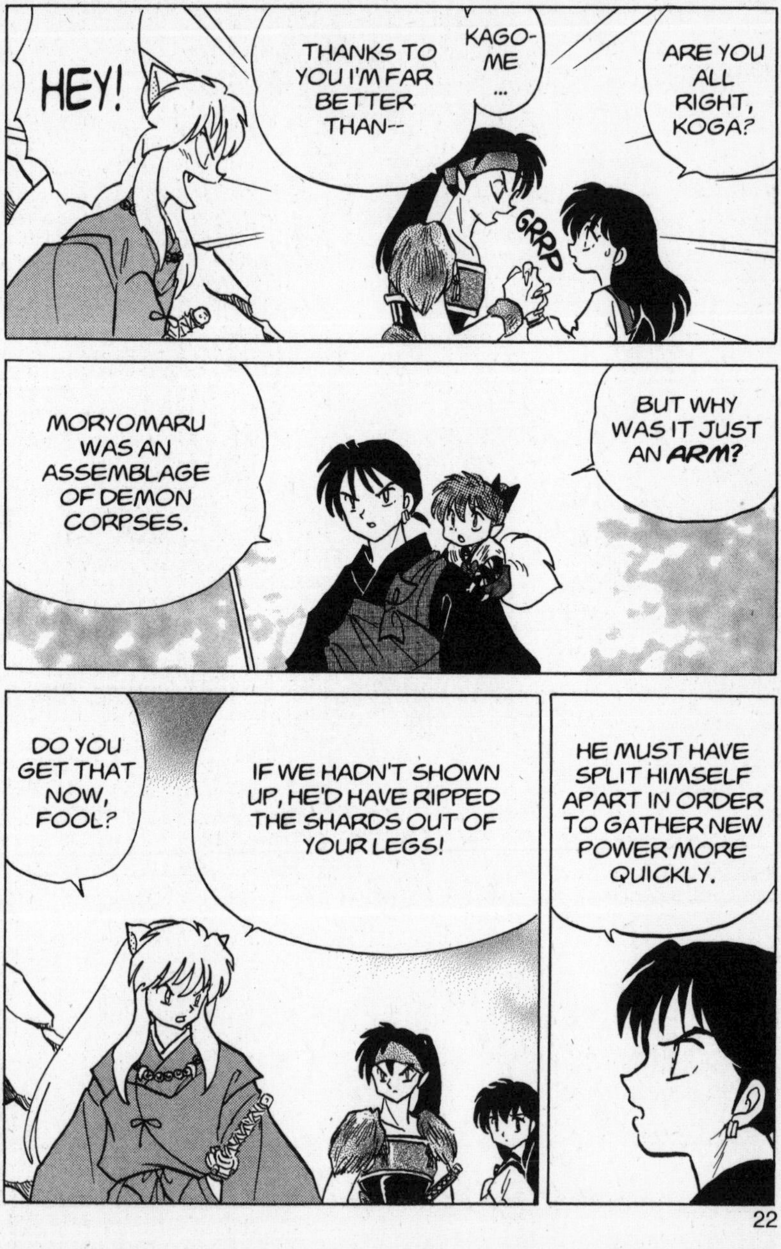
ARE YOU ALL RIGHT, KOGA?
KAGO-ME ...
THANKS TO YOU I'M FAR BETTER THAN--
GRRP
HEY!
BUT WHY WAS IT JUST AN ARM?
MORYOMARU WAS AN ASSEMBLAGE OF DEMON CORPSES.
HE MUST HAVE SPLIT HIMSELF APART IN ORDER TO GATHER NEW POWER MORE QUICKLY.
IF WE HADN'T SHOWN UP, HE'D HAVE RIPPED THE SHARDS OUT OF YOUR LEGS!
DO YOU GET THAT NOW, FOOL?

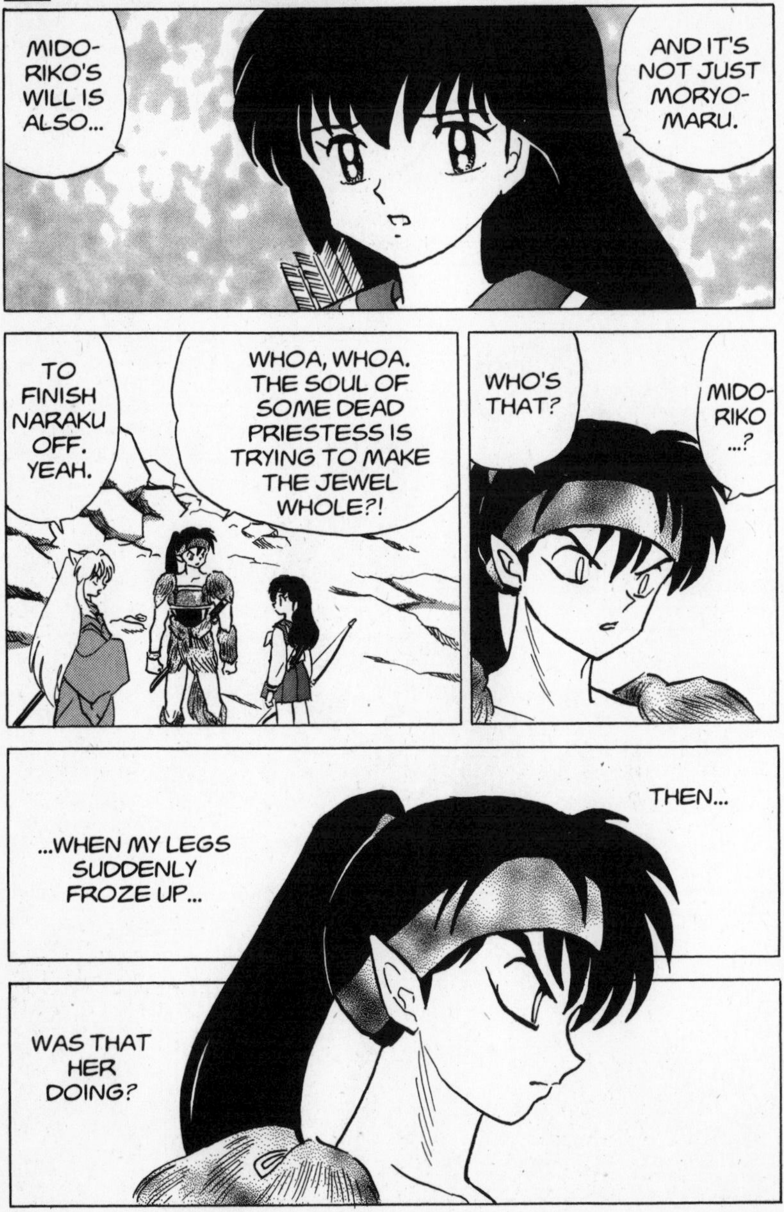
AND IT'S NOT JUST MORYO-MARU.
MIDO-RIKO'S WILL IS ALSO...
MIDO-RIKO ...?
WHO'S THAT?
WHOA, WHOA. THE SOUL OF SOME DEAD PRIESTESS IS TRYING TO MAKE THE JEWEL WHOLE?!
TO FINISH NARAKU OFF. YEAH.
THEN...
...WHEN MY LEGS SUDDENLY FROZE UP...
WAS THAT HER DOING?

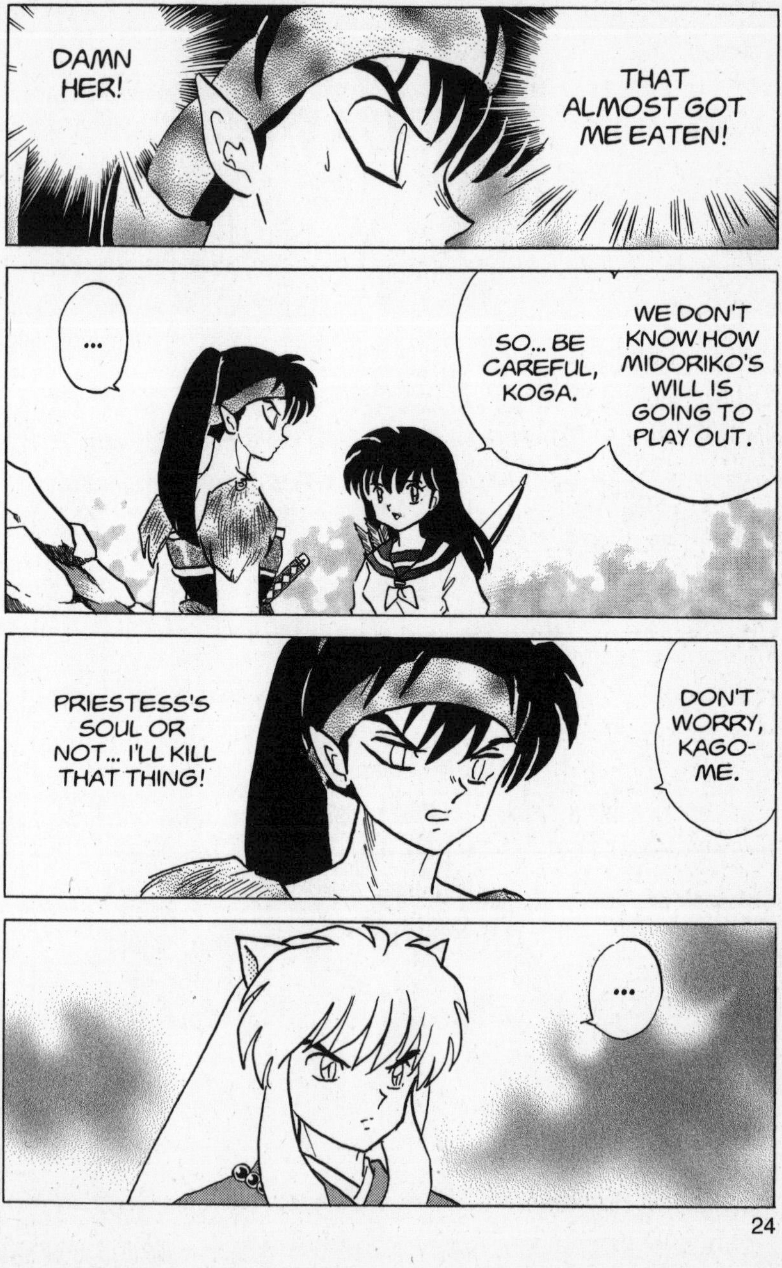
THAT ALMOST GOT ME EATEN!
DAMN HER!
WE DON'T KNOW HOW MIDORIKO'S WILL IS GOING TO PLAY OUT.
SO... BE CAREFUL, KOGA.
...
DON'T WORRY, KAGO-ME.
PRIESTESS'S SOUL OR NOT... I'LL KILL THAT THING!
...

SCROLL 2

THE BURIAL GROUND OF THE WOLVES

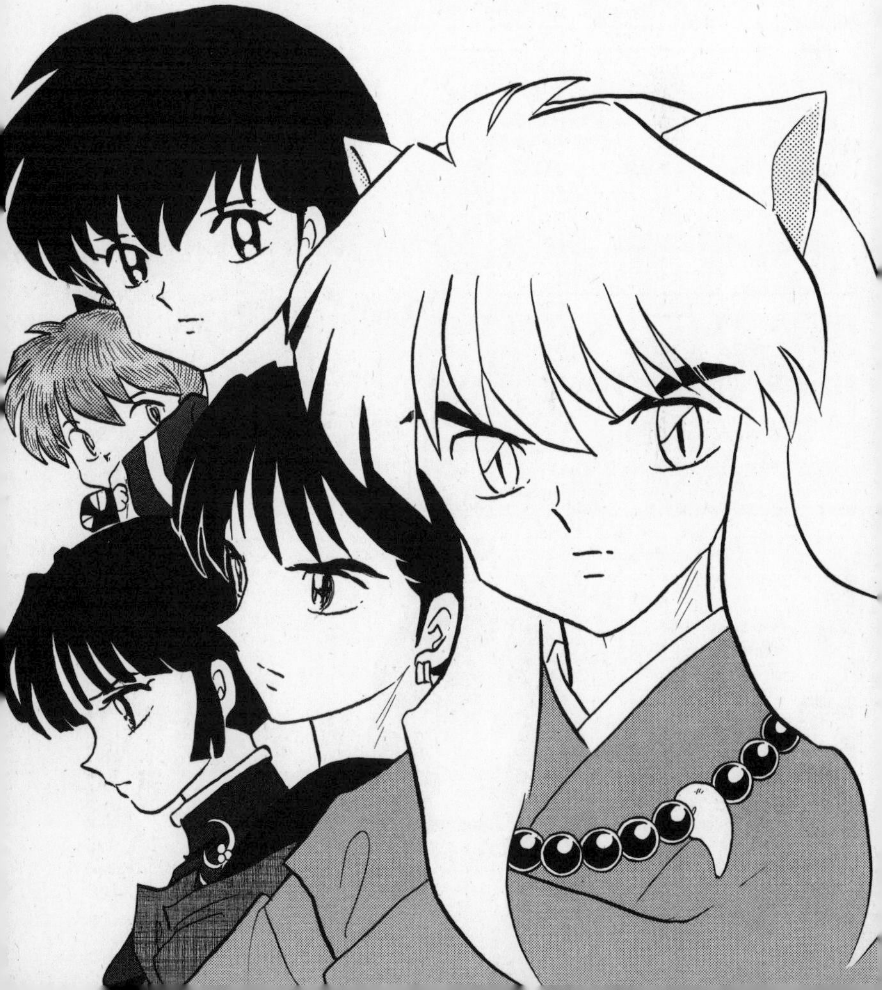

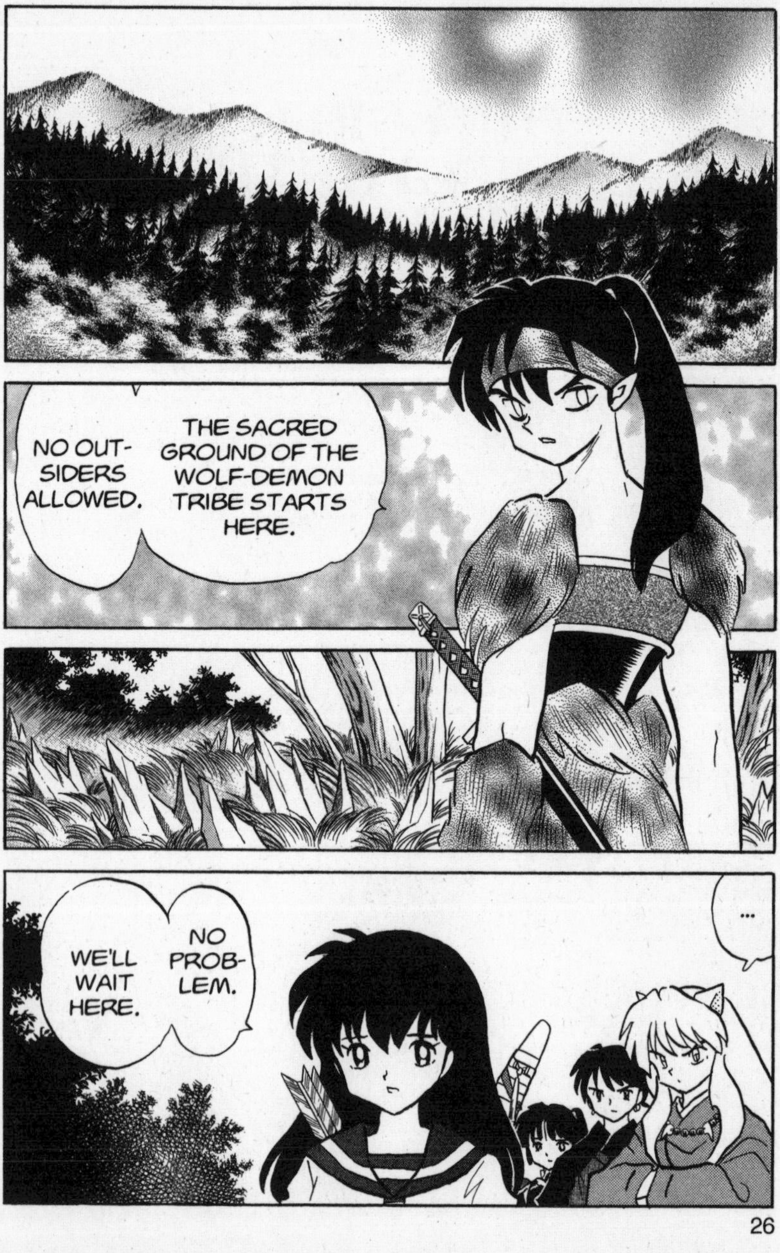
THE SACRED GROUND OF THE WOLF-DEMON TRIBE STARTS HERE.
NO OUT-SIDERS ALLOWED.
...
NO PROB-LEM.
WE'LL WAIT HERE.

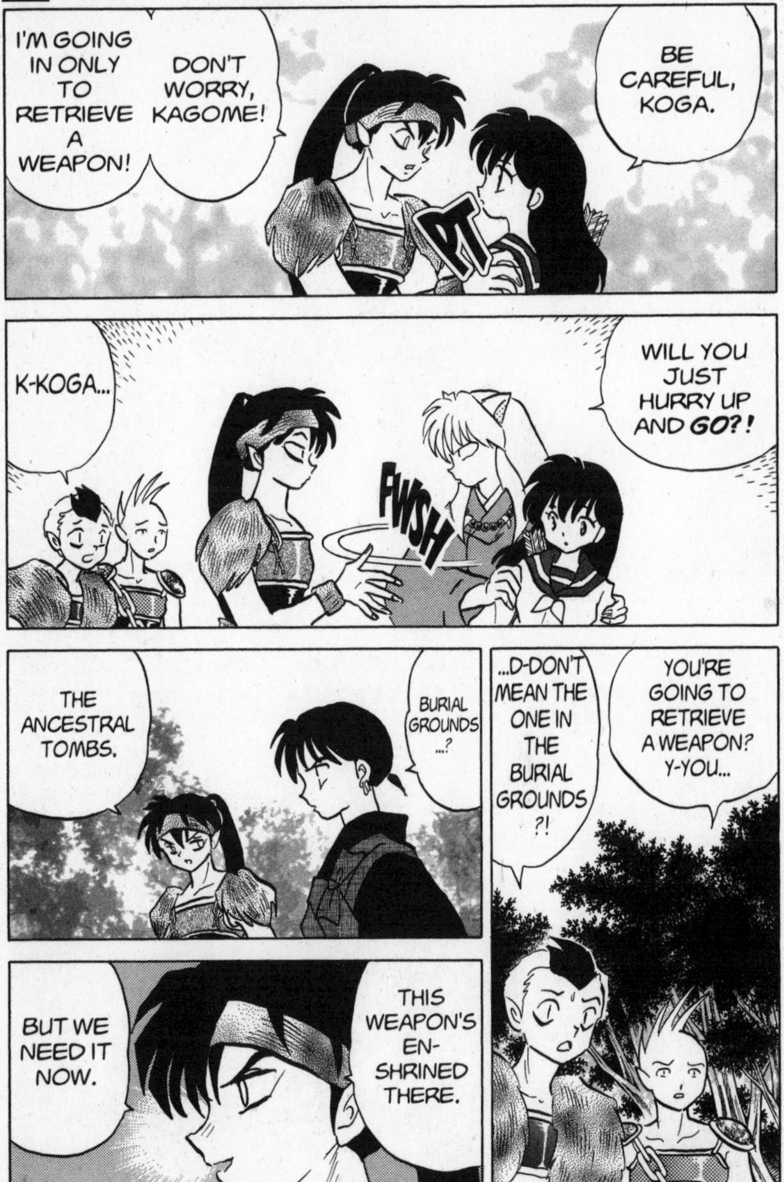
BE CAREFUL, KOGA.
DON'T WORRY, KAGOME!
I'M GOING IN ONLY TO RETRIEVE A WEAPON!
PT
WILL YOU JUST HURRY UP AND **GO?!**
FWSH
K-KOGA...
YOU'RE GOING TO RETRIEVE A WEAPON? Y-YOU...
...D-DON'T MEAN THE ONE IN THE BURIAL GROUNDS ?!
BURIAL GROUNDS ...?
THE ANCESTRAL TOMBS.
THIS WEAPON'S EN-SHRINED THERE.
BUT WE NEED IT NOW.

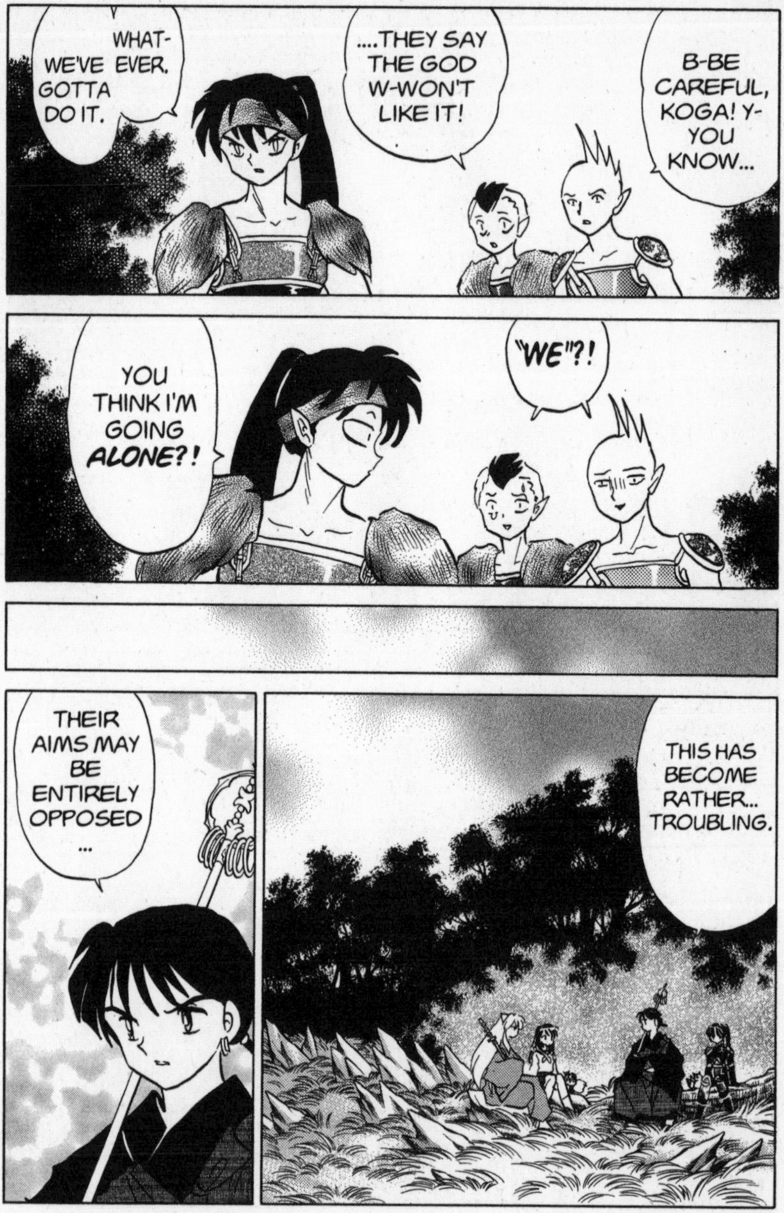
B-BE CAREFUL, KOGA! Y-YOU KNOW...
....THEY SAY THE GOD W-WON'T LIKE IT!
WHAT-EVER. WE'VE GOTTA DO IT.
"WE"?!
YOU THINK I'M GOING ALONE?!
THIS HAS BECOME RATHER... TROUBLING.
THEIR AIMS MAY BE ENTIRELY OPPOSED ...

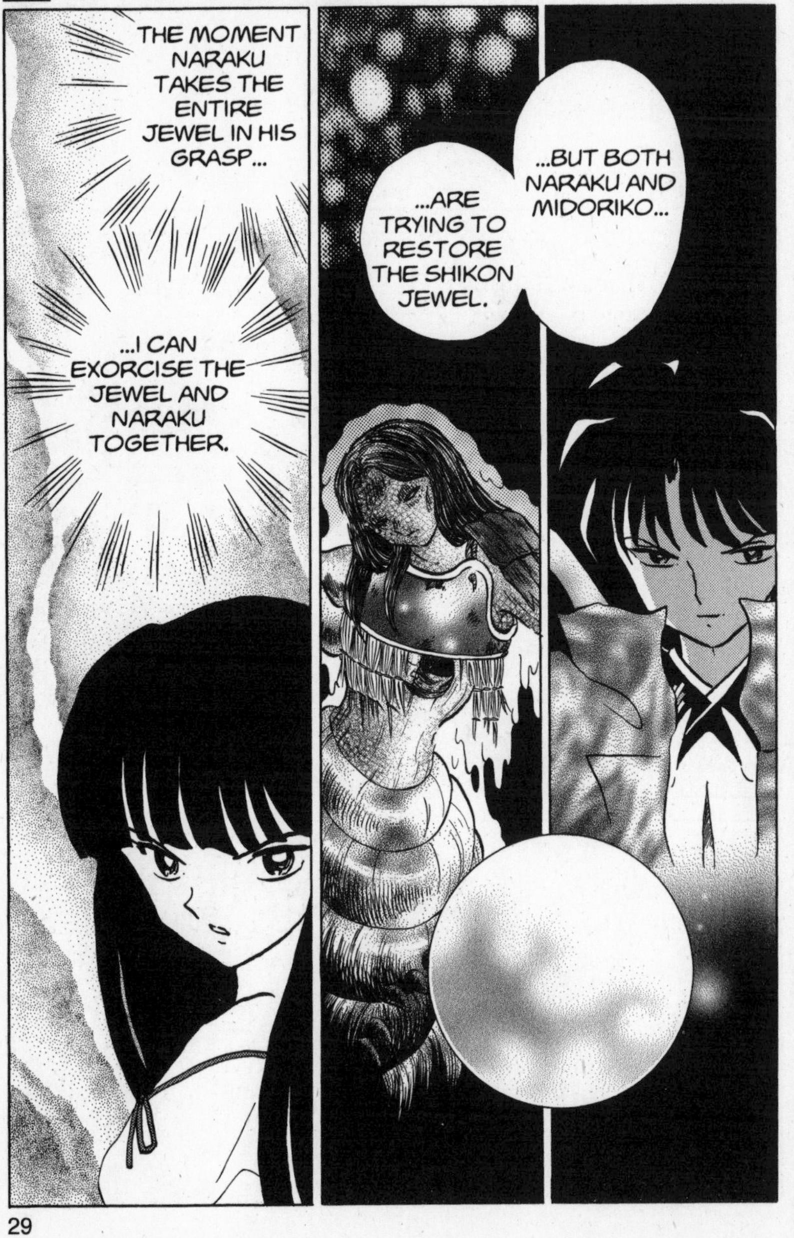
...BUT BOTH NARAKU AND MIDORIKO...
...ARE TRYING TO RESTORE THE SHIKON JEWEL.
THE MOMENT NARAKU TAKES THE ENTIRE JEWEL IN HIS GRASP...
...I CAN EXORCISE THE JEWEL AND NARAKU TOGETHER.

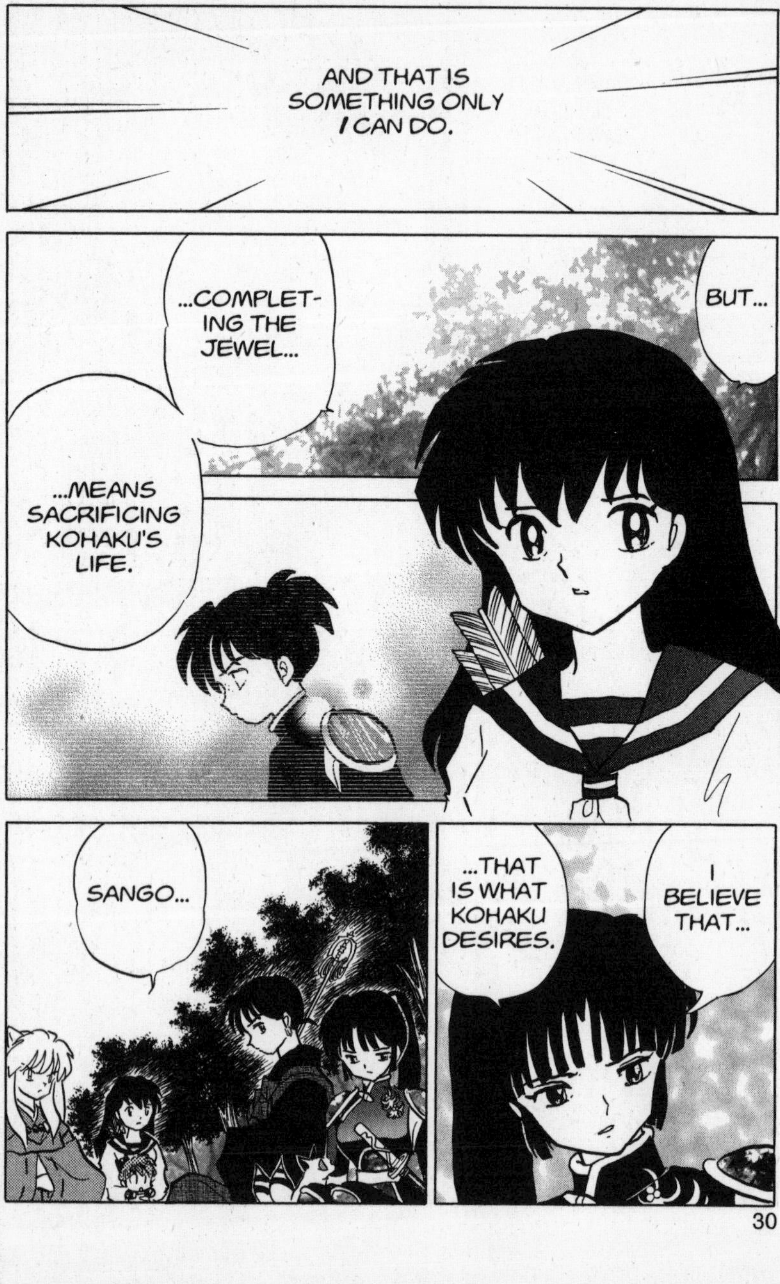
AND THAT IS SOMETHING ONLY I CAN DO.
BUT...
...COMPLETING THE JEWEL...
...MEANS SACRIFICING KOHAKU'S LIFE.
I BELIEVE THAT...
...THAT IS WHAT KOHAKU DESIRES.
SANGO...

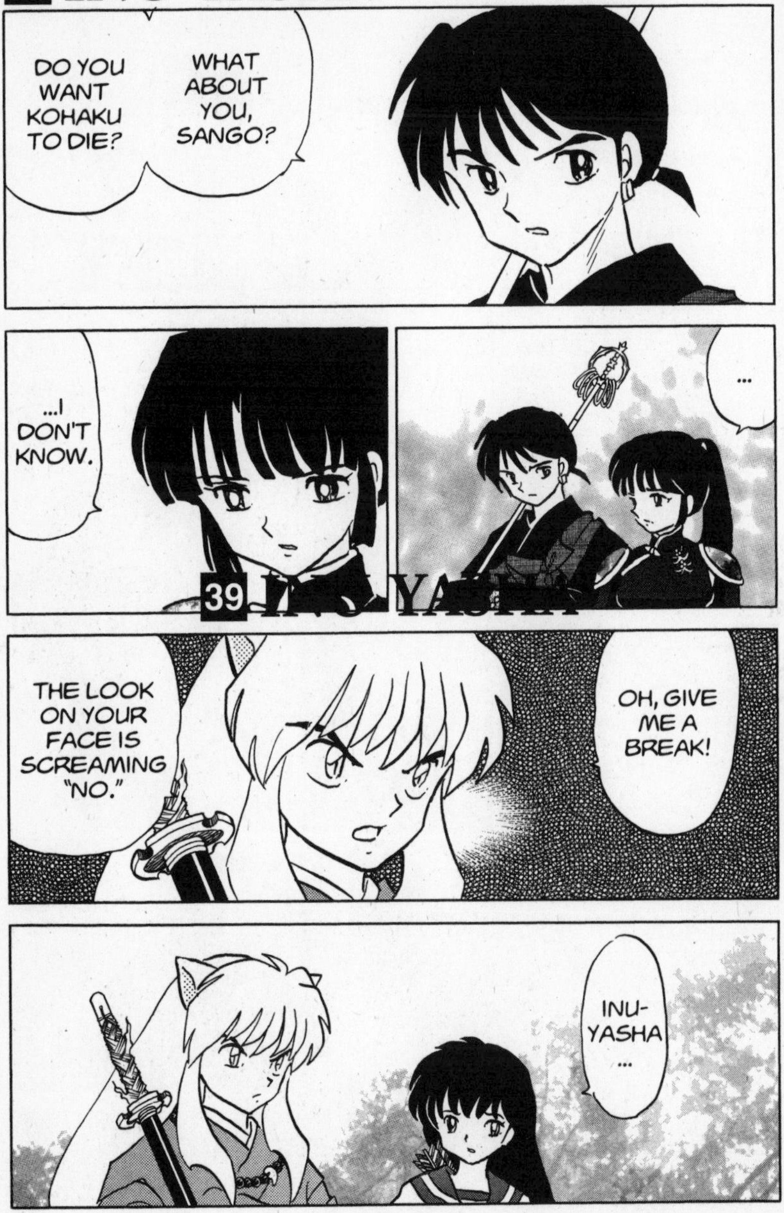
WHAT ABOUT YOU, SANGO?
DO YOU WANT KOHAKU TO DIE?
...
...I DON'T KNOW.
OH, GIVE ME A BREAK!
THE LOOK ON YOUR FACE IS SCREAMING "NO."
INU-YASHA ...

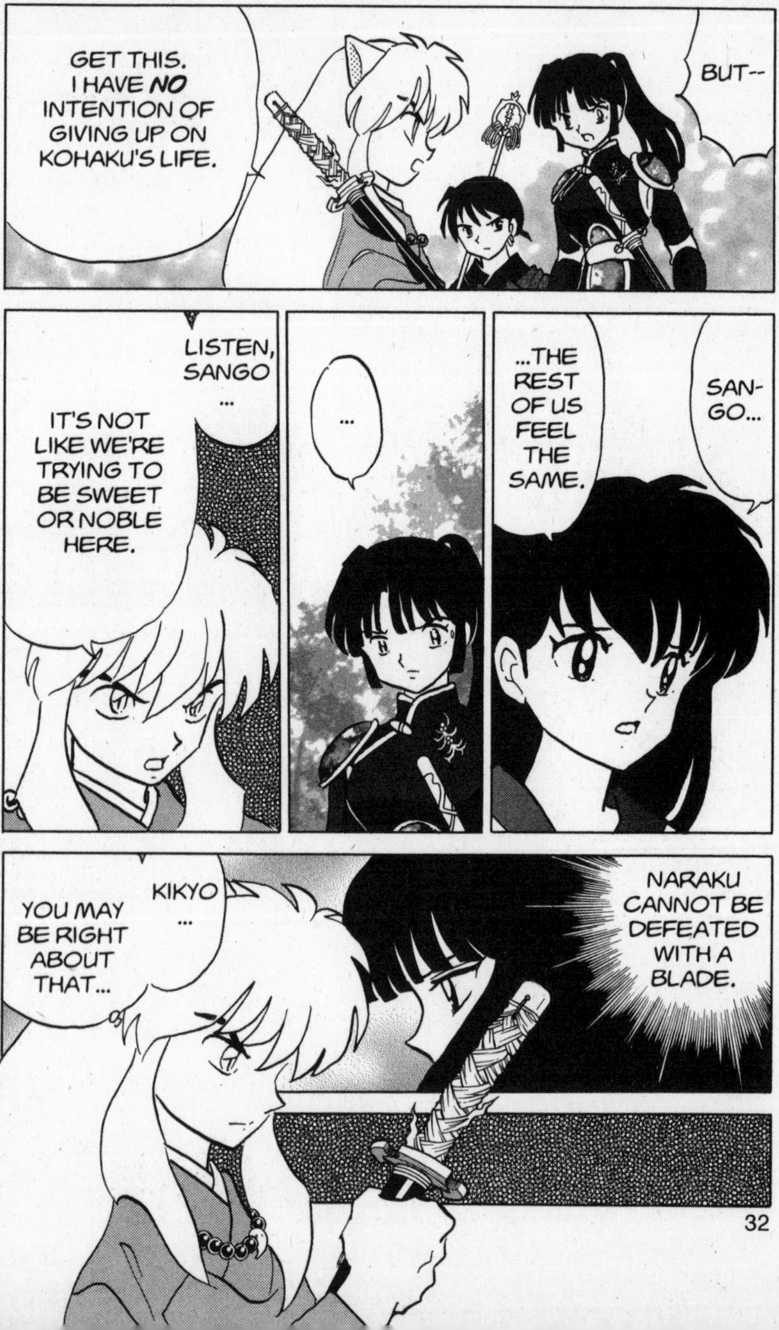
BUT--
GET THIS. I HAVE **NO** INTENTION OF GIVING UP ON KOHAKU'S LIFE.
SAN-GO...
...THE REST OF US FEEL THE SAME.
...
LISTEN, SANGO ...
IT'S NOT LIKE WE'RE TRYING TO BE SWEET OR NOBLE HERE.
NARAKU CANNOT BE DEFEATED WITH A BLADE.
KIKYO ...
YOU MAY BE RIGHT ABOUT THAT...

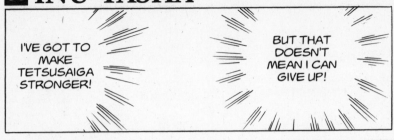

I'VE GOT TO MAKE TETSUSAIGA STRONGER!

BUT THAT DOESN'T MEAN I CAN GIVE UP!

JUST THE FIVE OF US!

WE'VE GOT TO TAKE NARAKU DOWN BEFORE THE JEWEL IS RESTORED--

THE RESTORATION OF THE JEWEL MUST BE STOPPED.

WE ARE AGREED.

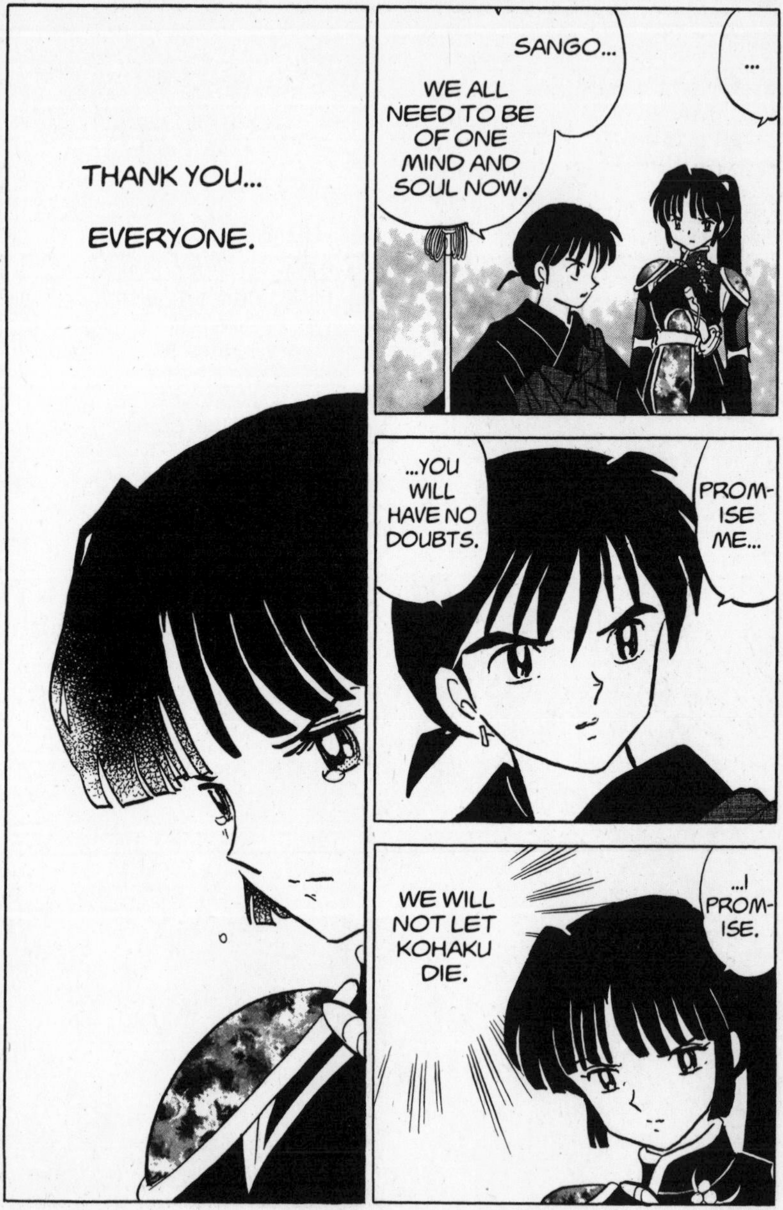
...
SANGO... WE ALL NEED TO BE OF ONE MIND AND SOUL NOW.
PROMISE ME...
...YOU WILL HAVE NO DOUBTS.
...I PROMISE.
WE WILL NOT LET KOHAKU DIE.
THANK YOU...
EVERYONE.

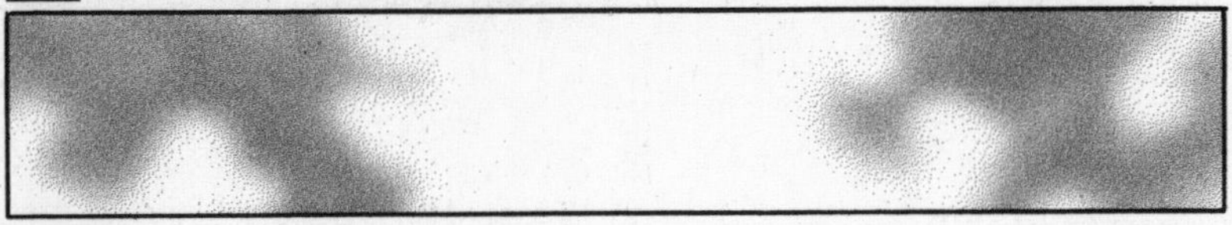

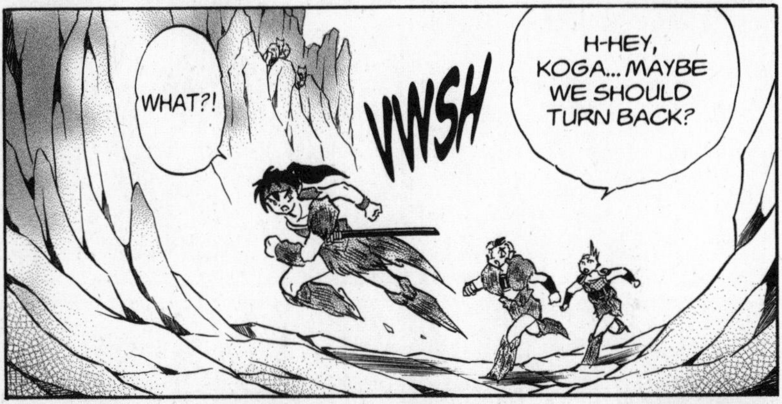
H-HEY, KOGA... MAYBE WE SHOULD TURN BACK?
VWSH
WHAT?!

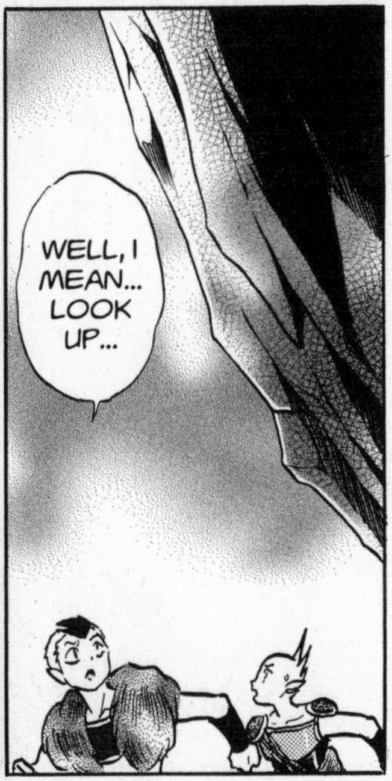
WELL, I MEAN... LOOK UP...

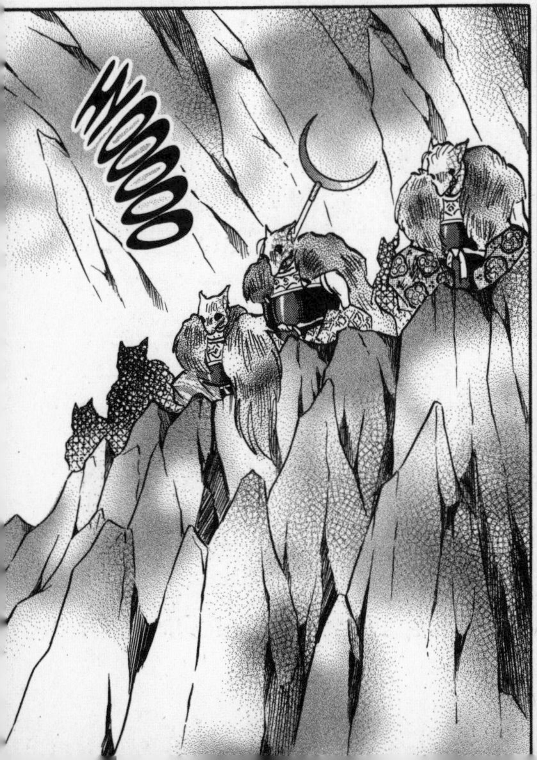
HNOOOOO

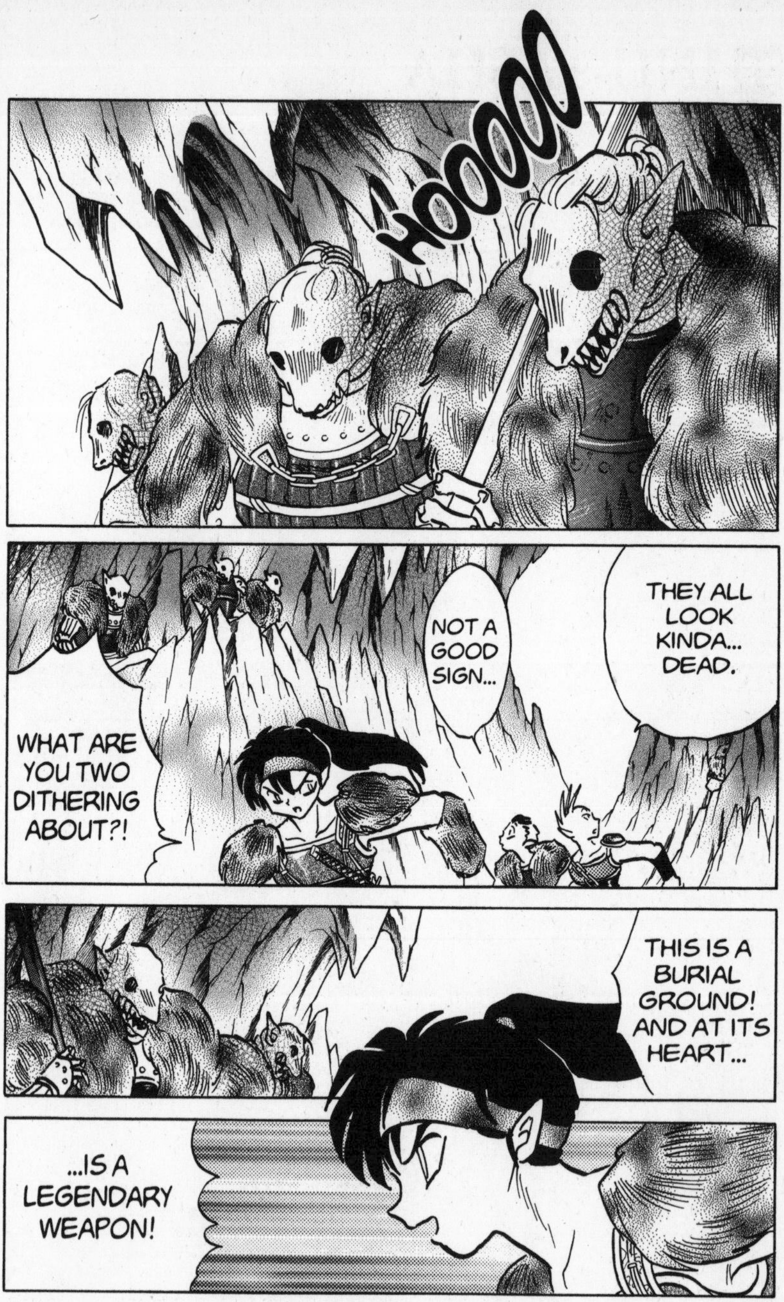
HOOOOO
THEY ALL LOOK KINDA... DEAD.
NOT A GOOD SIGN...
WHAT ARE YOU TWO DITHERING ABOUT?!
THIS IS A BURIAL GROUND! AND AT ITS HEART...
...IS A LEGENDARY WEAPON!

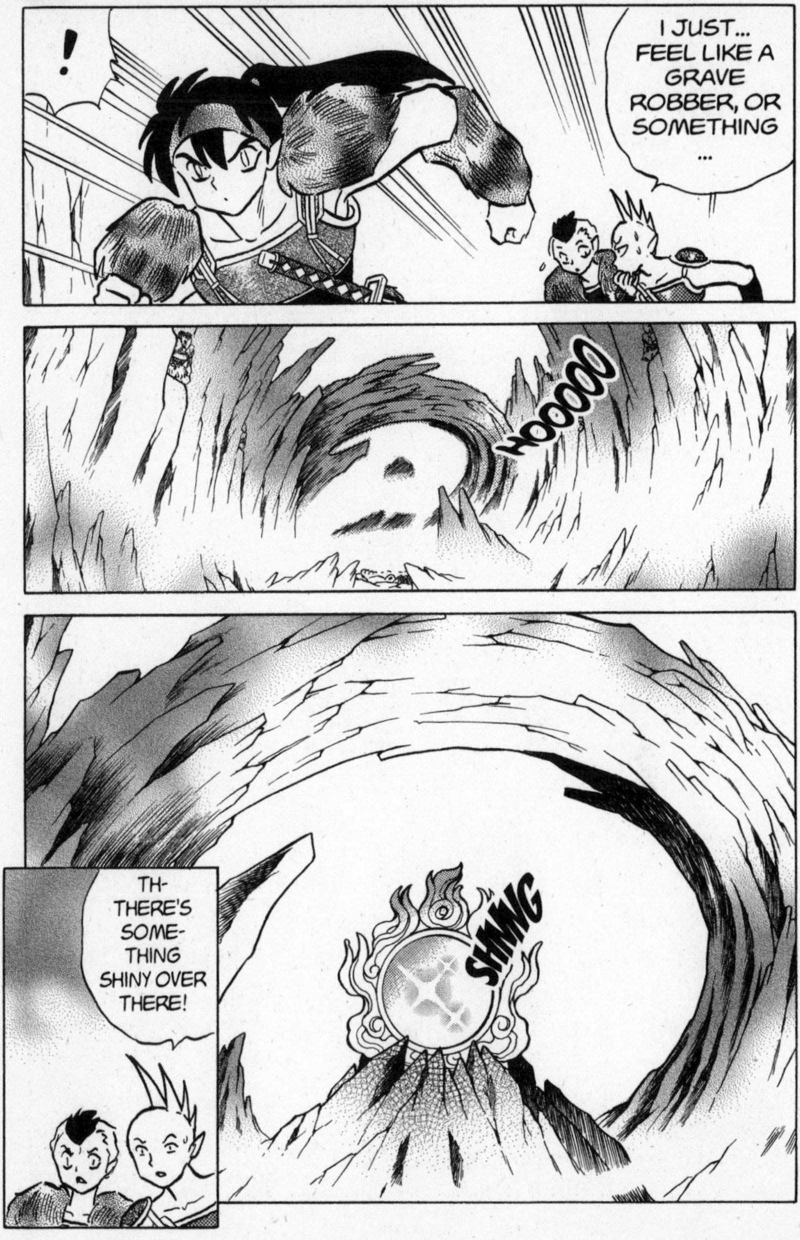
I JUST... FEEL LIKE A GRAVE ROBBER, OR SOMETHING ...
!
HOOOOO
SHNNG
TH- THERE'S SOME- THING SHINY OVER THERE!

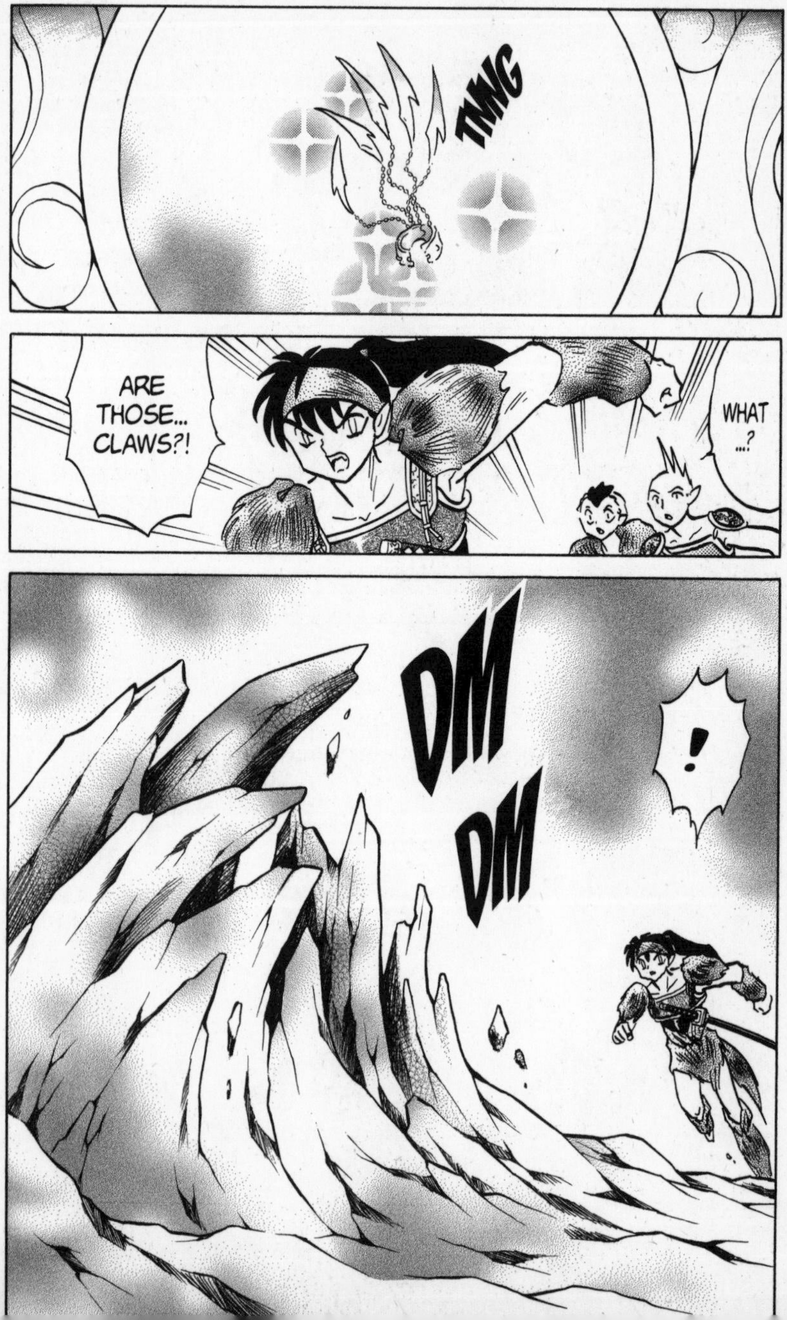
TWNG
WHAT ...?
ARE THOSE... CLAWS?!
DM
DM
!

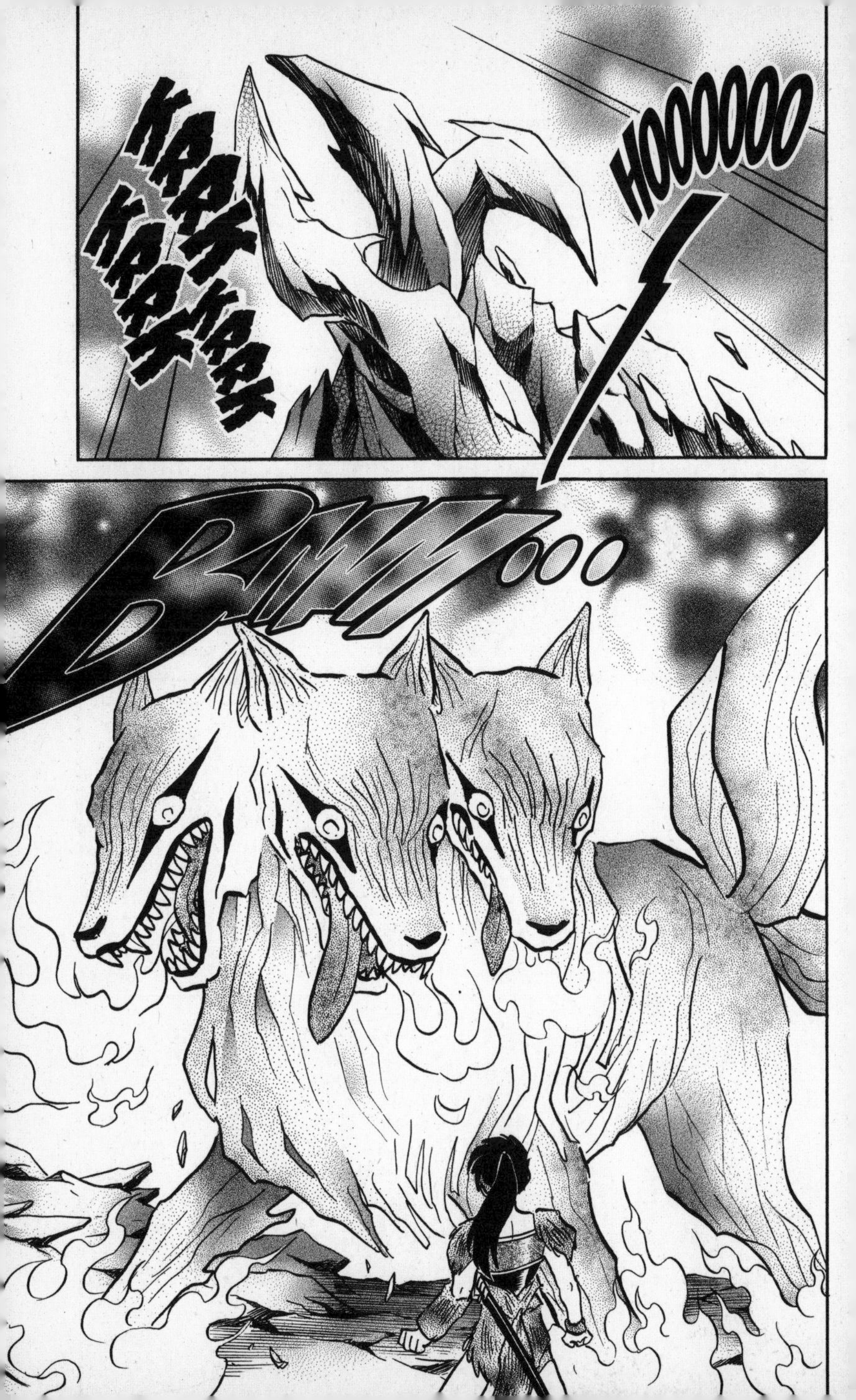
HOOOOOO
KRAK KRAK KRAK KRAK
BAM...

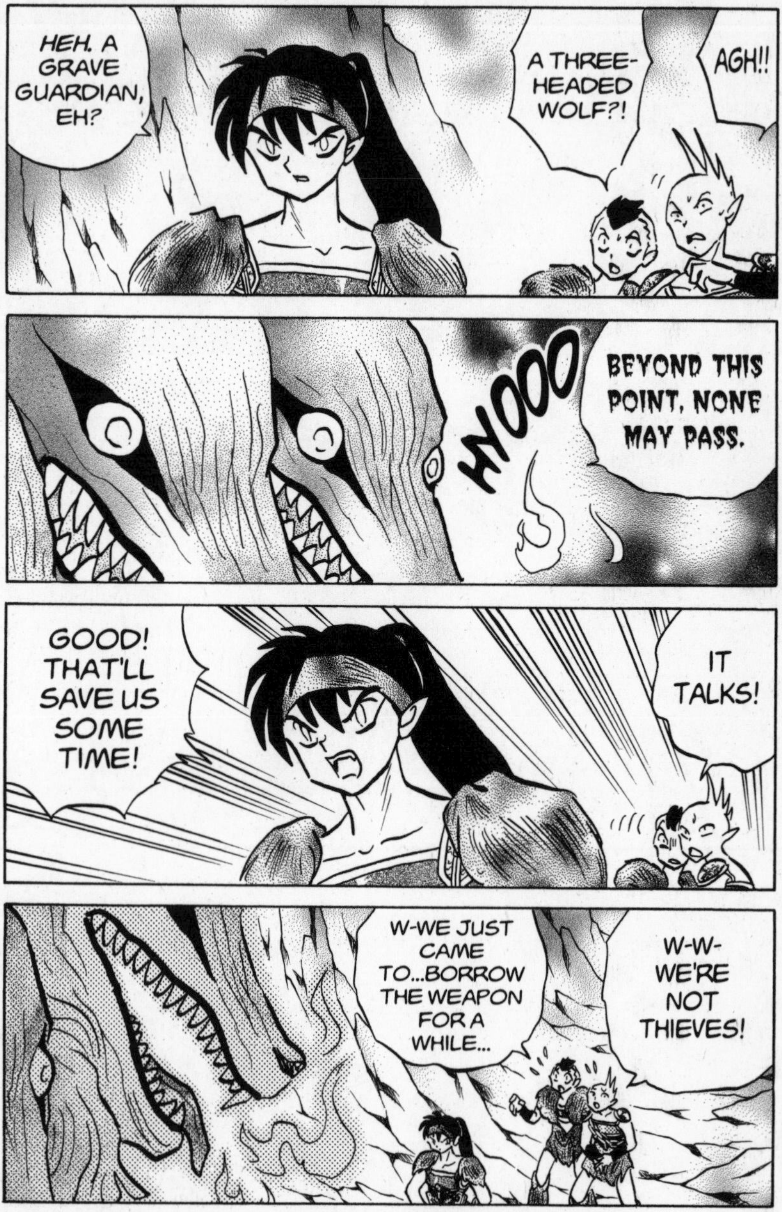
AGH!!
A THREE-HEADED WOLF?!
HEH. A GRAVE GUARDIAN, EH?
BEYOND THIS POINT, NONE MAY PASS.
HYOOO
IT TALKS!
GOOD! THAT'LL SAVE US SOME TIME!
W-W-WE'RE NOT THIEVES!
W-WE JUST CAME TO...BORROW THE WEAPON FOR A WHILE...

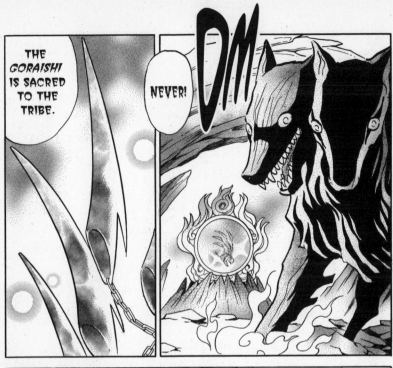

THE *GORAISHI* IS SACRED TO THE TRIBE.

NEVER!

ITS CLAWS ARE IMBUED WITH THE SOULS OF GENERATIONS GONE.

IF YOU WISH TO WIELD THEM...

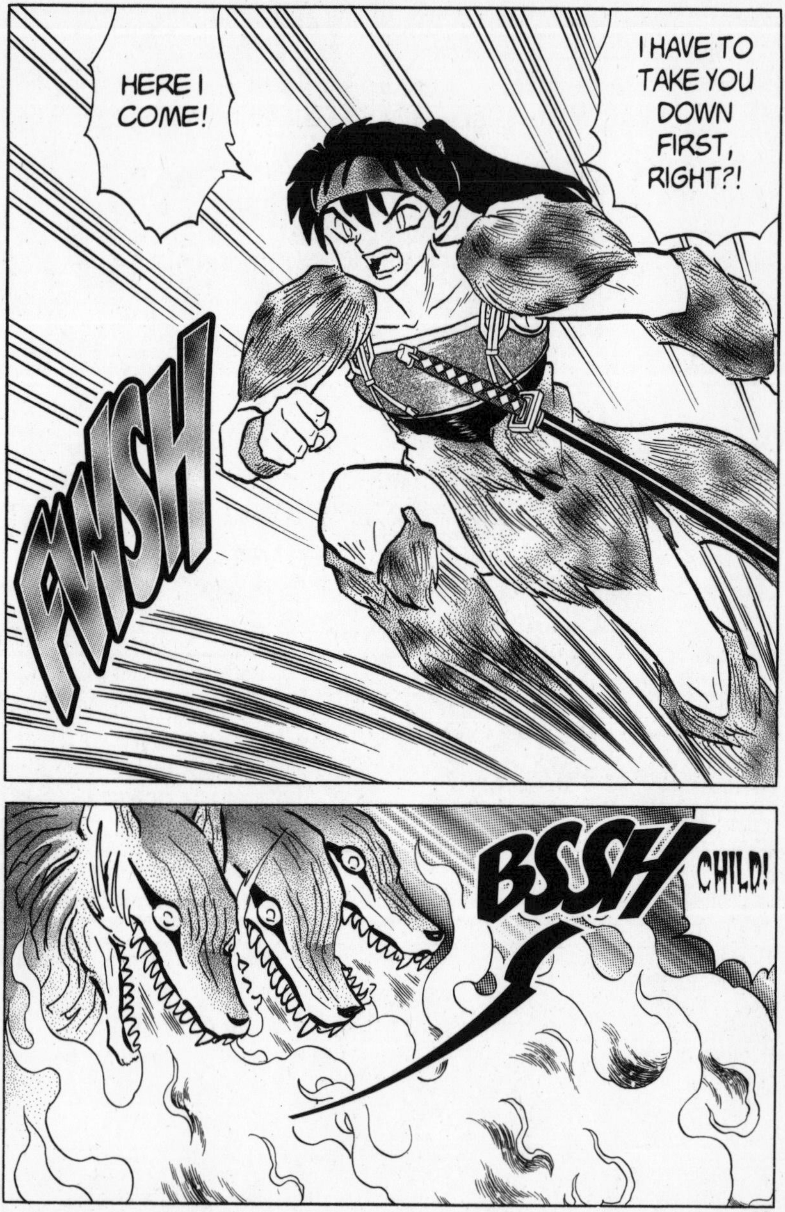
I HAVE TO TAKE YOU DOWN FIRST, RIGHT?!
HERE I COME!
FWISH
CHILD!
BSSH

SCROLL 3

THE GUARDIAN OF THE TREASURE

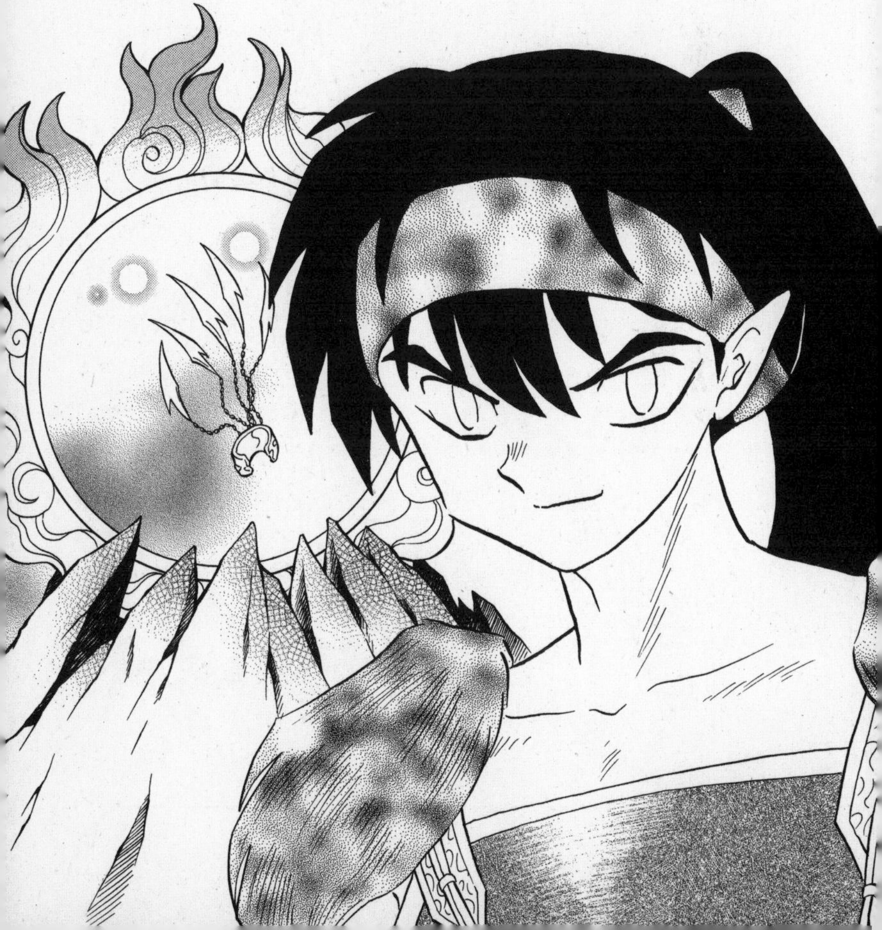

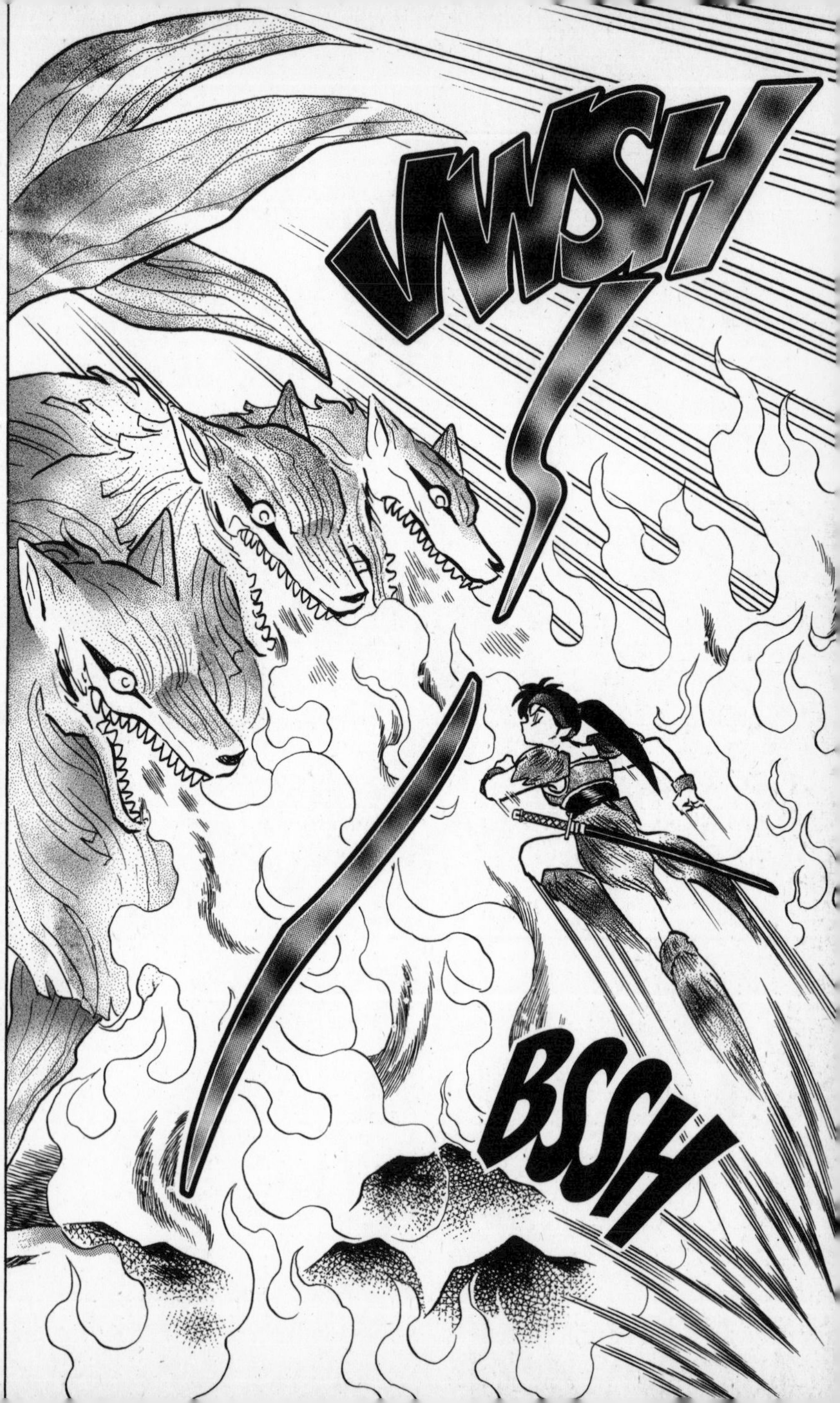
VWSH
BSSH

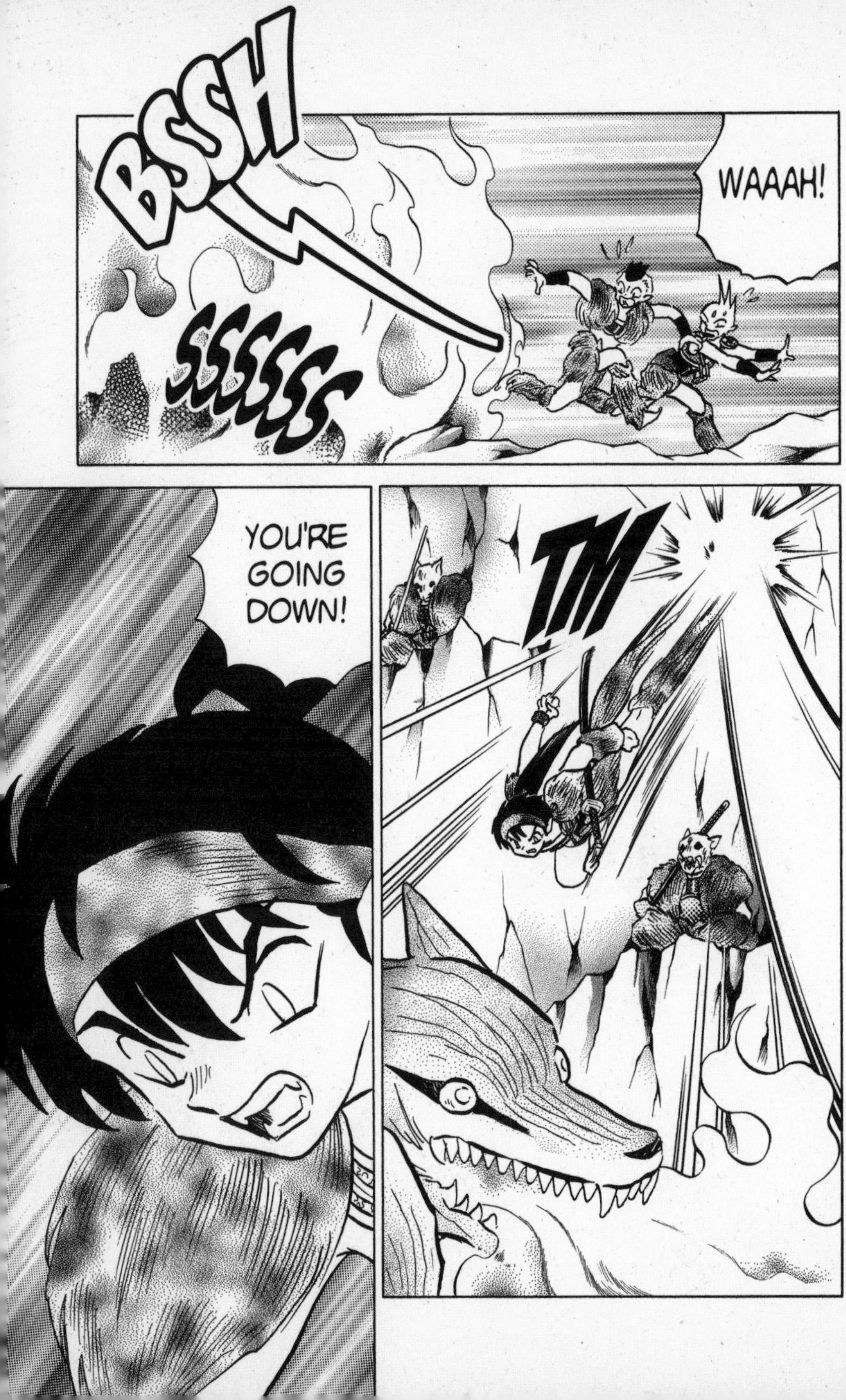
WAAAH!
BSSH
SSSSSS
TM
YOU'RE GOING DOWN!

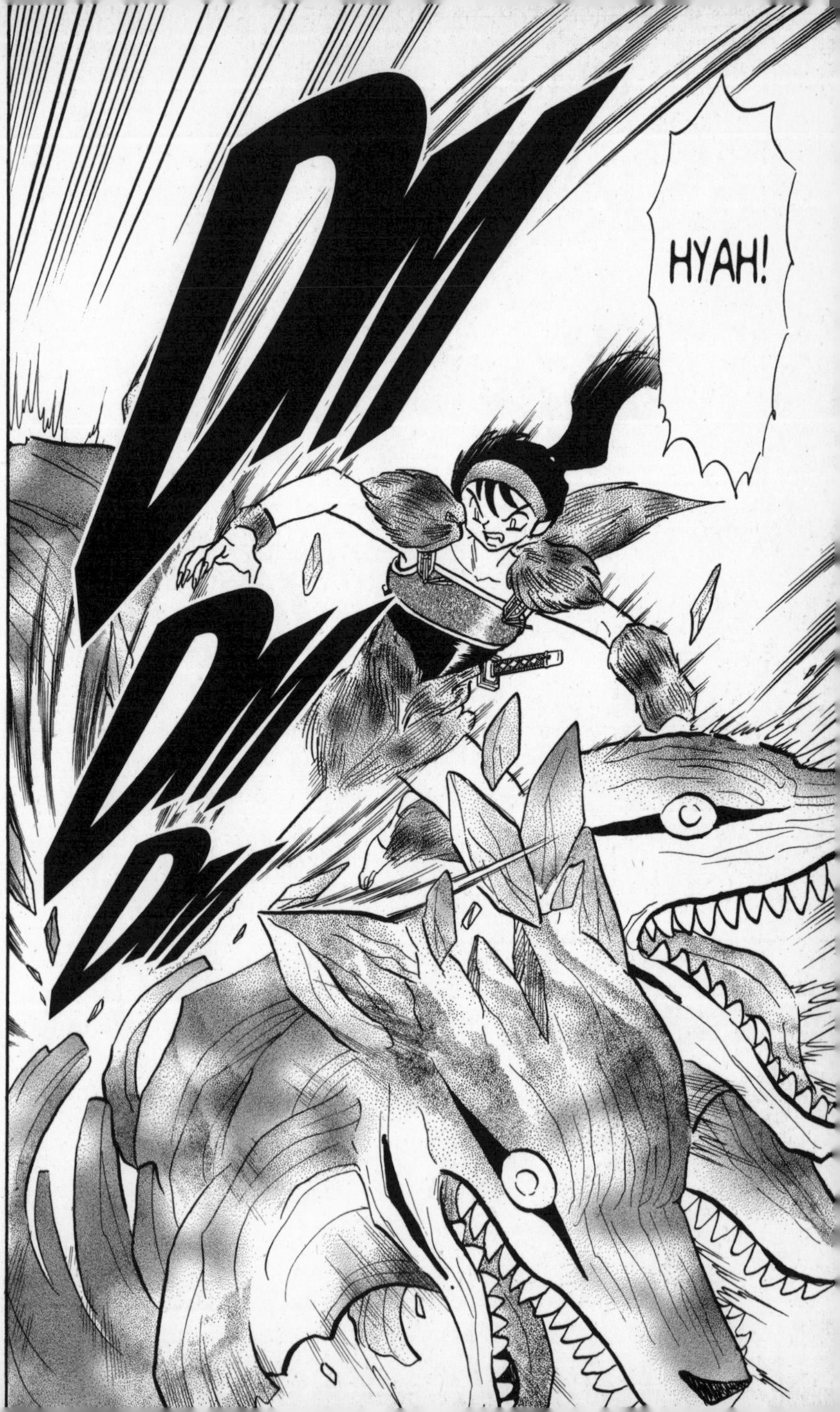
HYAH!

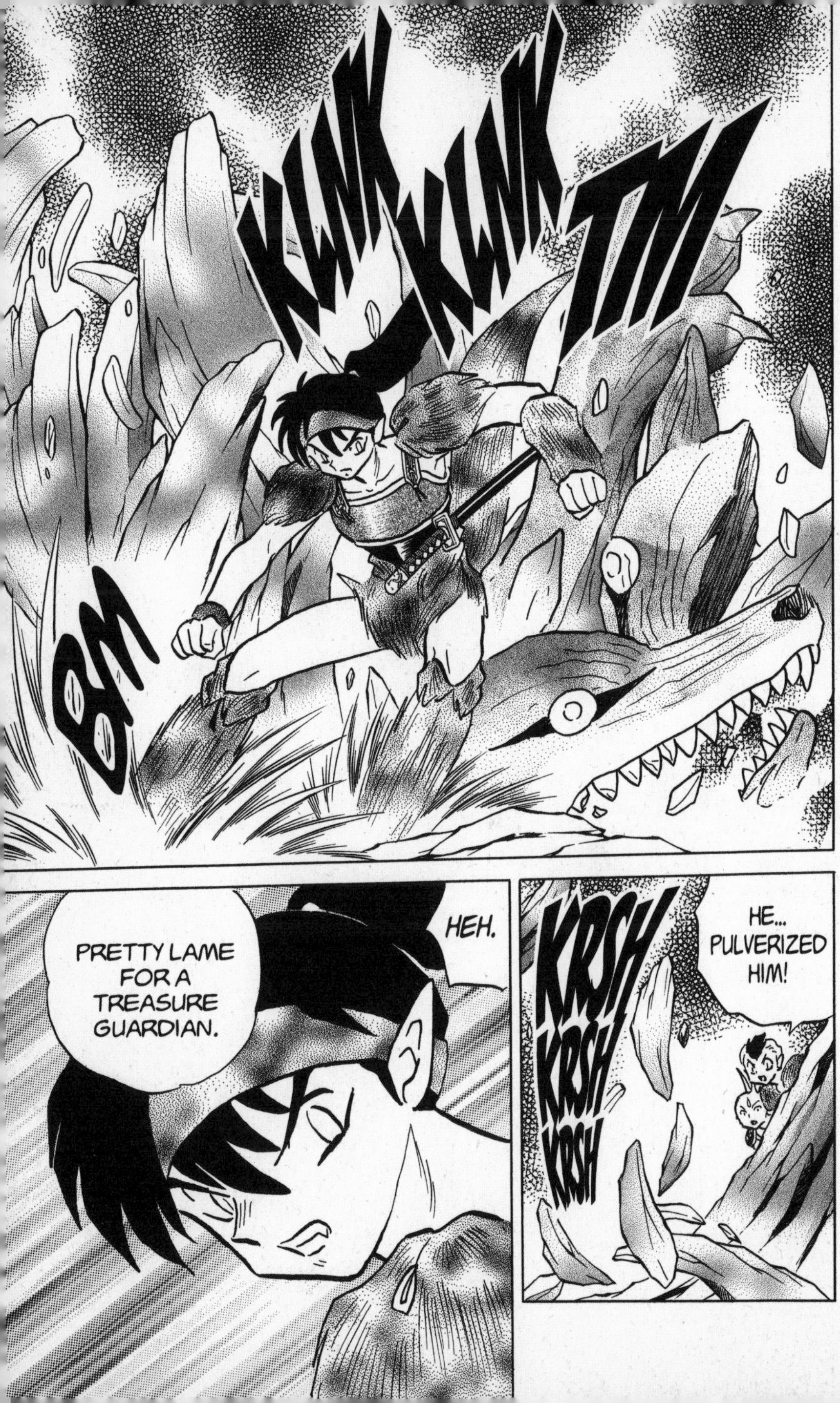
KLINK KLINK TIN
BAM
KRSH KRSH KRSH
HE... PULVERIZED HIM!
HEH.
PRETTY LAME FOR A TREASURE GUARDIAN.

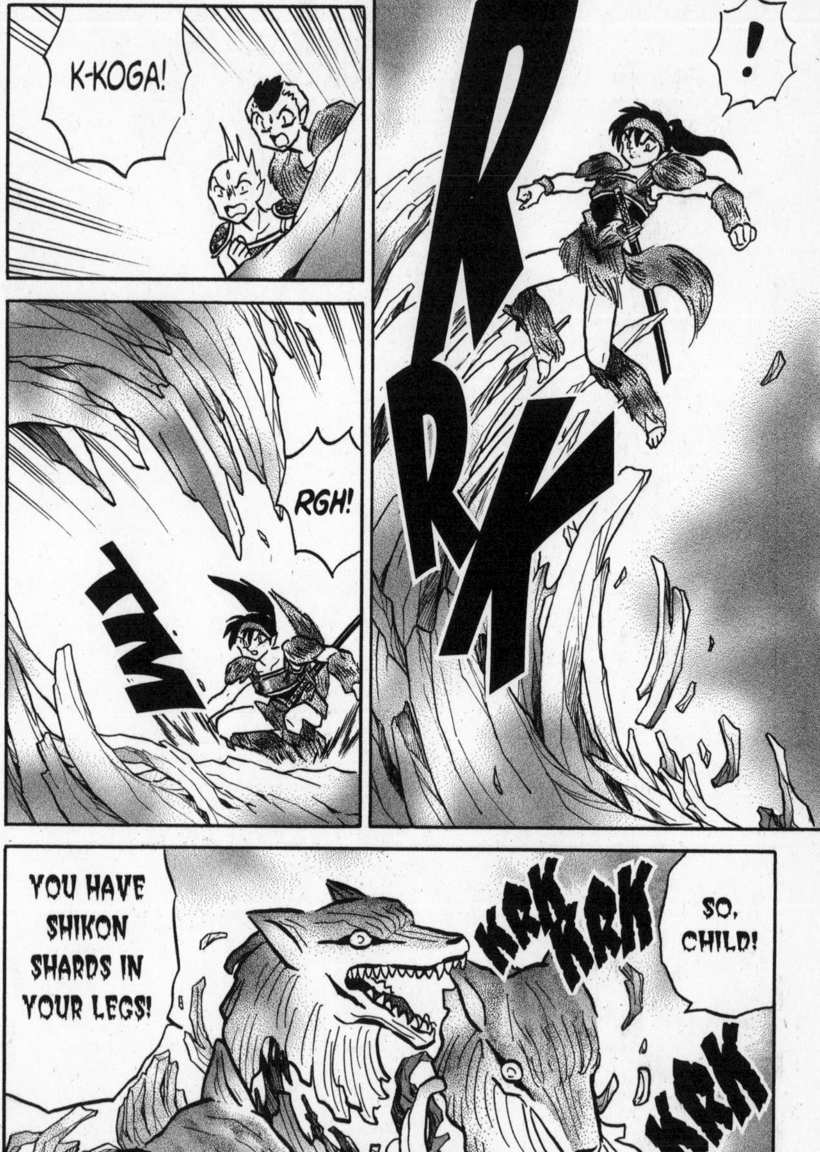
!
RRK
K-KOGA!
RGH!
TWM
SO, CHILD!
KRK KRK
KRK
YOU HAVE SHIKON SHARDS IN YOUR LEGS!

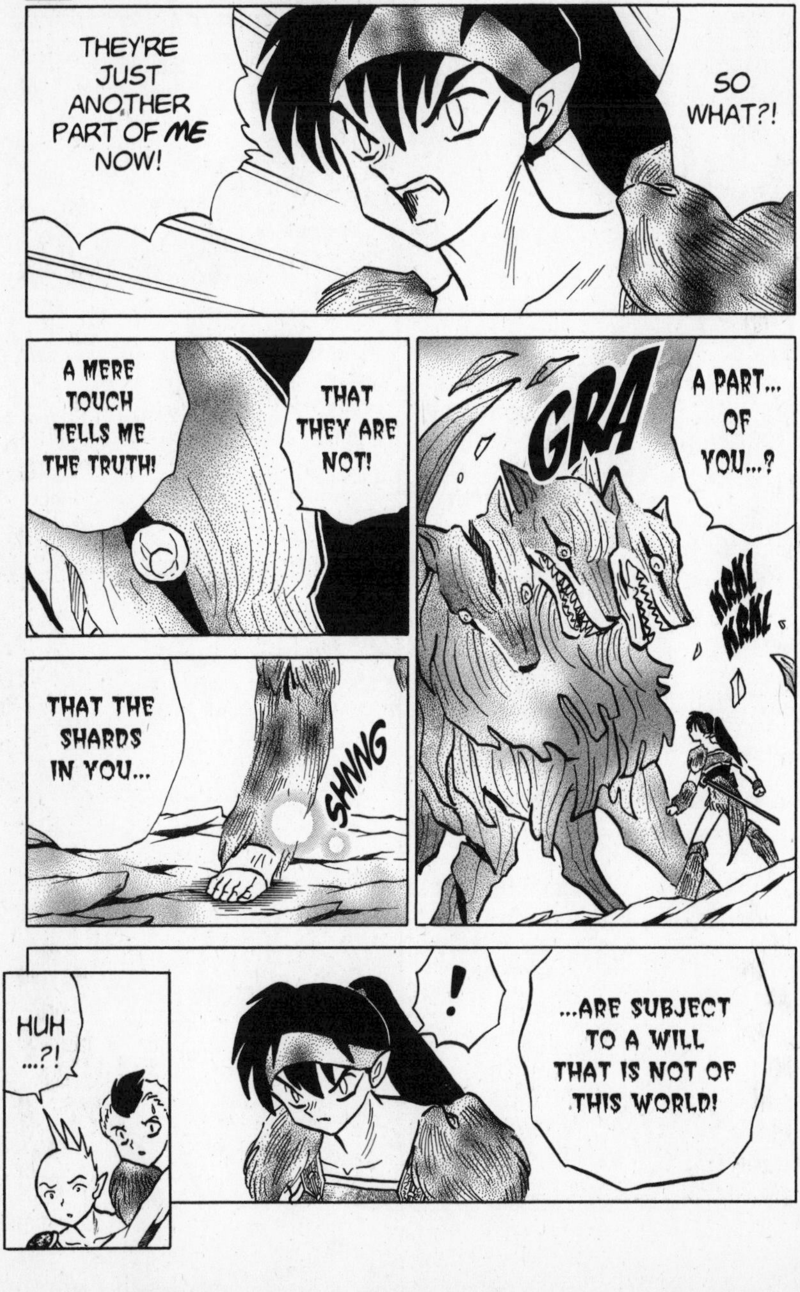
SO WHAT?!
THEY'RE JUST ANOTHER PART OF ME NOW!
A PART... OF YOU...?
GRA
KRAK KRAK
A MERE TOUCH TELLS ME THE TRUTH!
THAT THEY ARE NOT!
THAT THE SHARDS IN YOU...
SHING
...ARE SUBJECT TO A WILL THAT IS NOT OF THIS WORLD!
!
HUH ...?!

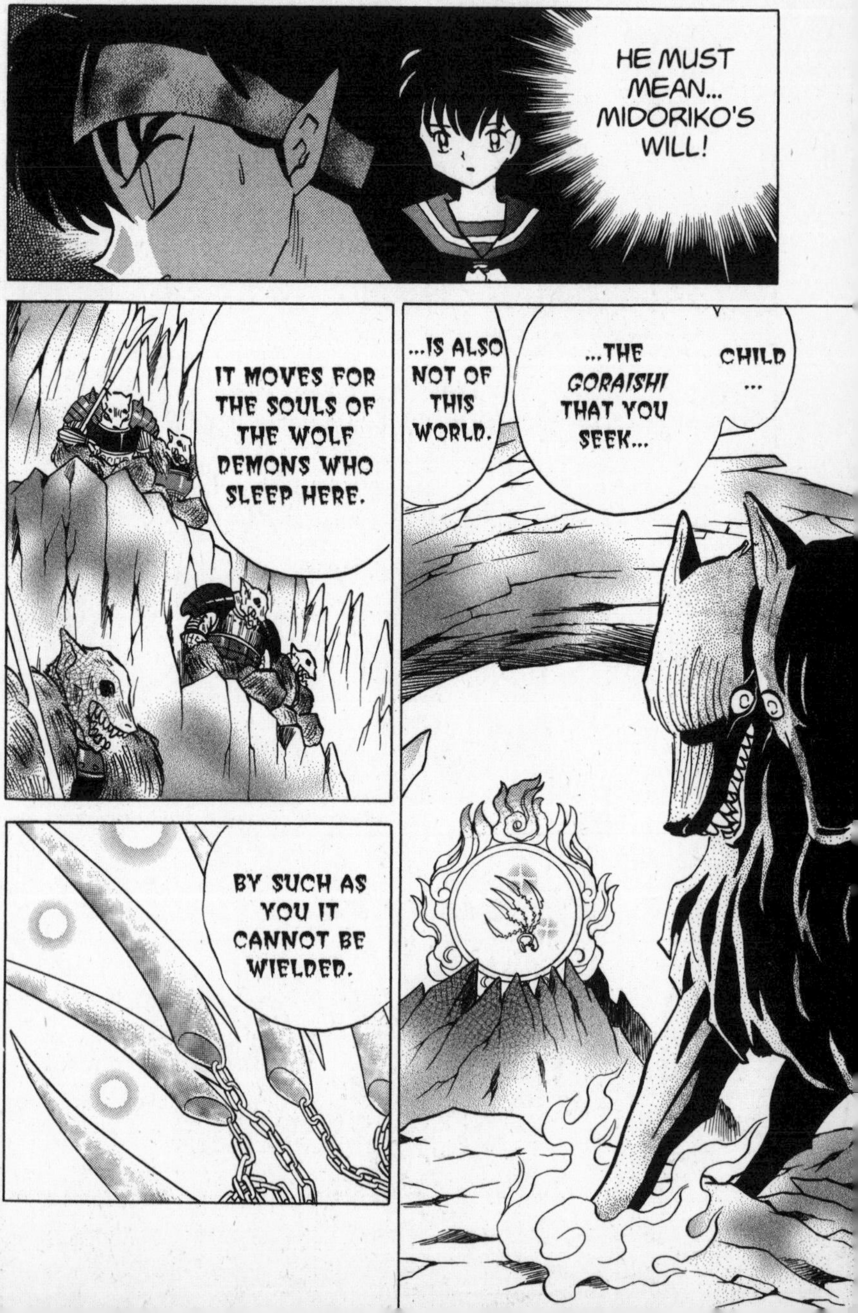
HE MUST MEAN... MIDORIKO'S WILL!
CHILD ...
...THE *GORAISHI* THAT YOU SEEK...
...IS ALSO NOT OF THIS WORLD.
IT MOVES FOR THE SOULS OF THE WOLF DEMONS WHO SLEEP HERE.
BY SUCH AS YOU IT CANNOT BE WIELDED.

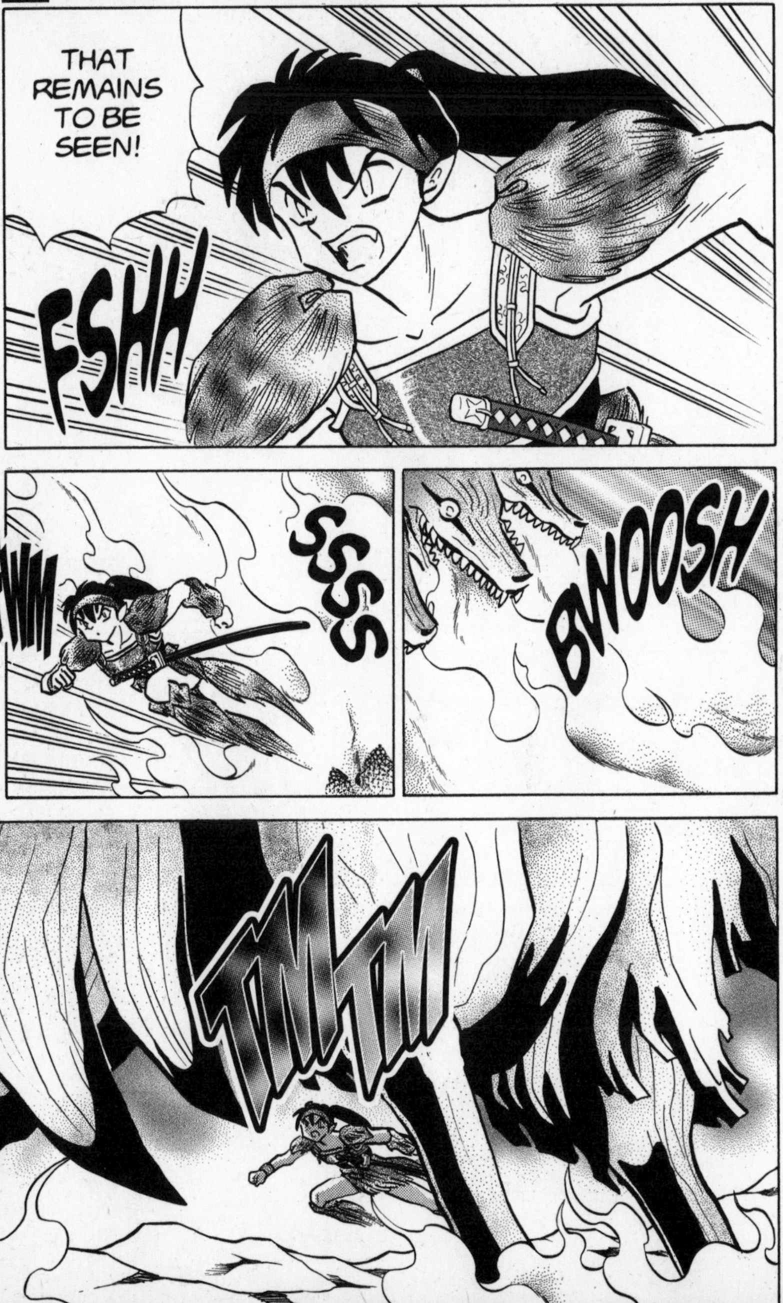
THAT REMAINS TO BE SEEN!
FSHH
BWOOSH
SSSS
FWM
TMTM

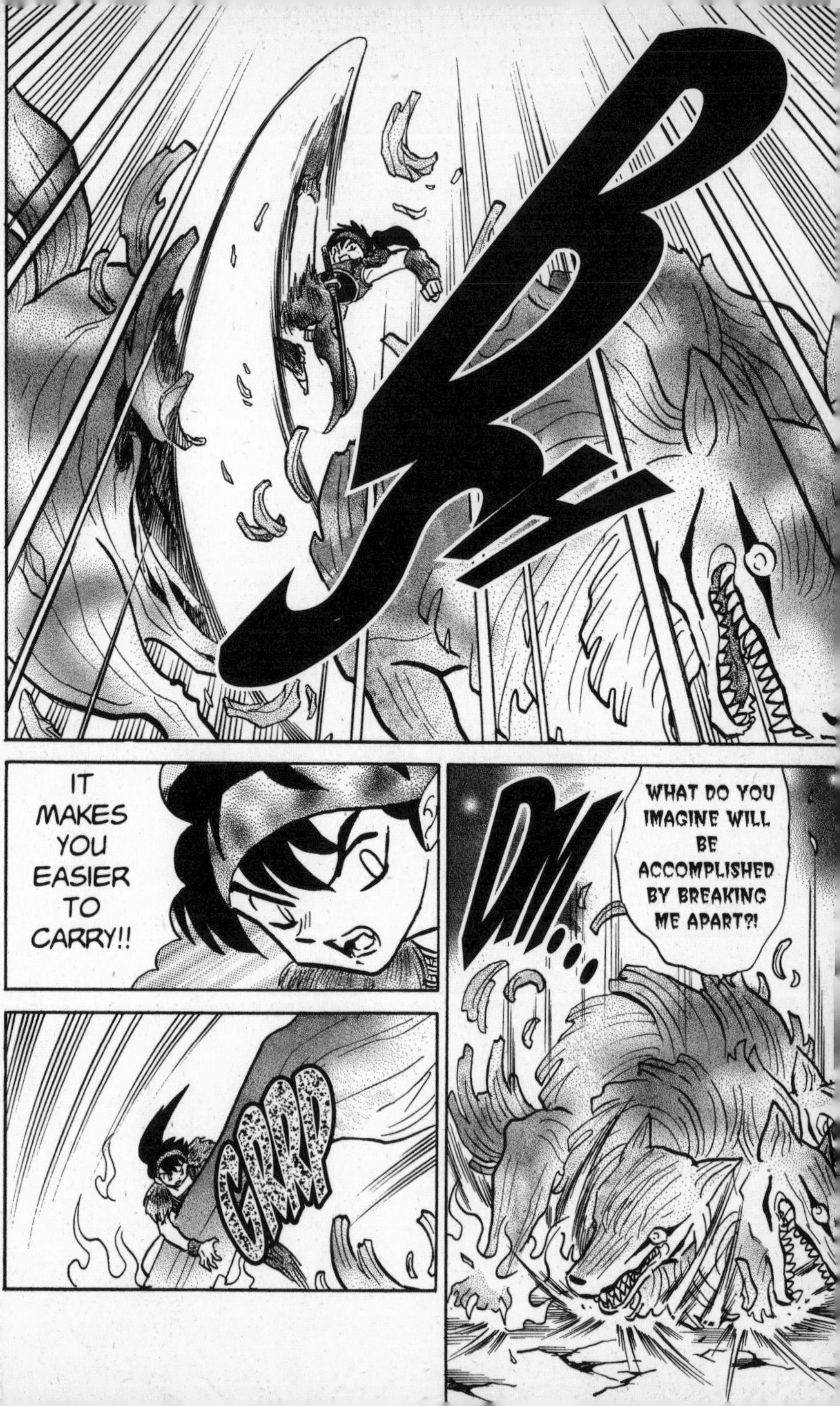
WHAT DO YOU IMAGINE WILL BE ACCOMPLISHED BY BREAKING ME APART?!
IT MAKES YOU EASIER TO CARRY!!

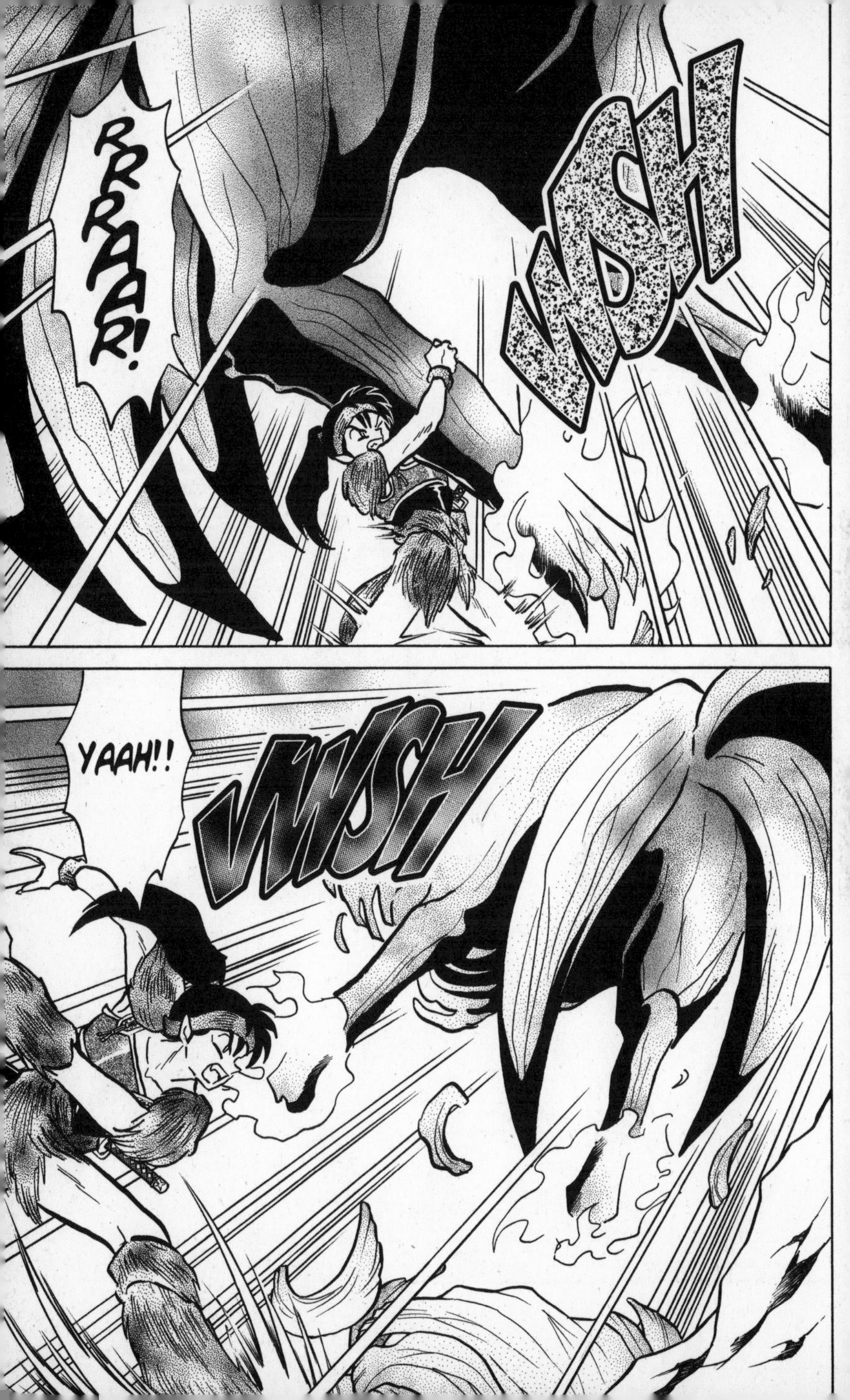
WOSH
RRRAAAR!
YAAH!!
WHOSH

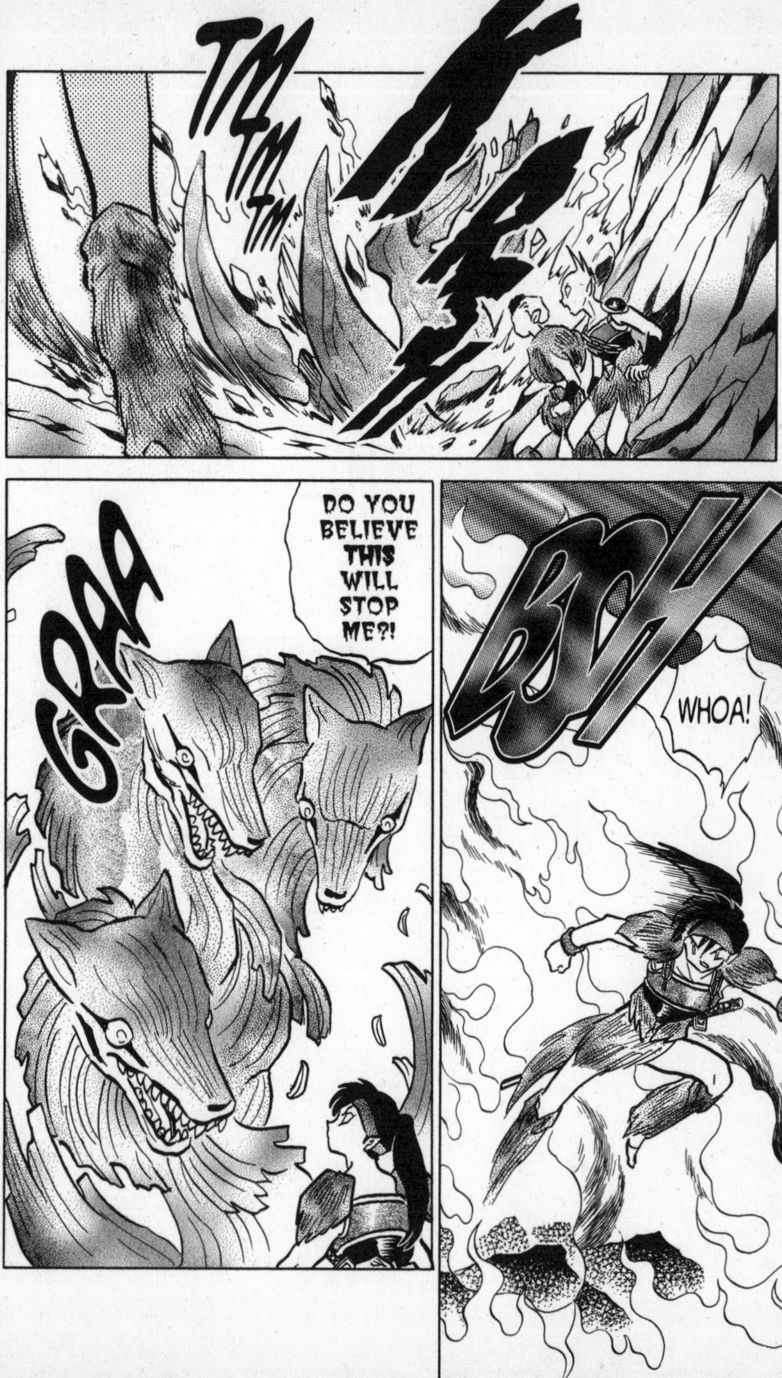
TM TM TM
BSH
WHOA!
DO YOU BELIEVE THIS WILL STOP ME?!
GRAA

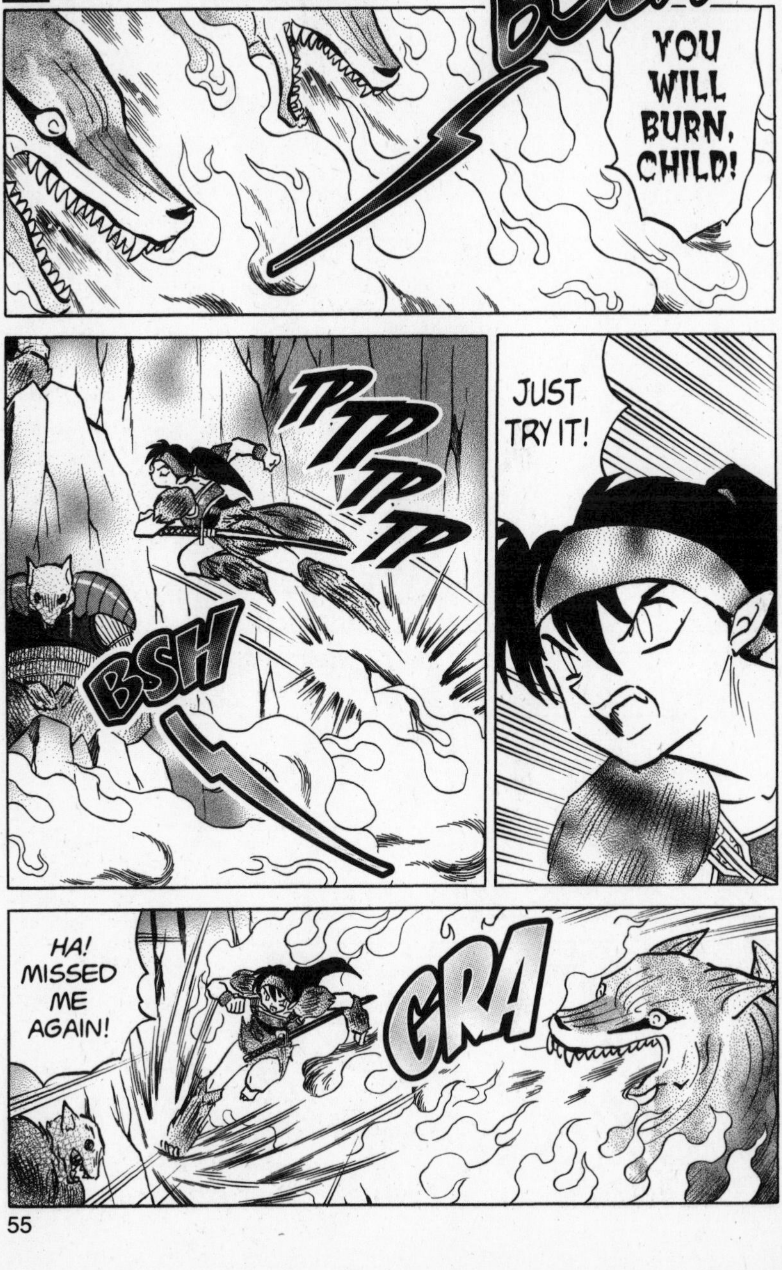
BSSH
YOU WILL BURN, CHILD!
JUST TRY IT!
TP TP TP TP TP
BSH
GRA
HA! MISSED ME AGAIN!

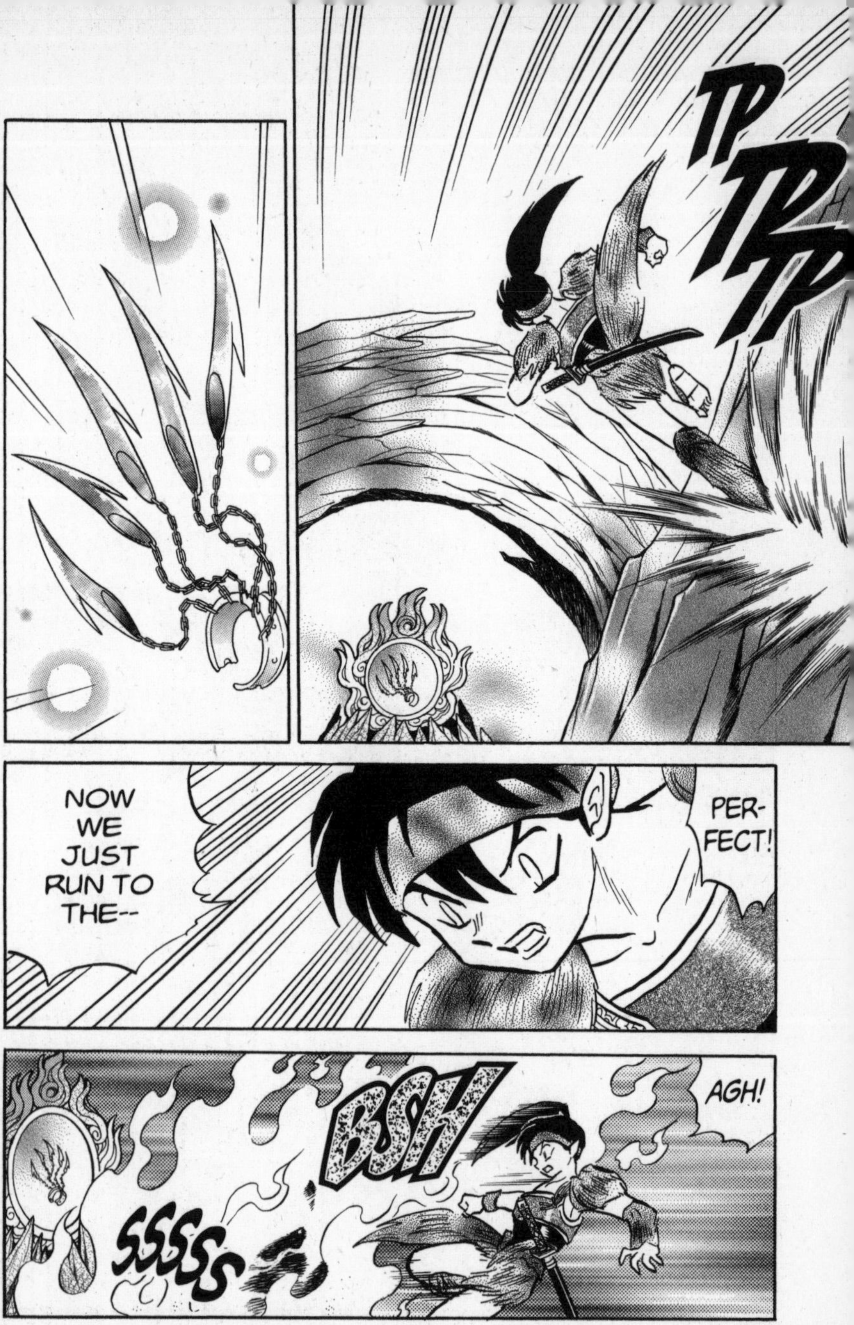
TP TP TP
PER-FECT!
NOW WE JUST RUN TO THE--
AGH!
BSH
SSSSS

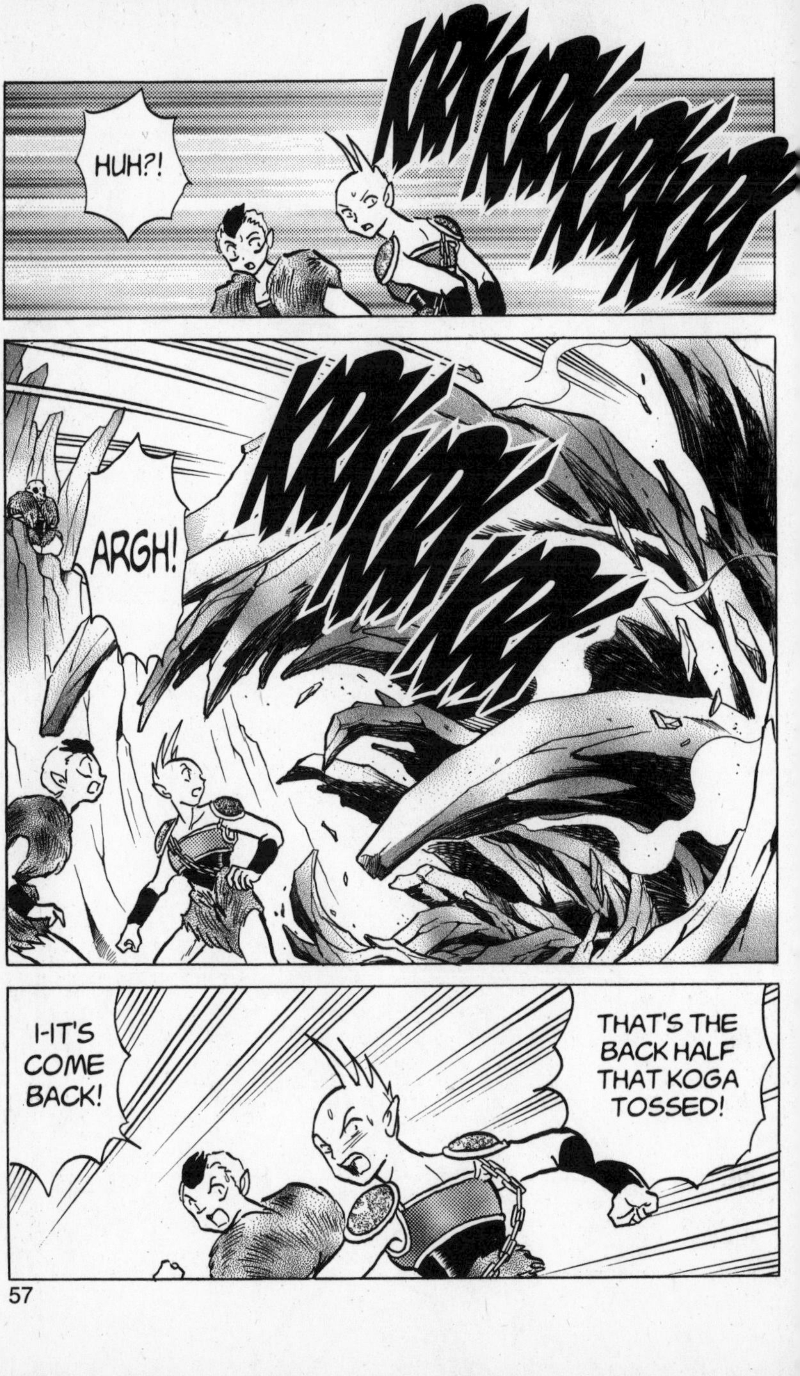
HUH?!
ARGH!
THAT'S THE BACK HALF THAT KOGA TOSSED!
I-IT'S COME BACK!

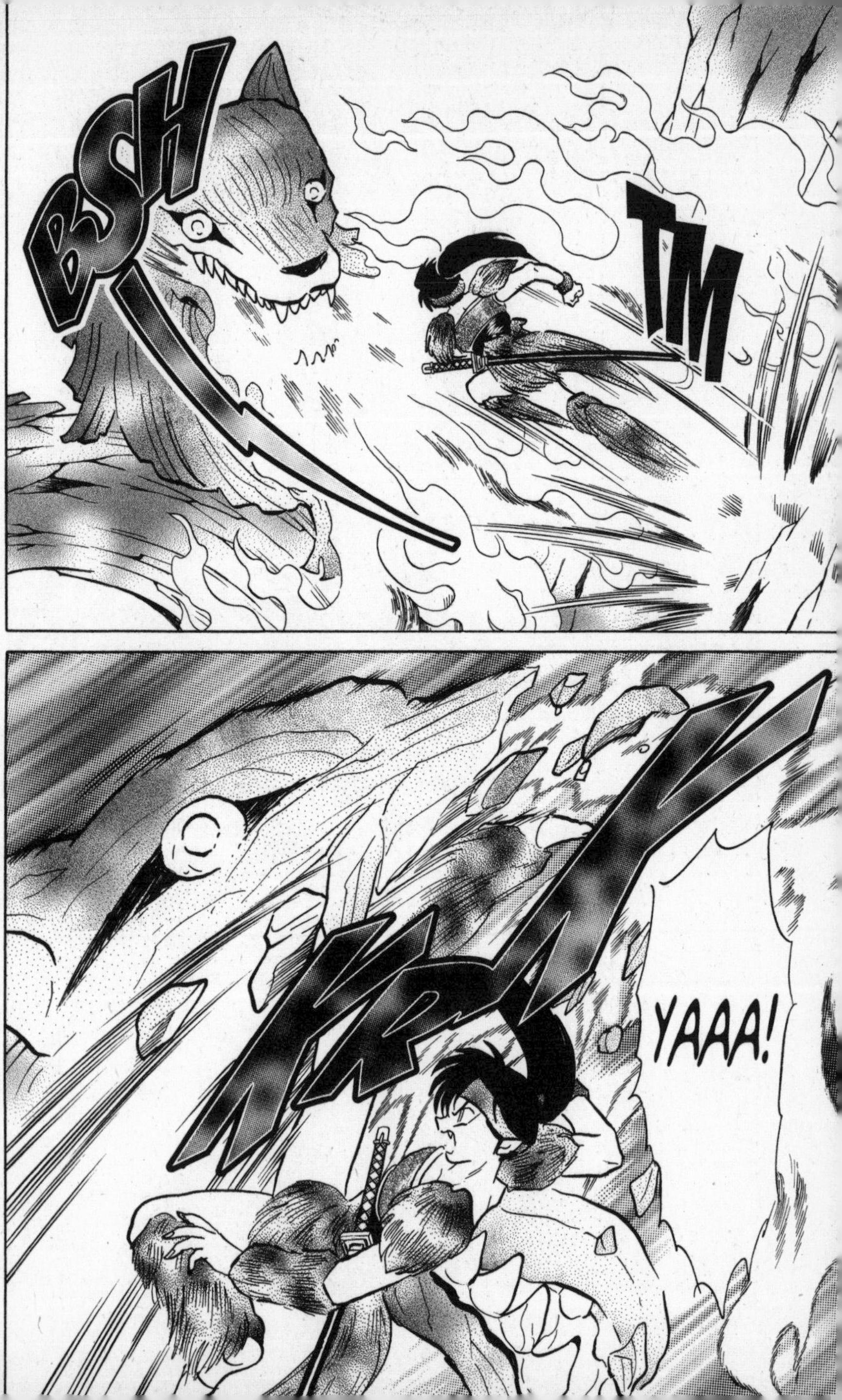
TM
BSH
YAAA!

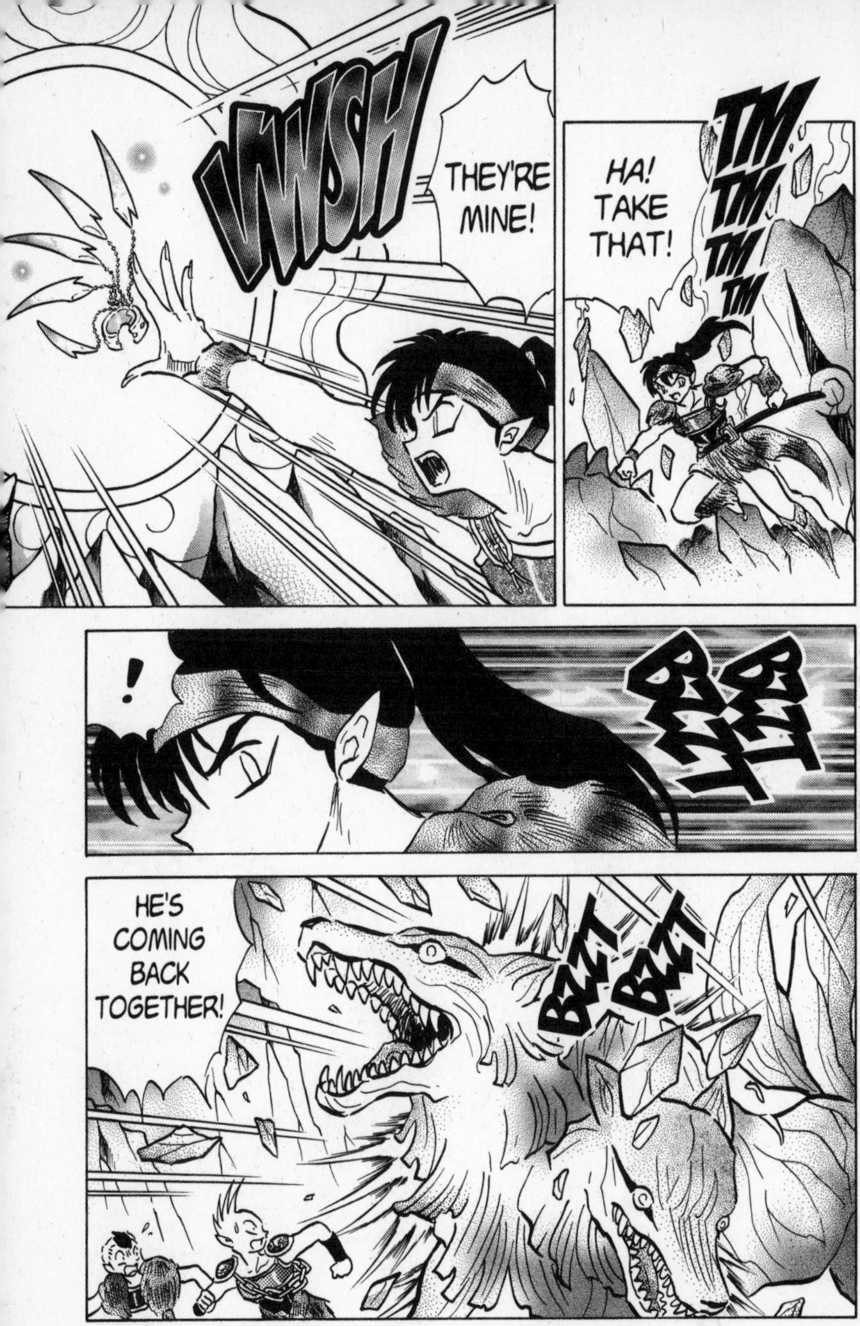
HA! TAKE THAT!
TM TM TM TM
VWSH
THEY'RE MINE!
BZZT BZZT
!
HE'S COMING BACK TOGETHER!
BZZT BZZT

!

MMG....

HURRY UP AND GRAB THE THING!

KOGA!

GRA

SCROLL 4

THE CLAWS

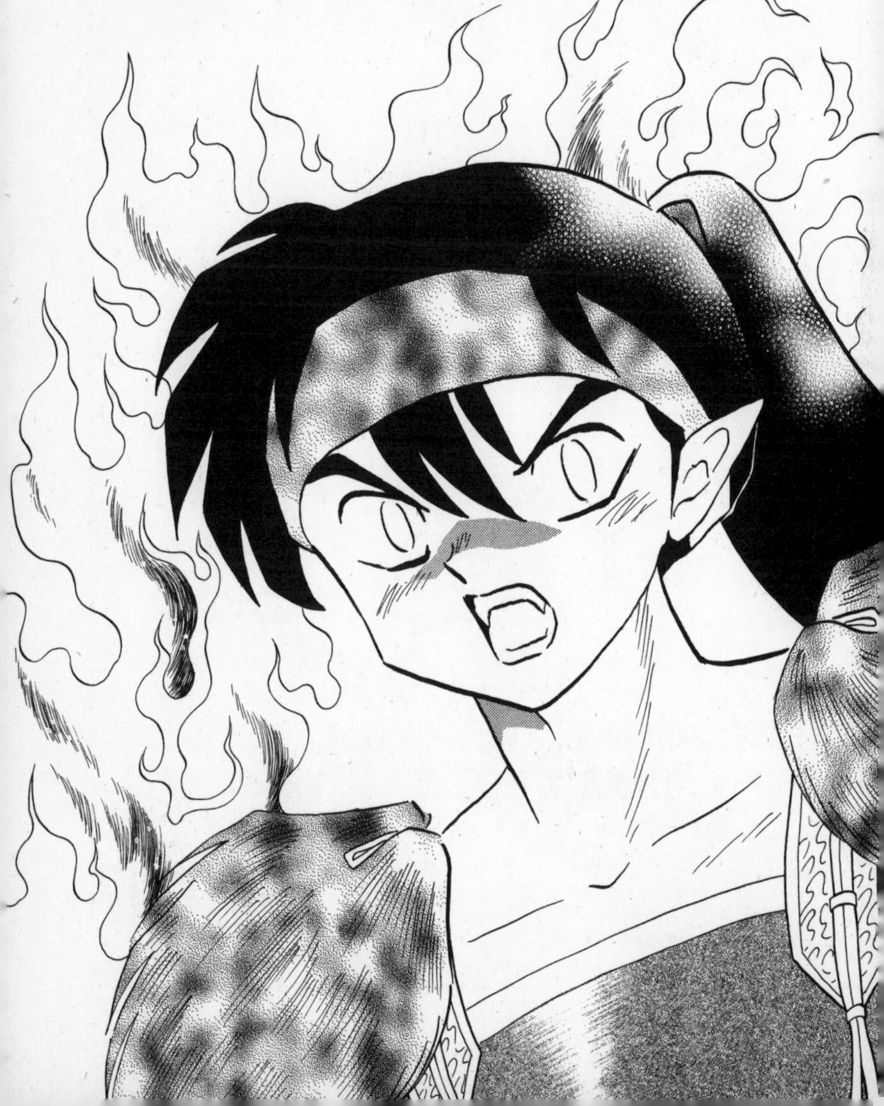

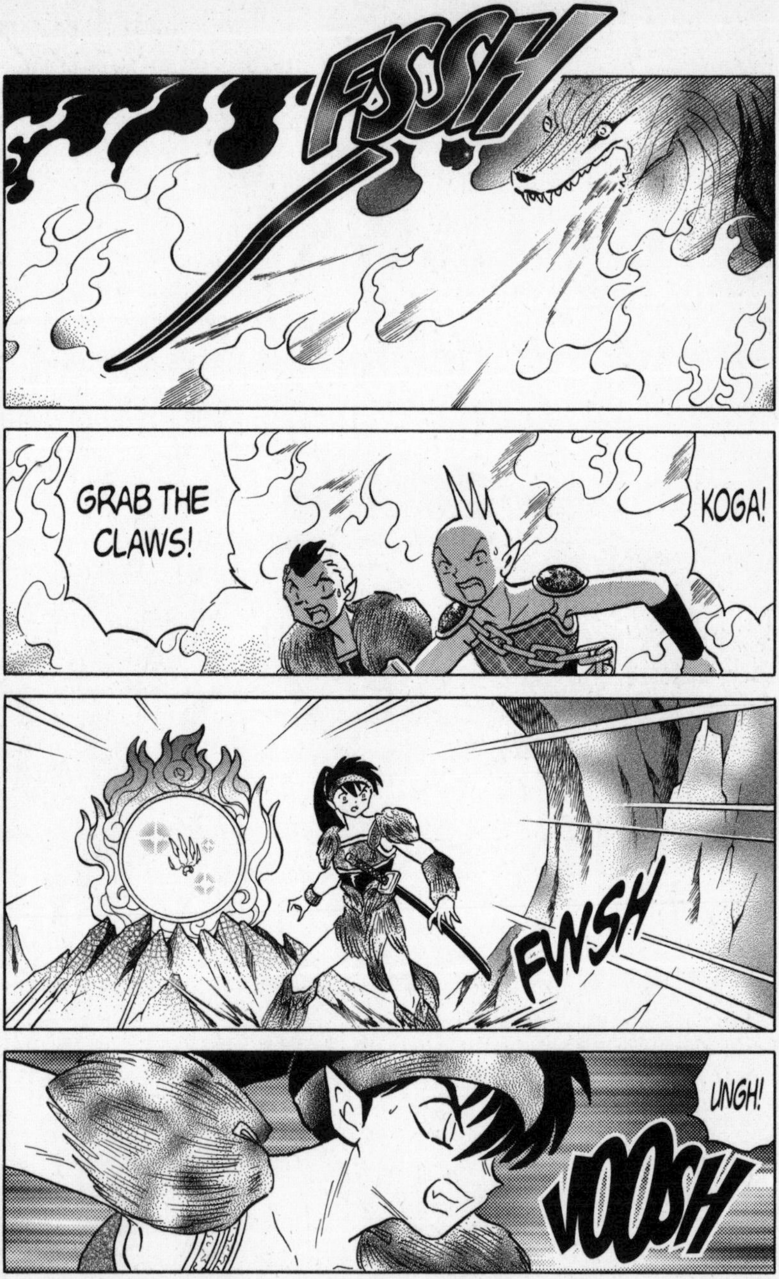
FSSH
KOGA!
GRAB THE CLAWS!
FWSH
UNGH!
VOOSH

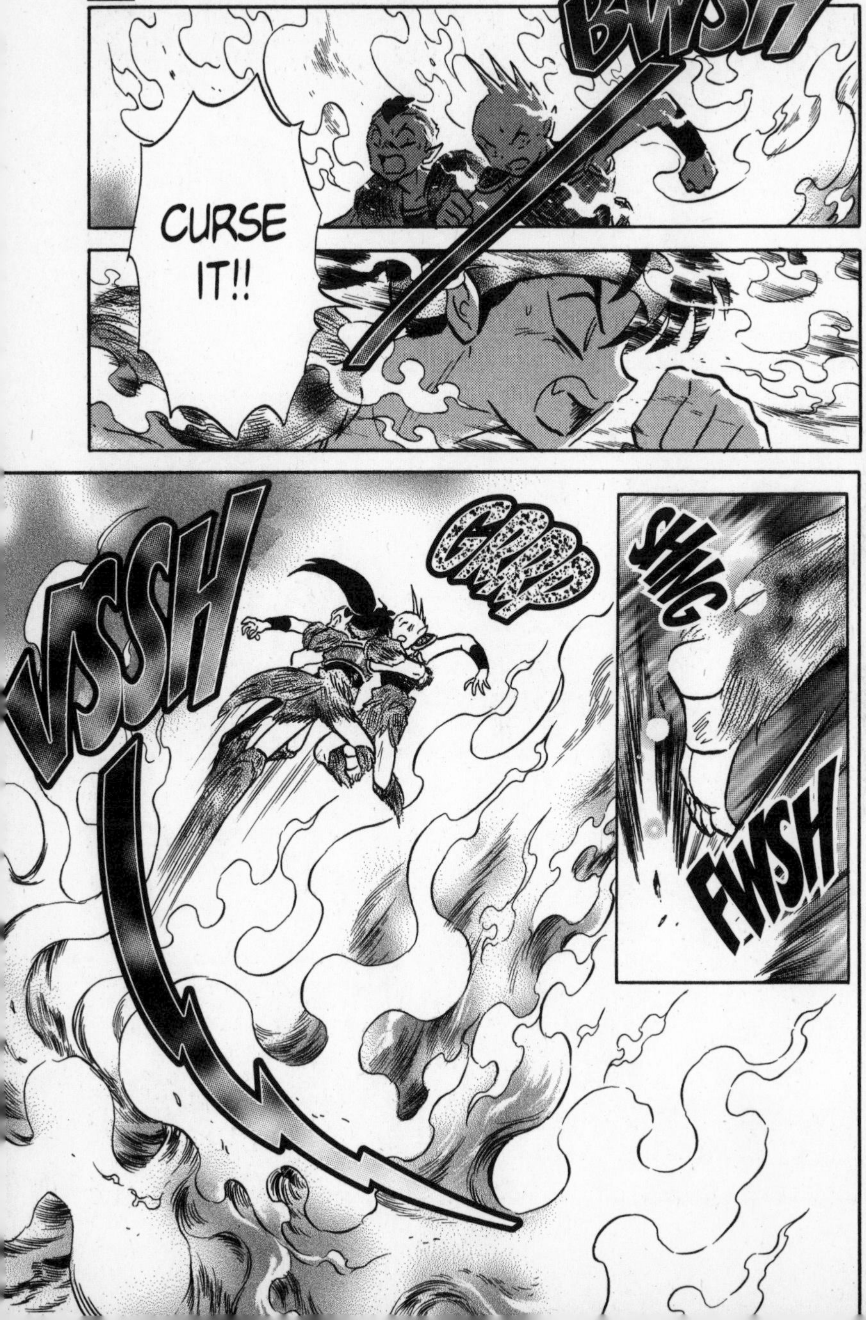
BWSH
CURSE IT!!
SHING
FWSH
GRIP
VSSH

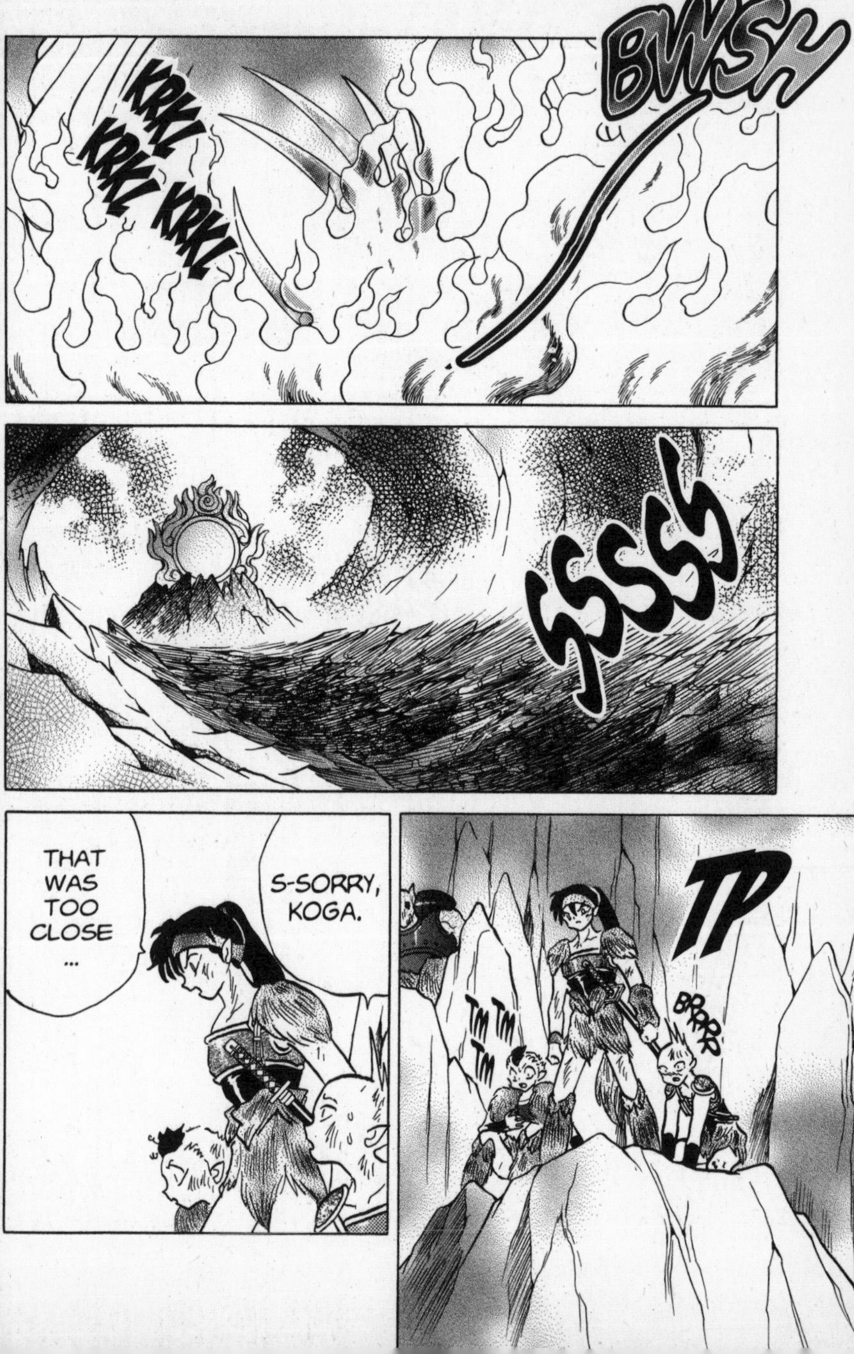
BWSH
KRKL KRKL KRKL
SSSS
TP
TM TM TM TM
BRRRR
S-SORRY, KOGA.
THAT WAS TOO CLOSE ...

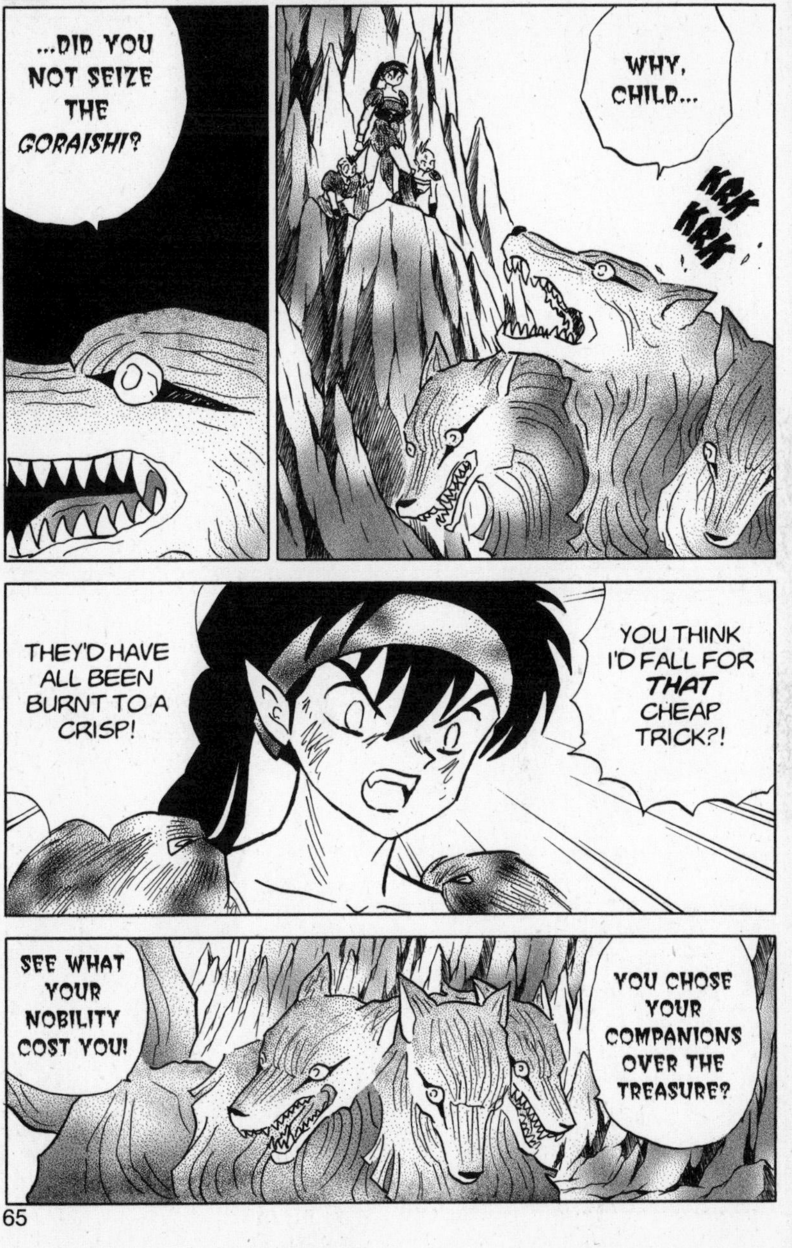
WHY, CHILD...
KRK KRK
...DID YOU NOT SEIZE THE GORAISHI?
YOU THINK I'D FALL FOR THAT CHEAP TRICK?!
THEY'D HAVE ALL BEEN BURNT TO A CRISP!
YOU CHOSE YOUR COMPANIONS OVER THE TREASURE?
SEE WHAT YOUR NOBILITY COST YOU!

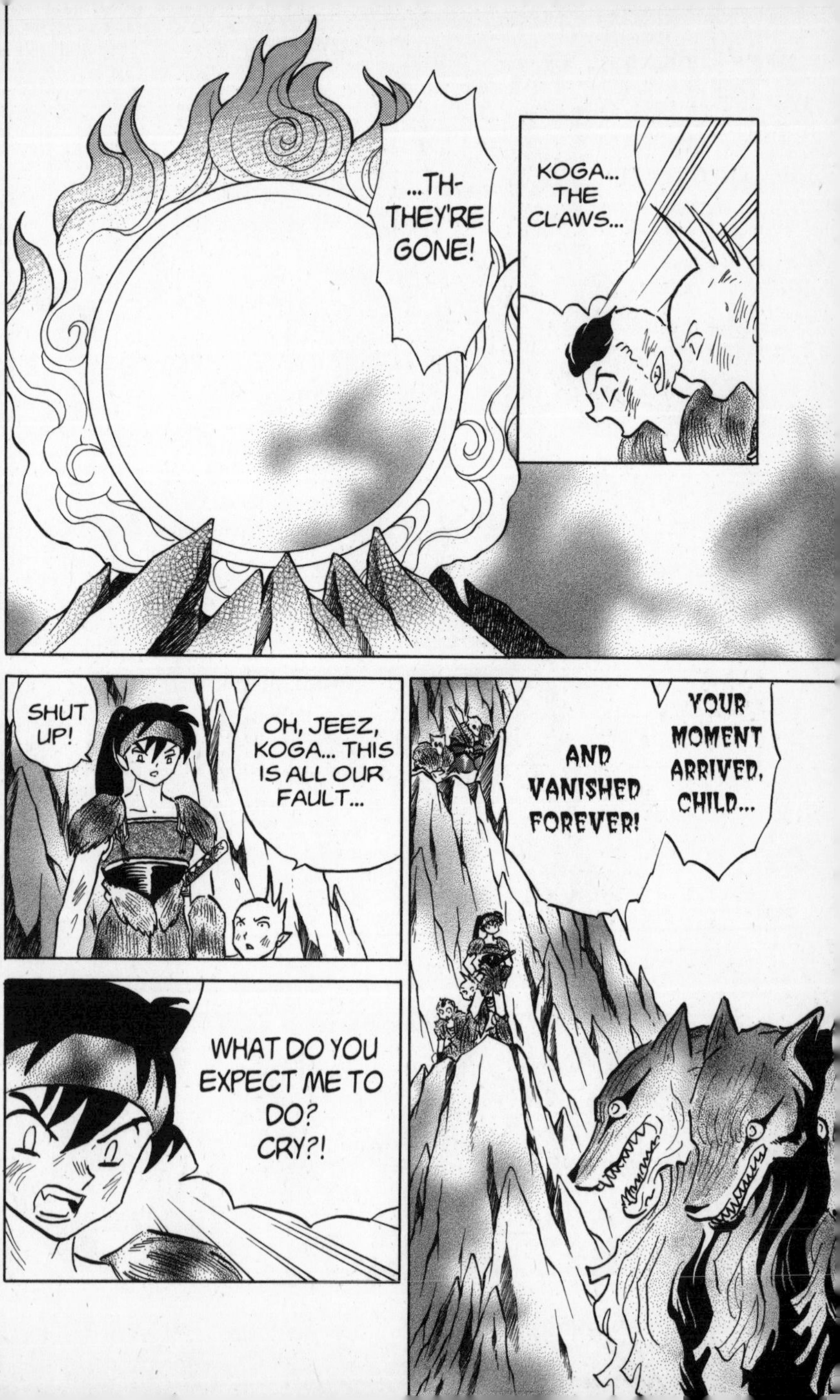
KOGA... THE CLAWS...
...TH- THEY'RE GONE!
YOUR MOMENT ARRIVED, CHILD...
AND VANISHED FOREVER!
OH, JEEZ, KOGA... THIS IS ALL OUR FAULT...
SHUT UP!
WHAT DO YOU EXPECT ME TO DO? CRY?!

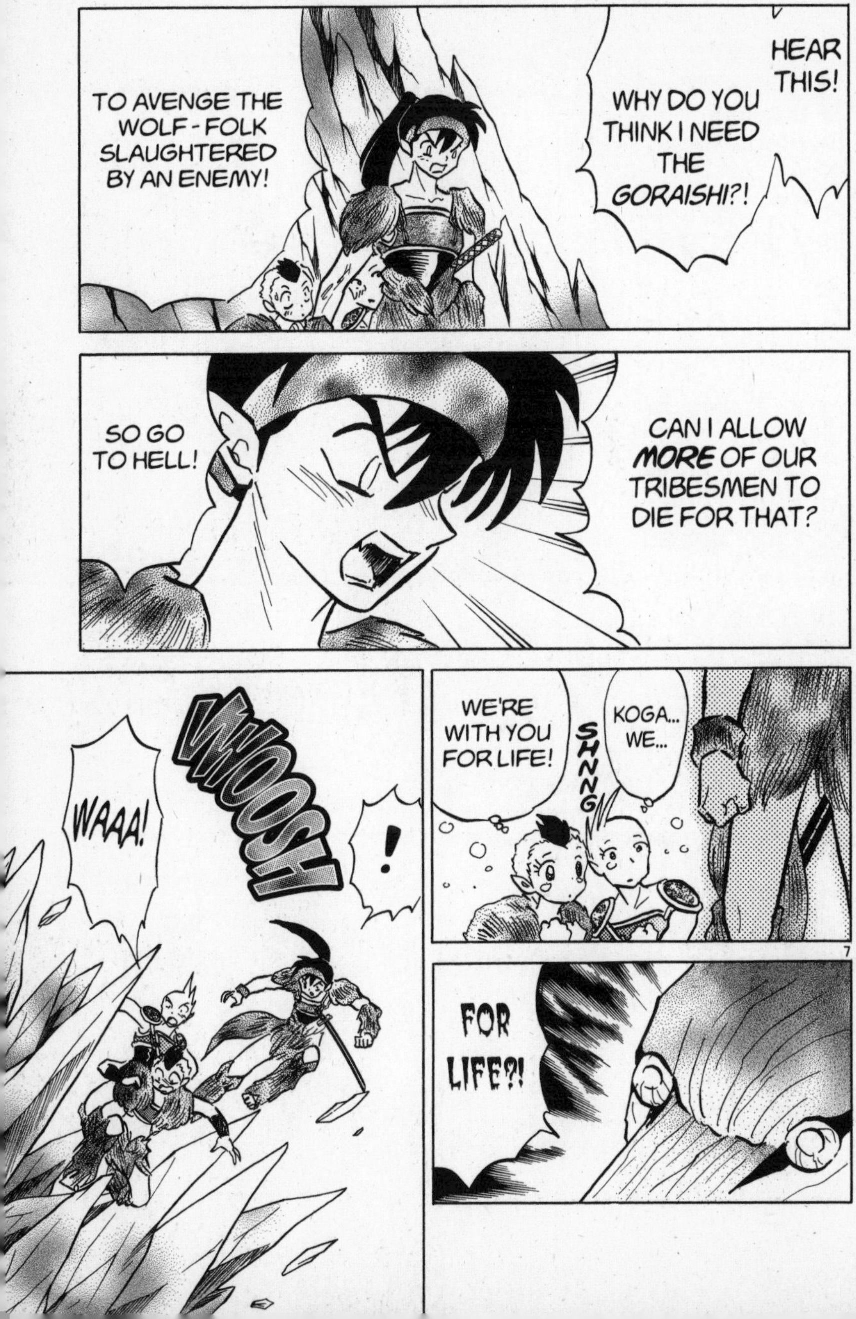
HEAR THIS!
WHY DO YOU THINK I NEED THE GORAISHI?!
TO AVENGE THE WOLF-FOLK SLAUGHTERED BY AN ENEMY!
CAN I ALLOW MORE OF OUR TRIBESMEN TO DIE FOR THAT?
SO GO TO HELL!
KOGA... WE...
SHNNG
WE'RE WITH YOU FOR LIFE!
FOR LIFE?!
!
WHOOSH
WAAA!

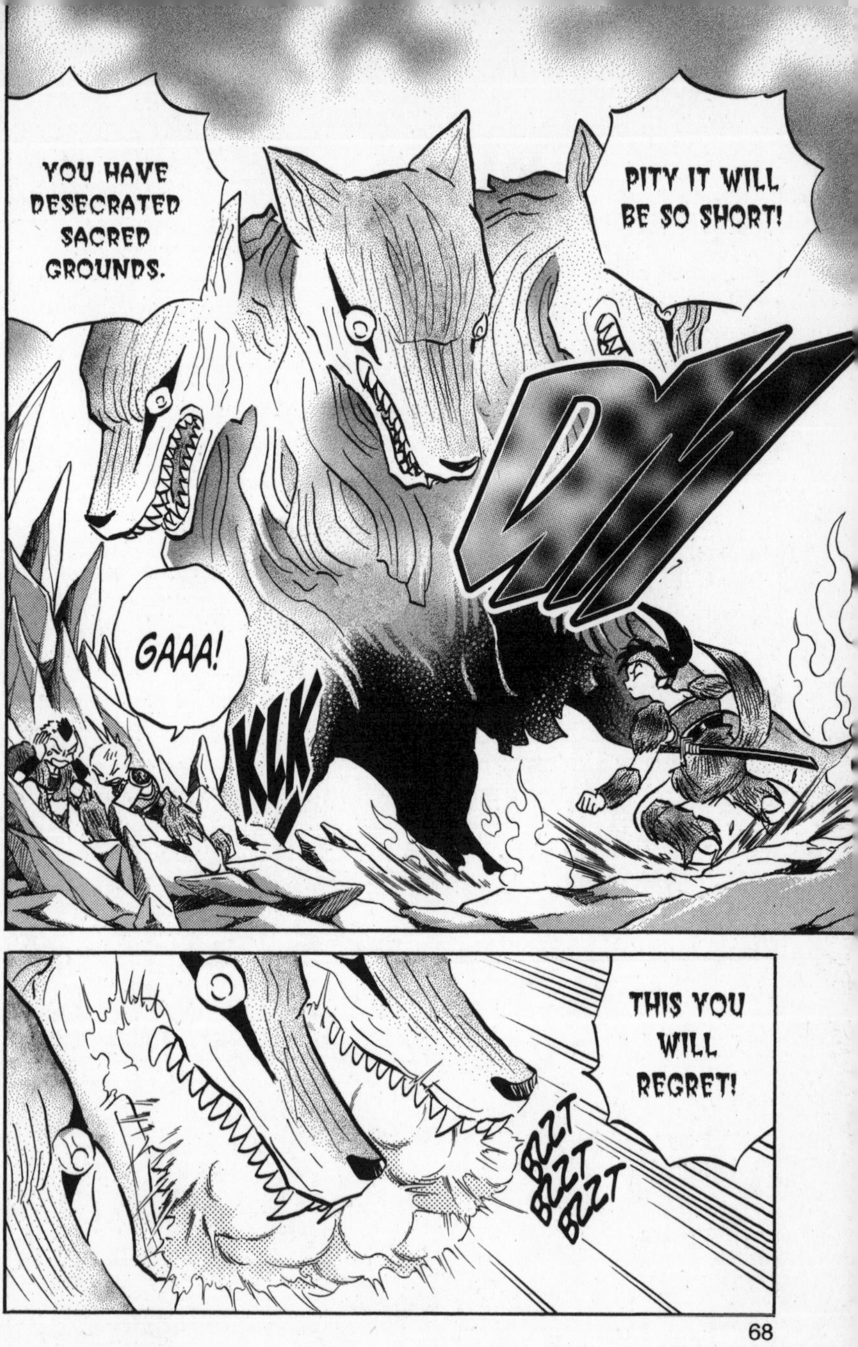
PITY IT WILL BE SO SHORT!
YOU HAVE DESECRATED SACRED GROUNDS.
DM
GAAA!
KLK
THIS YOU WILL REGRET!
BZZT BZZT BZZT

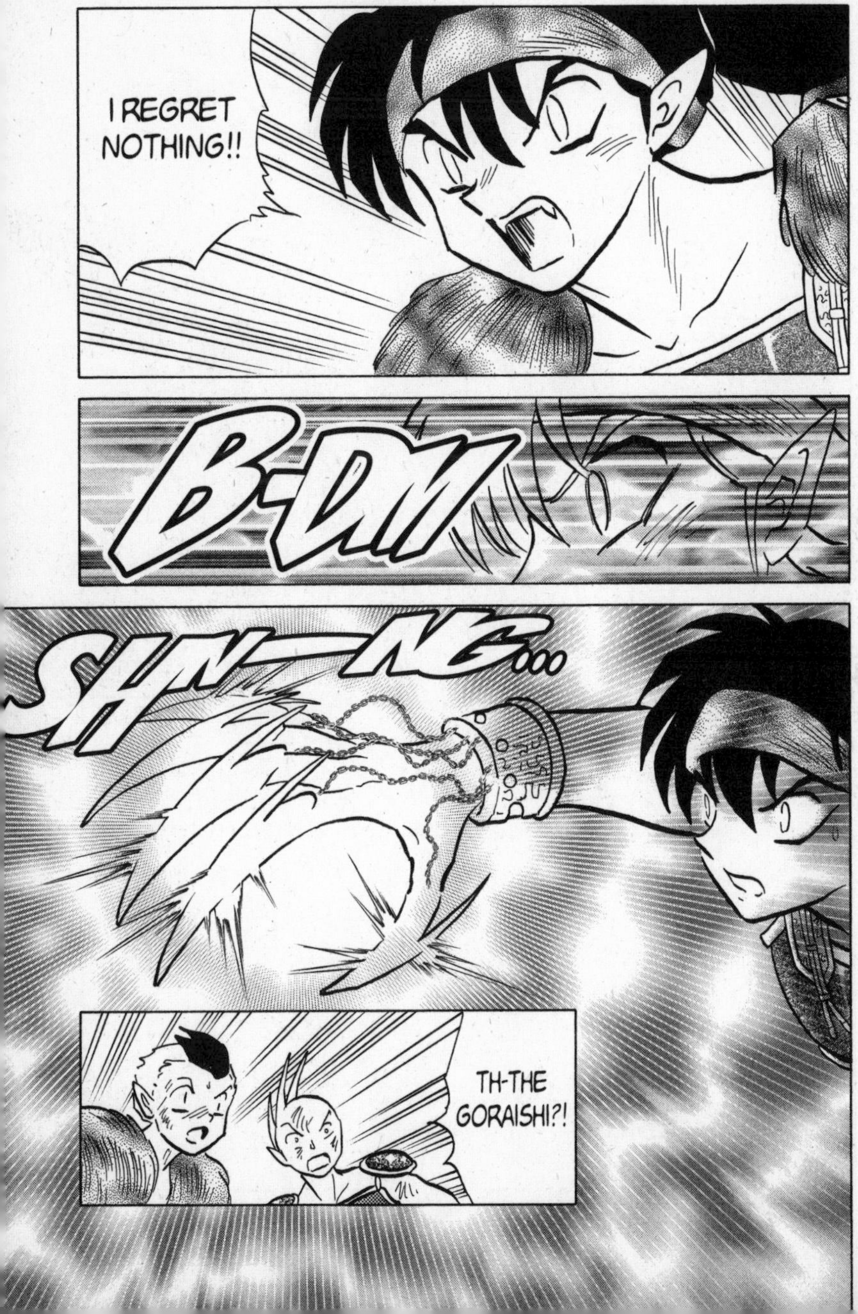
I REGRET NOTHING!!
B-DM
SHN—NG...
TH-THE GORAISHI?!

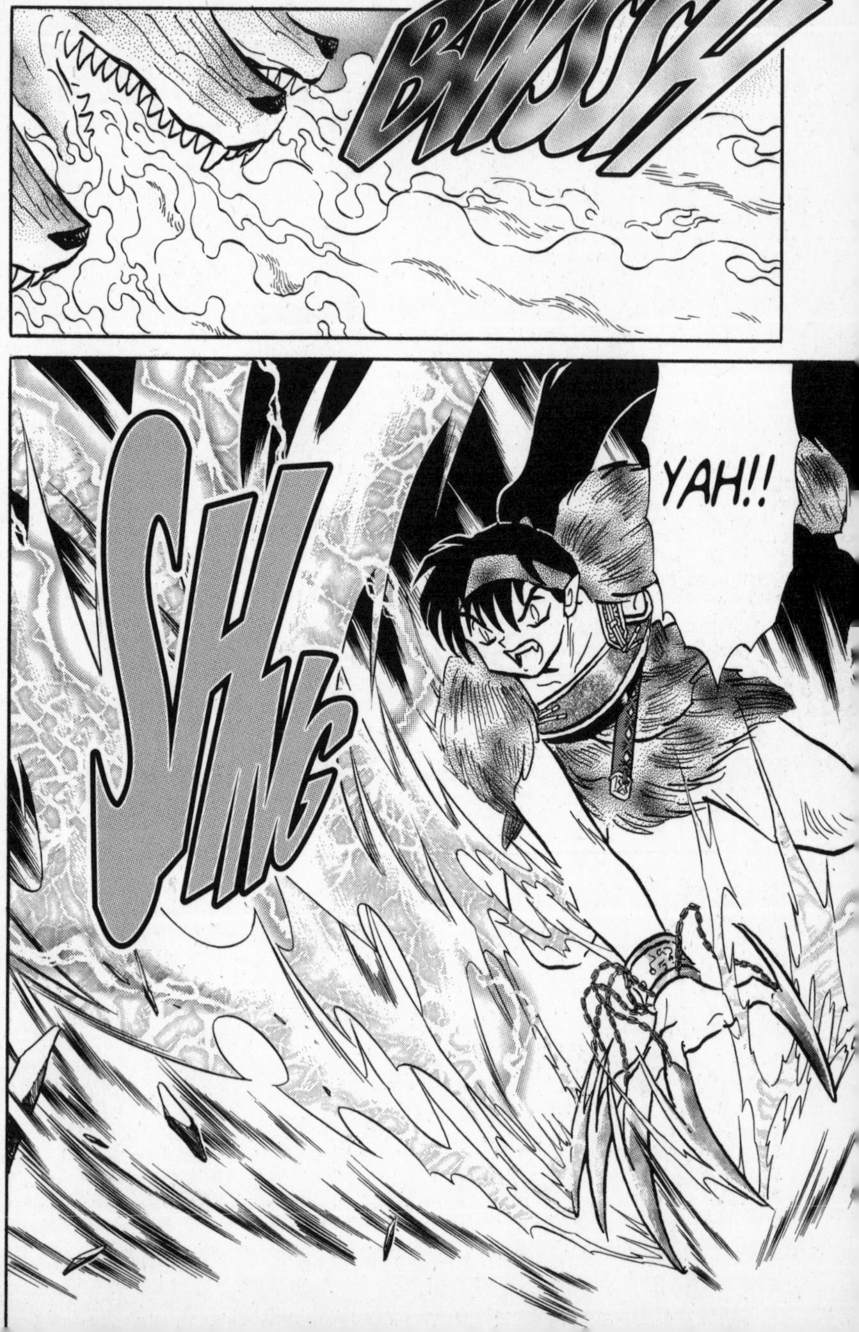
BAWOOSH
YAH!!
SHING

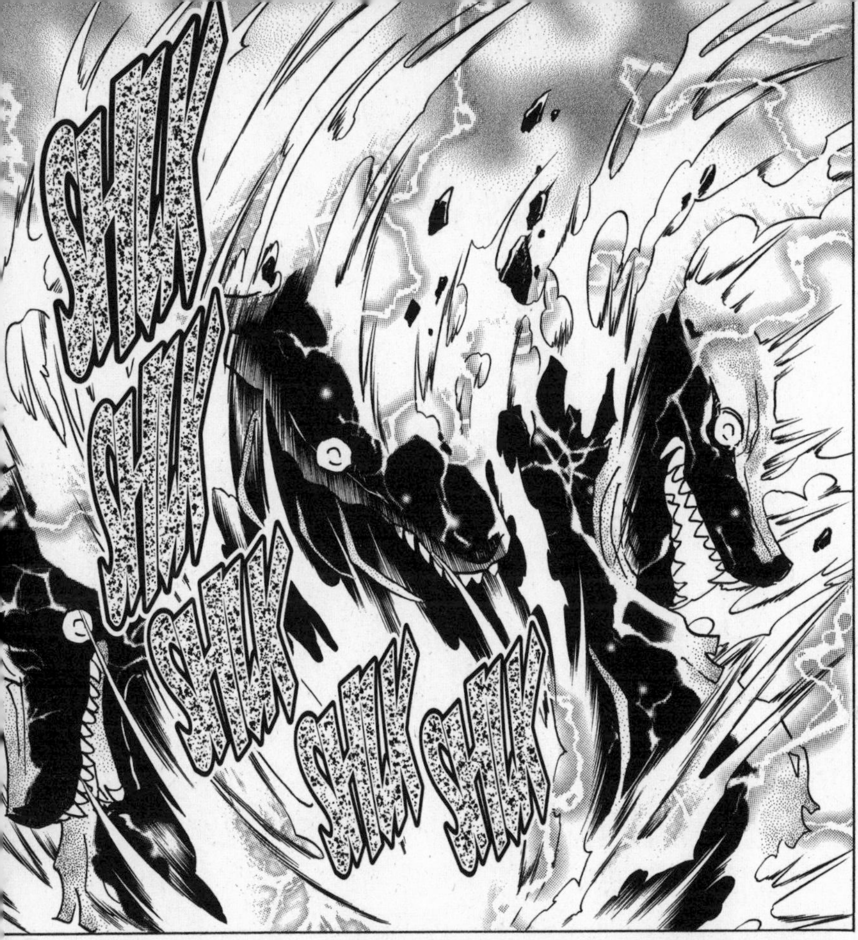
SHLK
SHLK
SHLK
SHLK
SHLK

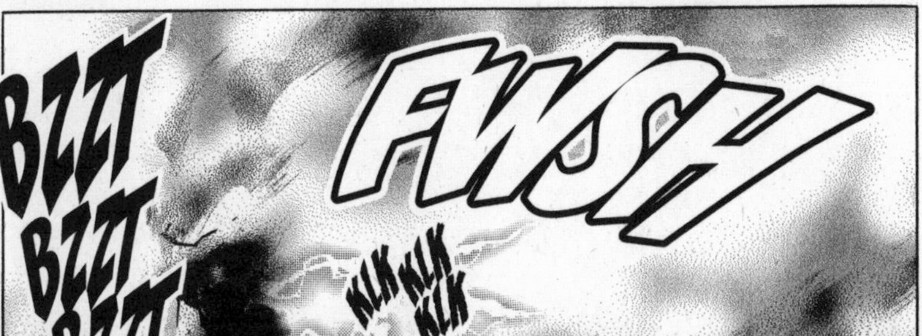
FWSH
KLK KLK KLK
BZZT BZZT BZZT

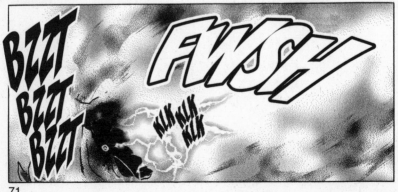

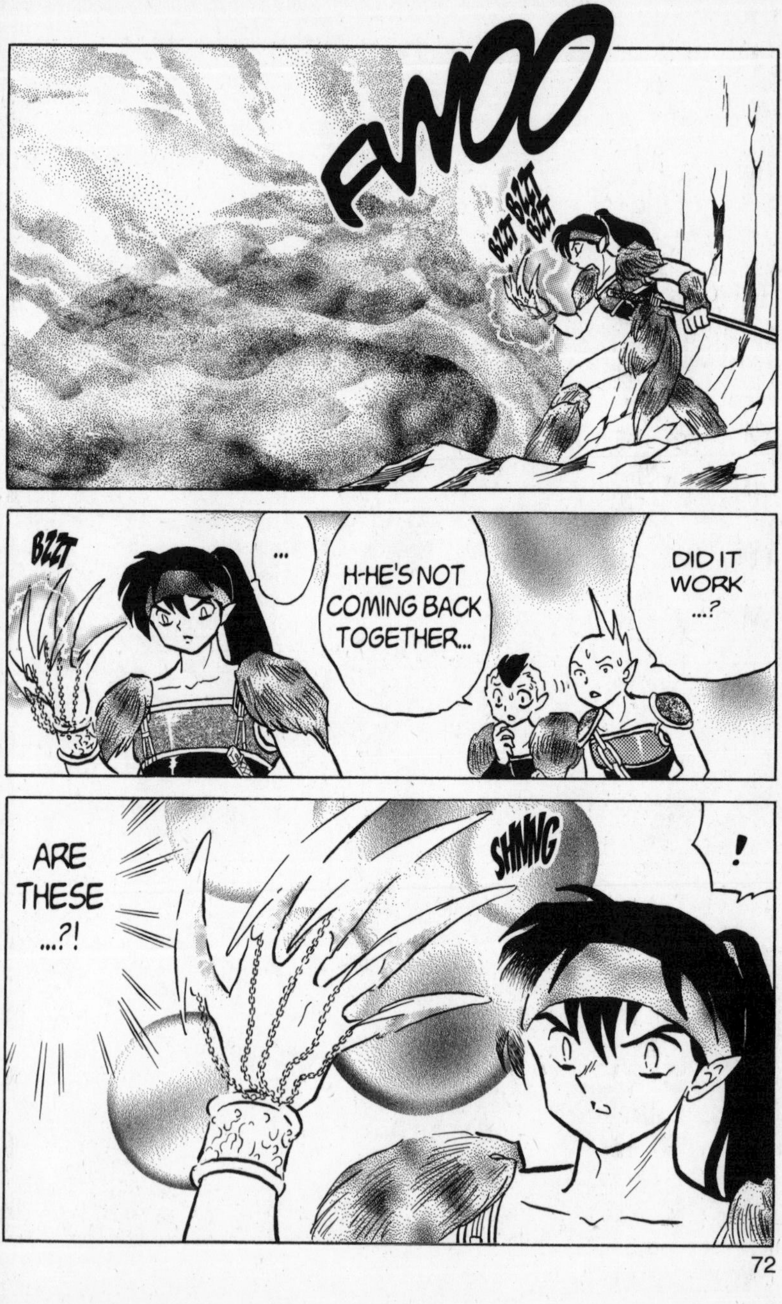
FWOO
BZZT BZZT BZZT
DID IT WORK ...?
H-HE'S NOT COMING BACK TOGETHER...
...
BZZT
!
SHNNG
ARE THESE ...?!

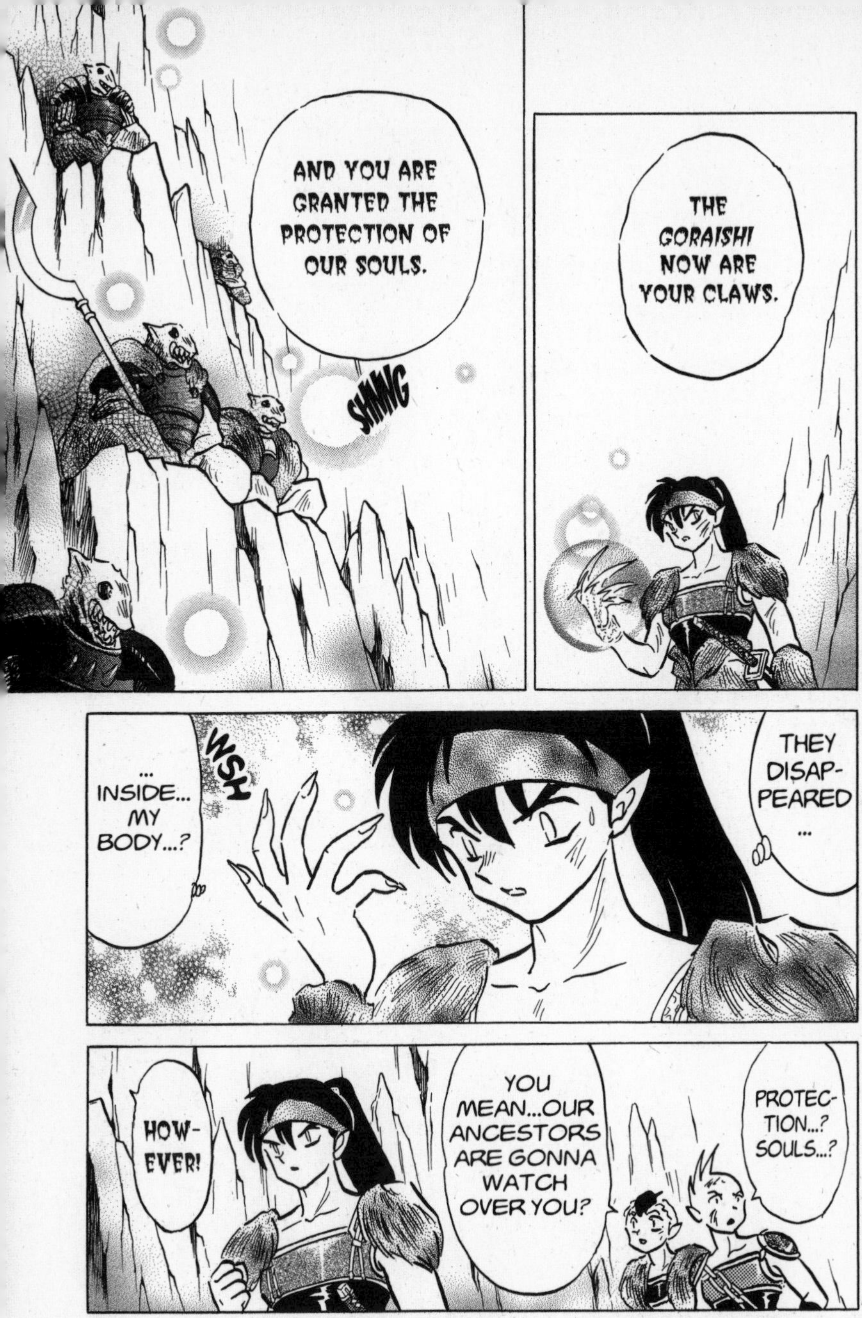
THE GORAISHI NOW ARE YOUR CLAWS.
AND YOU ARE GRANTED THE PROTECTION OF OUR SOULS.
SHING
THEY DISAP-PEARED...
WSH
...INSIDE... MY BODY...?
PROTEC-TION...? SOULS...?
YOU MEAN...OUR ANCESTORS ARE GONNA WATCH OVER YOU?
HOW-EVER!

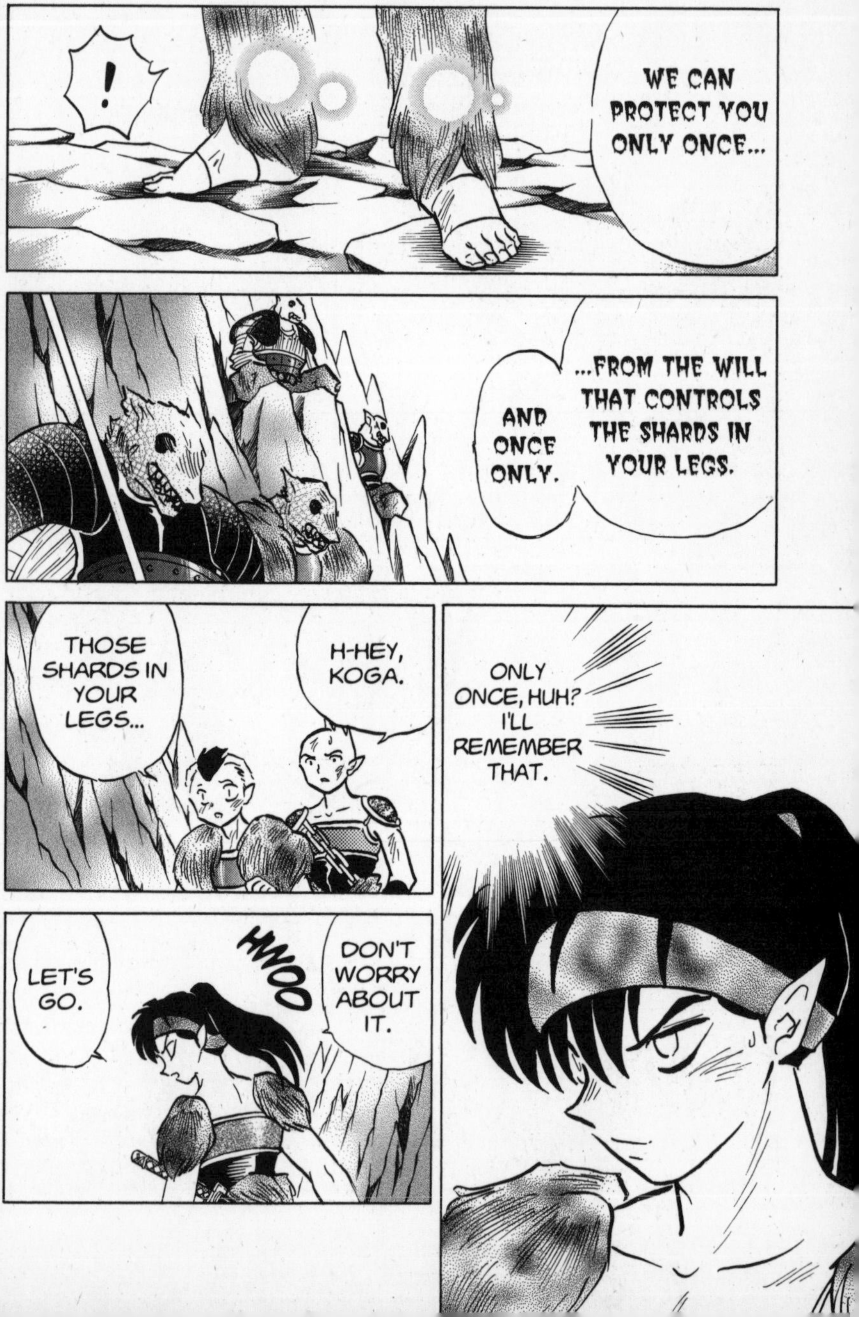
WE CAN PROTECT YOU ONLY ONCE...
!
...FROM THE WILL THAT CONTROLS THE SHARDS IN YOUR LEGS.
AND ONCE ONLY.
ONLY ONCE, HUH? I'LL REMEMBER THAT.
H-HEY, KOGA.
THOSE SHARDS IN YOUR LEGS...
DON'T WORRY ABOUT IT.
HWOO
LET'S GO.

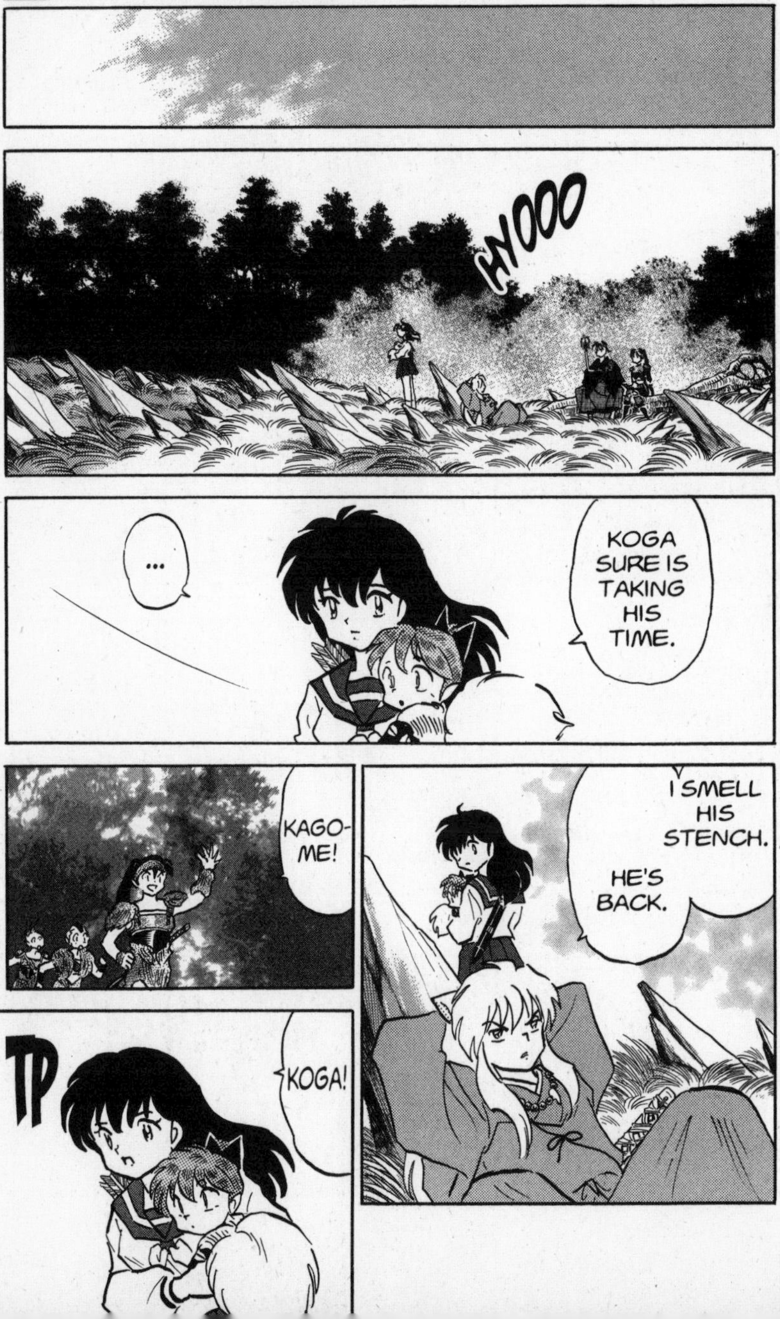
HYOOO
KOGA SURE IS TAKING HIS TIME.
...
I SMELL HIS STENCH.
HE'S BACK.
KAGO-ME!
TP
KOGA!

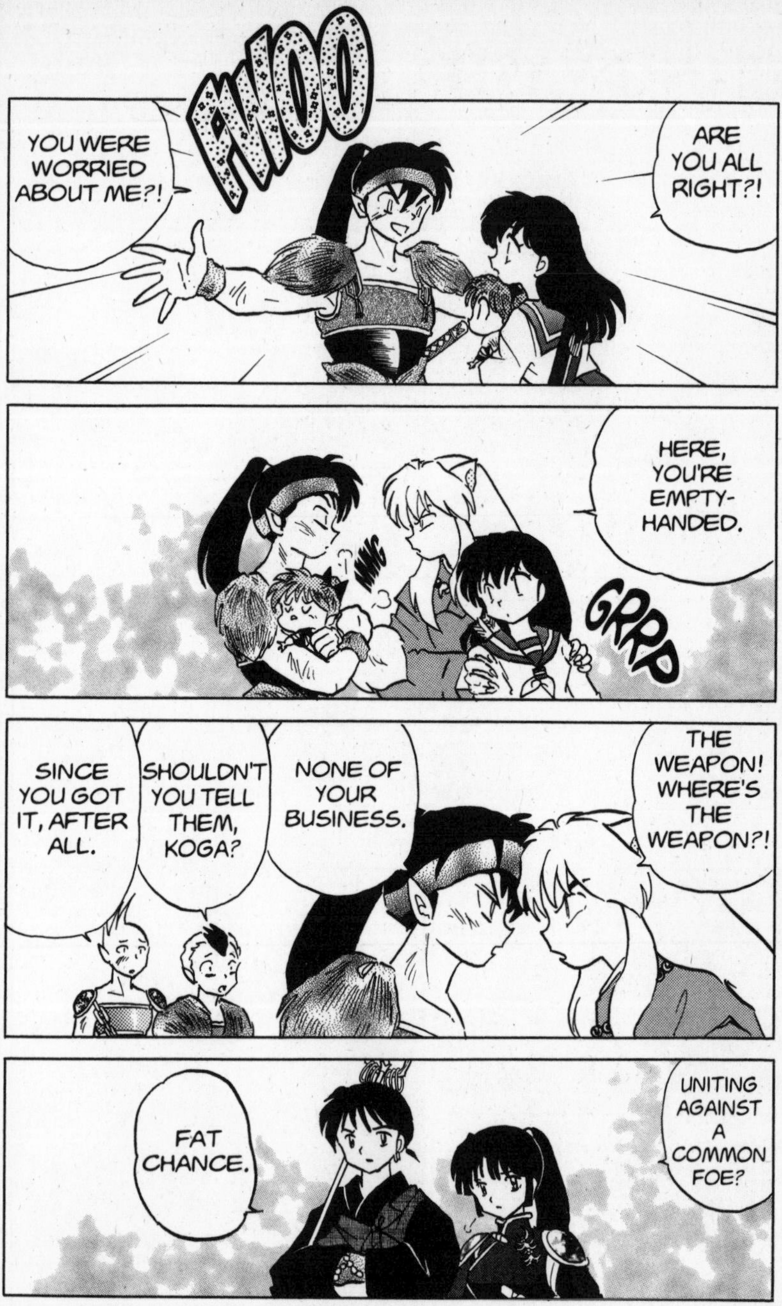
ARE YOU ALL RIGHT?!
PWOO
YOU WERE WORRIED ABOUT ME?!
HERE, YOU'RE EMPTY-HANDED.
GRRP
THE WEAPON! WHERE'S THE WEAPON?!
NONE OF YOUR BUSINESS.
SHOULDN'T YOU TELL THEM, KOGA?
SINCE YOU GOT IT, AFTER ALL.
UNITING AGAINST A COMMON FOE?
FAT CHANCE.

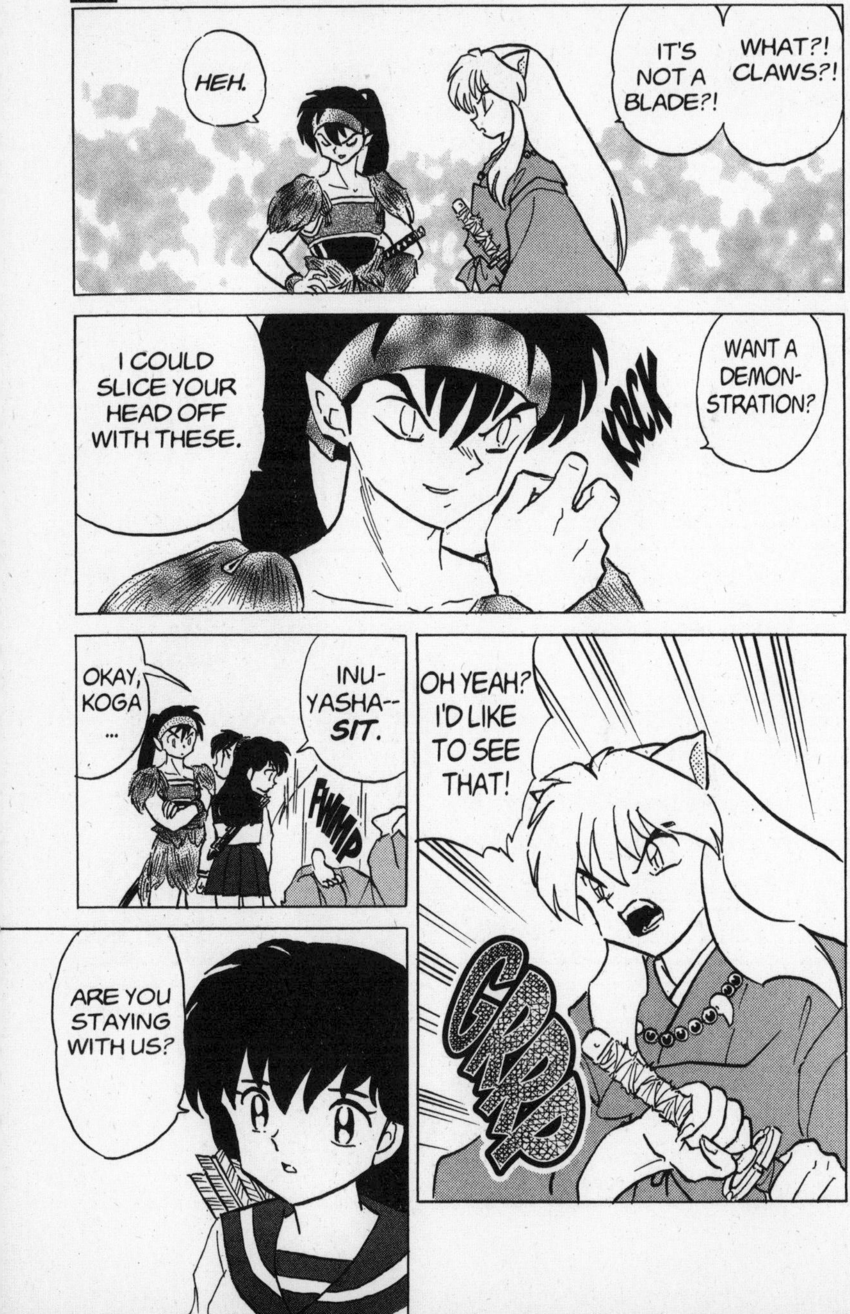
WHAT?! CLAWS?!
IT'S NOT A BLADE?!
HEH.
WANT A DEMONSTRATION?
KRCK
I COULD SLICE YOUR HEAD OFF WITH THESE.
OH YEAH? I'D LIKE TO SEE THAT!
GRIP
INU-YASHA-- SIT.
OKAY, KOGA ...
FWMP
ARE YOU STAYING WITH US?

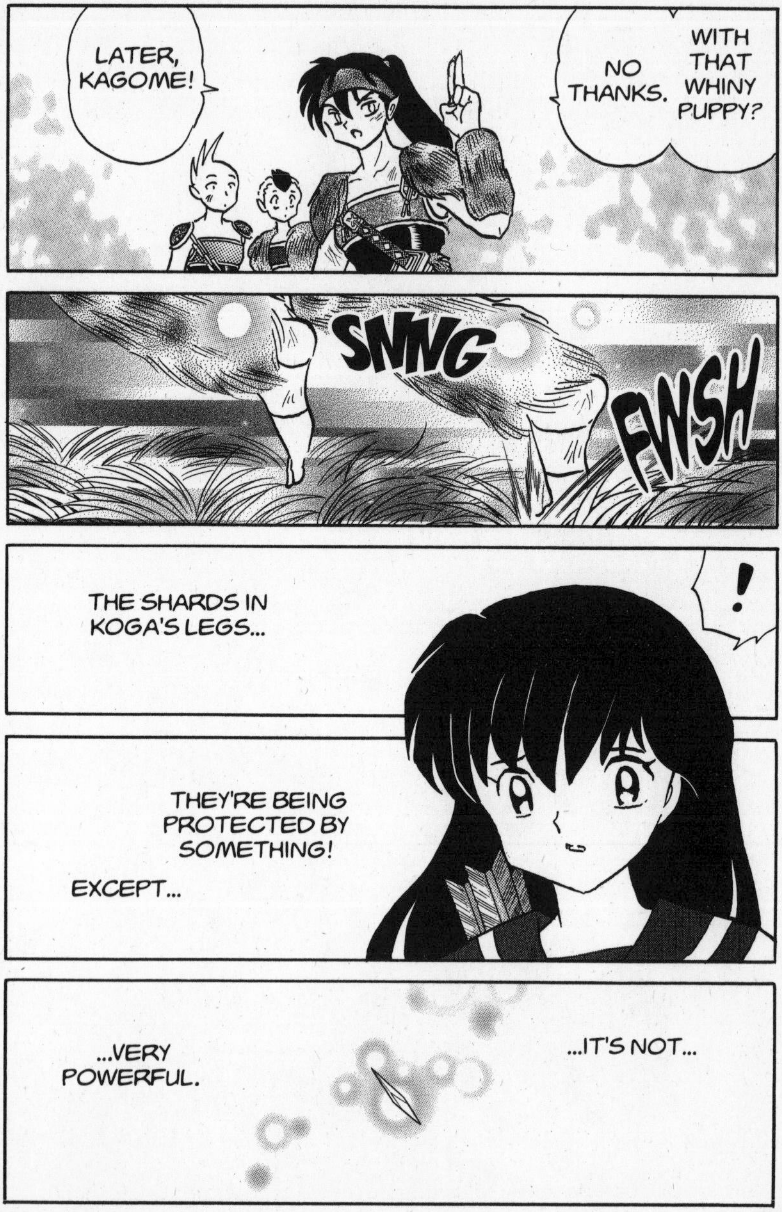
NO THANKS. WITH THAT WHINY PUPPY?
LATER, KAGOME!
FWSH
SNNG
!
THE SHARDS IN KOGA'S LEGS...
THEY'RE BEING PROTECTED BY SOMETHING!
EXCEPT...
...IT'S NOT...
...VERY POWERFUL.

SCROLL 5
MUJINA

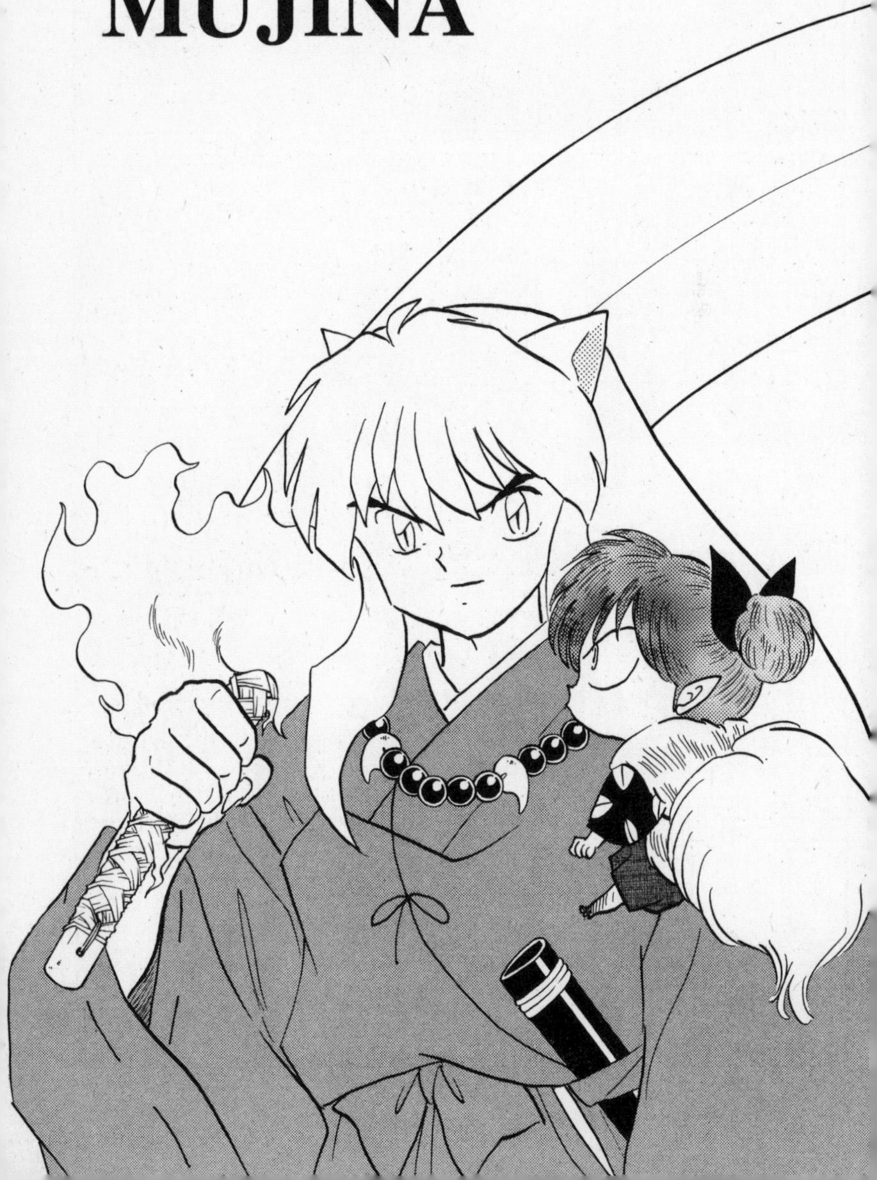

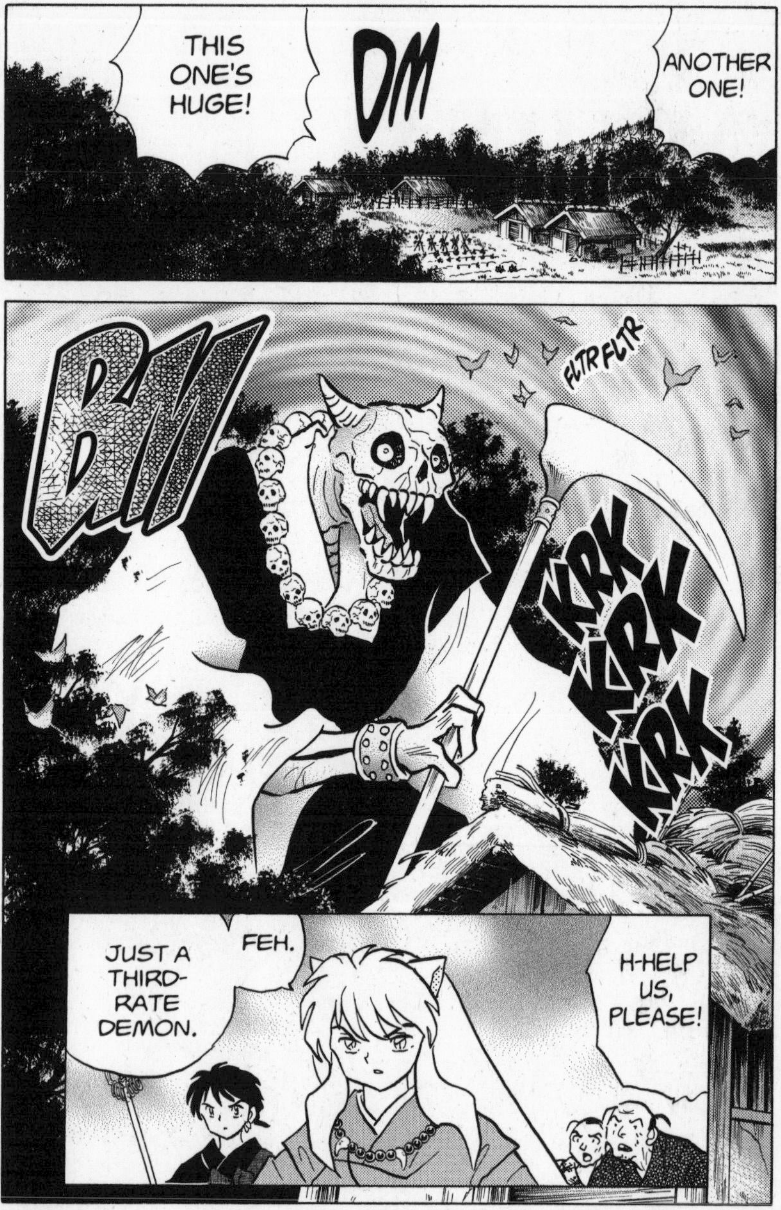
ANOTHER ONE!
DM
THIS ONE'S HUGE!
FLTR FLTR
BM
KRK KRK KRK
H-HELP US, PLEASE!
FEH.
JUST A THIRD-RATE DEMON.

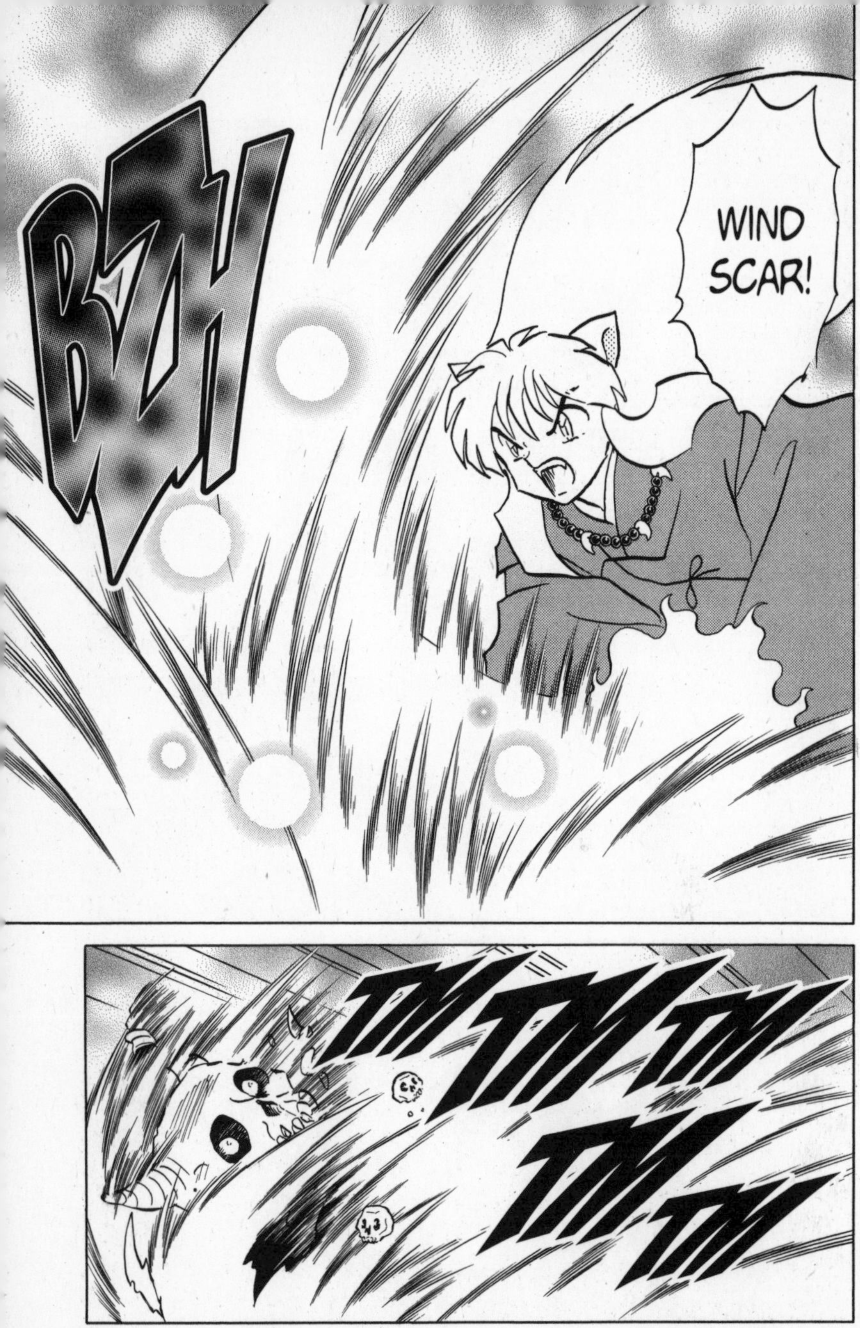
WIND SCAR!
BZZH
TMTMTM
TMTM

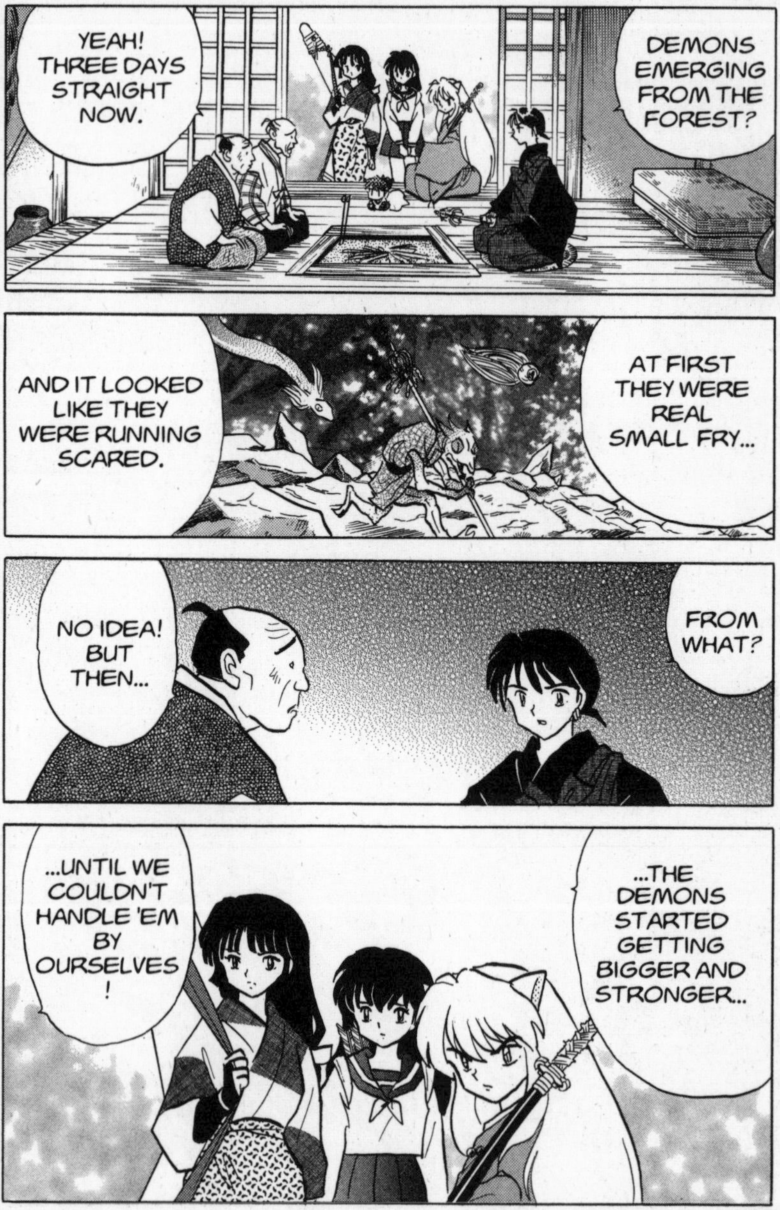
DEMONS EMERGING FROM THE FOREST?
YEAH! THREE DAYS STRAIGHT NOW.
AT FIRST THEY WERE REAL SMALL FRY...
AND IT LOOKED LIKE THEY WERE RUNNING SCARED.
FROM WHAT?
NO IDEA! BUT THEN...
...THE DEMONS STARTED GETTING BIGGER AND STRONGER...
...UNTIL WE COULDN'T HANDLE 'EM BY OURSELVES!

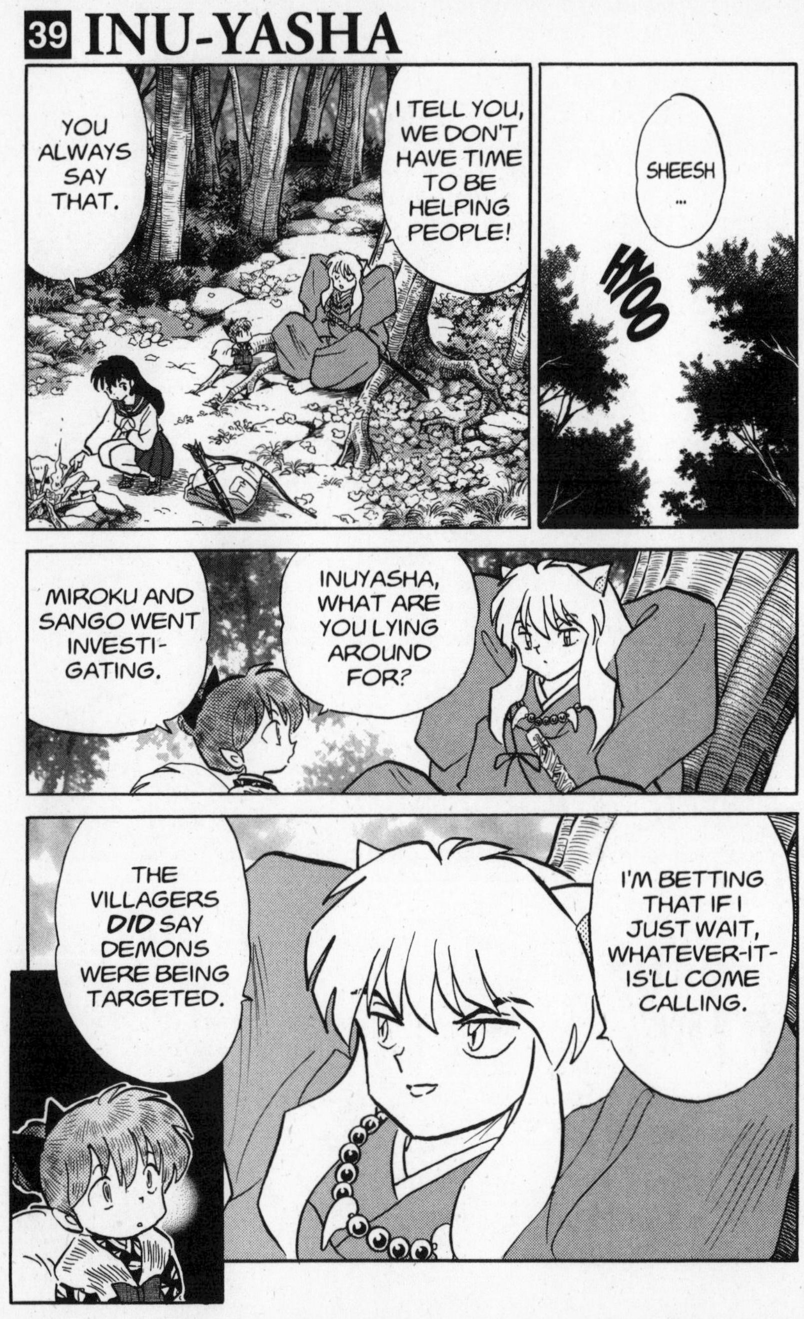
SHEESH ...
HYOO
I TELL YOU, WE DON'T HAVE TIME TO BE HELPING PEOPLE!
YOU ALWAYS SAY THAT.
INUYASHA, WHAT ARE YOU LYING AROUND FOR?
MIROKU AND SANGO WENT INVESTI-GATING.
I'M BETTING THAT IF I JUST WAIT, WHATEVER-IT-IS'LL COME CALLING.
THE VILLAGERS *DID* SAY DEMONS WERE BEING TARGETED.

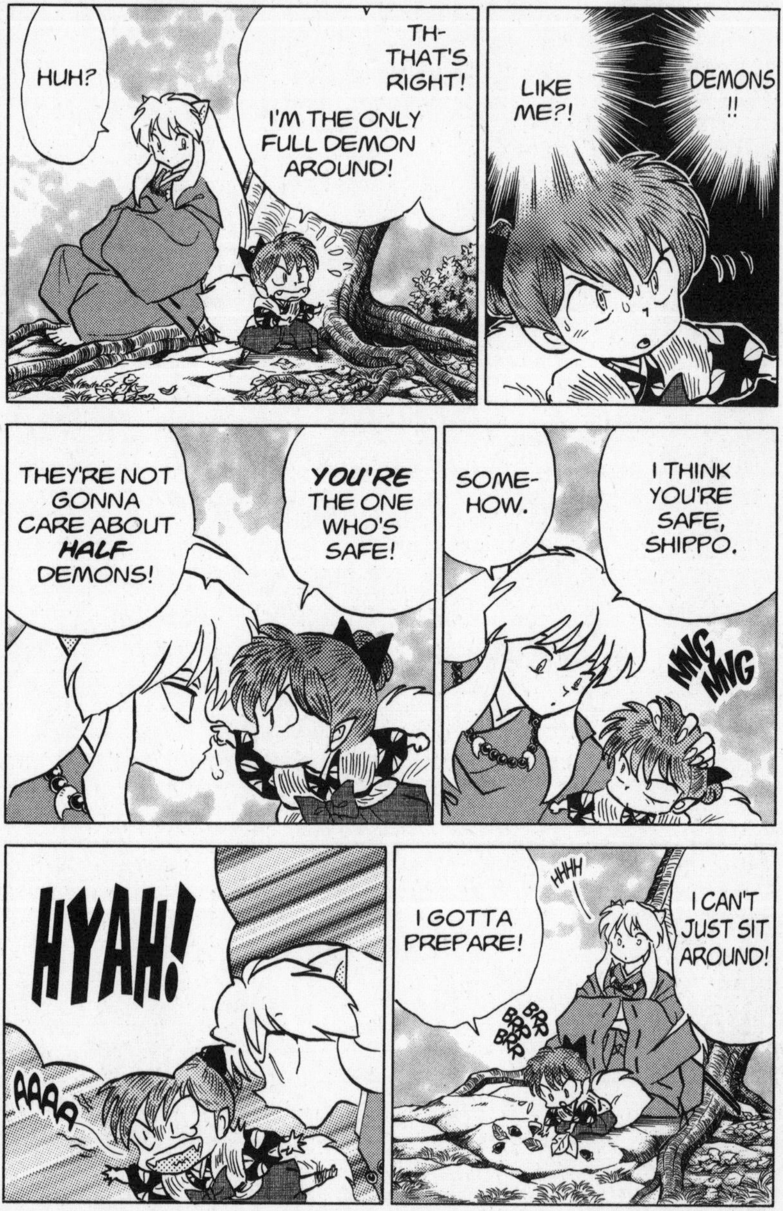
DEMONS !!
LIKE ME?!
TH- THAT'S RIGHT!
I'M THE ONLY FULL DEMON AROUND!
HUH?
I THINK YOU'RE SAFE, SHIPPO.
SOME- HOW.
MNG MNG
YOU'RE THE ONE WHO'S SAFE!
THEY'RE NOT GONNA CARE ABOUT HALF DEMONS!
I CAN'T JUST SIT AROUND!
HHHH
I GOTTA PREPARE!
BRR BRR BRR
HYAH!
AAAA

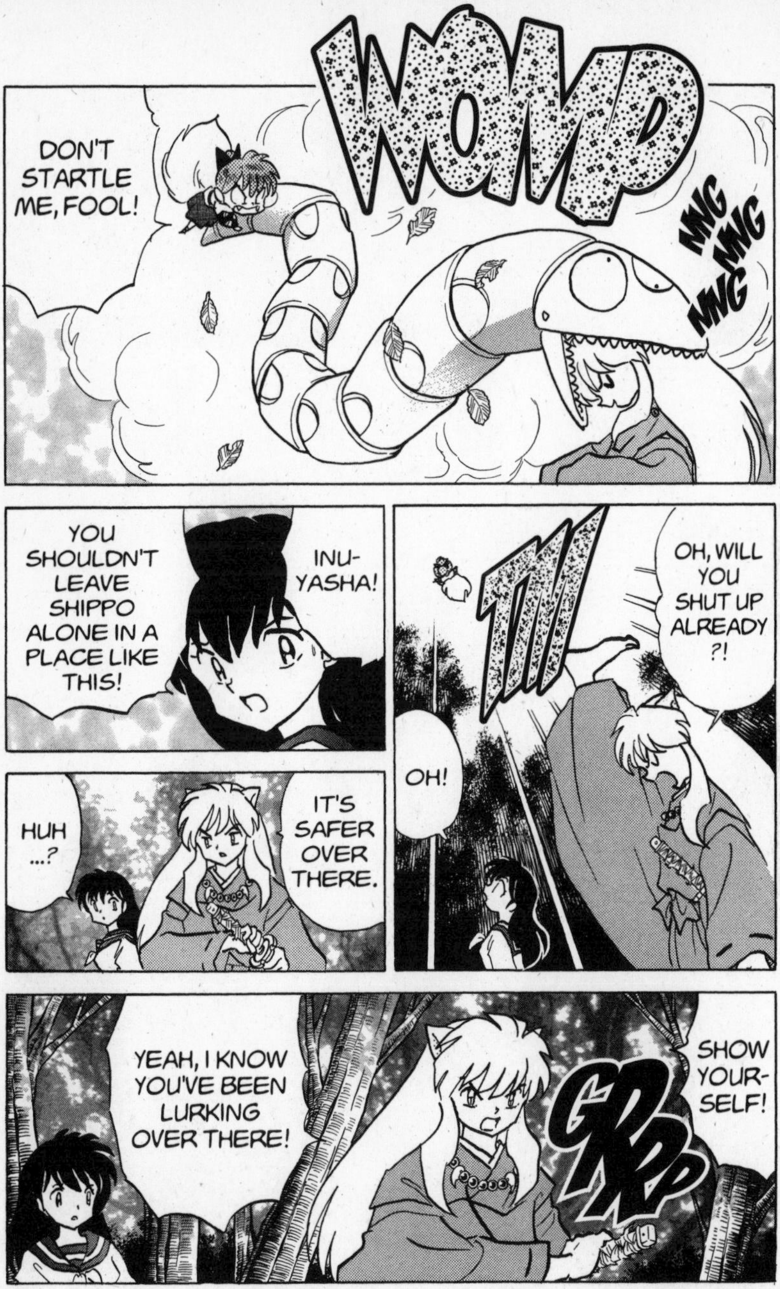
WOMP
MNG MNG MNG
DON'T STARTLE ME, FOOL!
OH, WILL YOU SHUT UP ALREADY ?!
OH!
INU-YASHA!
YOU SHOULDN'T LEAVE SHIPPO ALONE IN A PLACE LIKE THIS!
IT'S SAFER OVER THERE.
HUH ...?
SHOW YOUR-SELF!
YEAH, I KNOW YOU'VE BEEN LURKING OVER THERE!

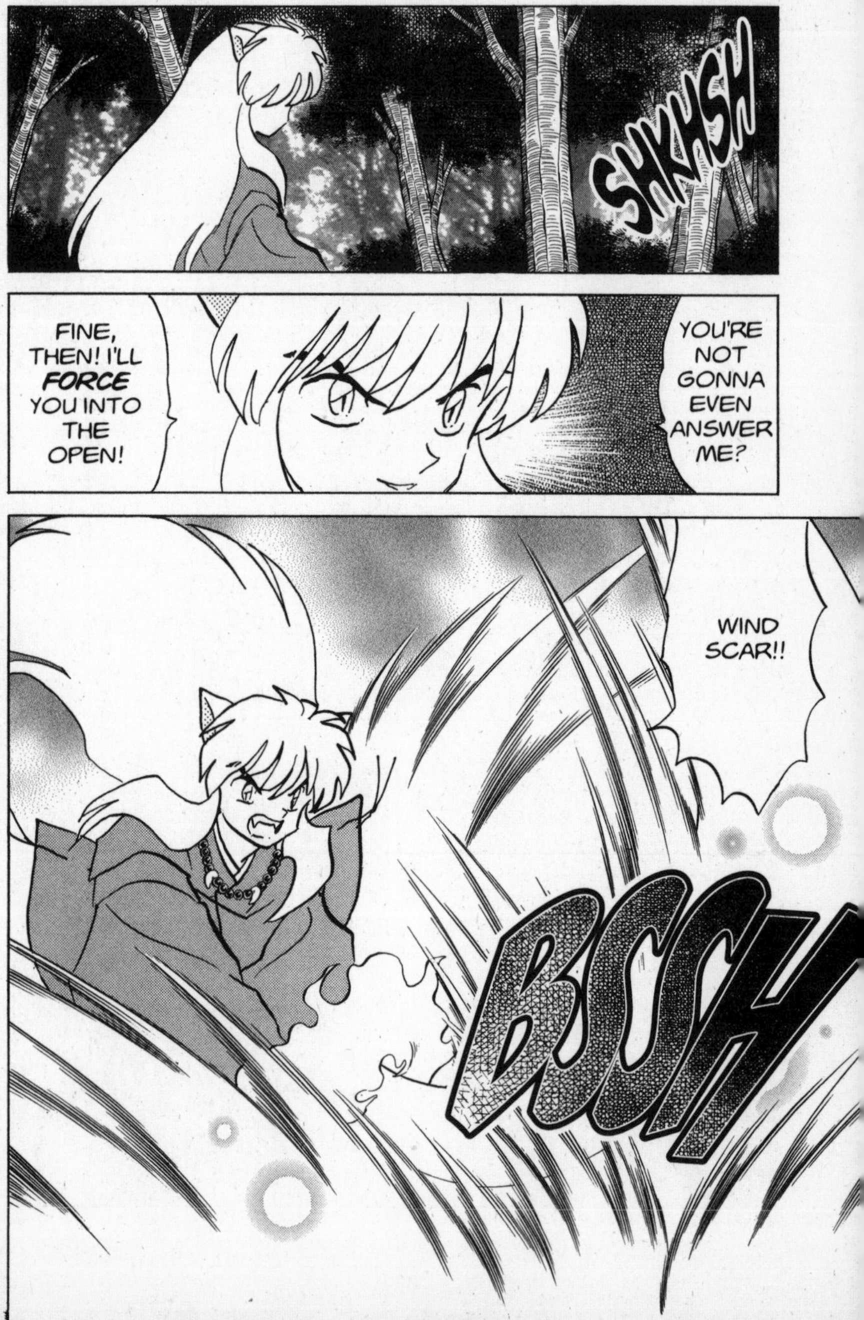
SHKSH
YOU'RE NOT GONNA EVEN ANSWER ME?
FINE, THEN! I'LL FORCE YOU INTO THE OPEN!
WIND SCAR!!
BSCH

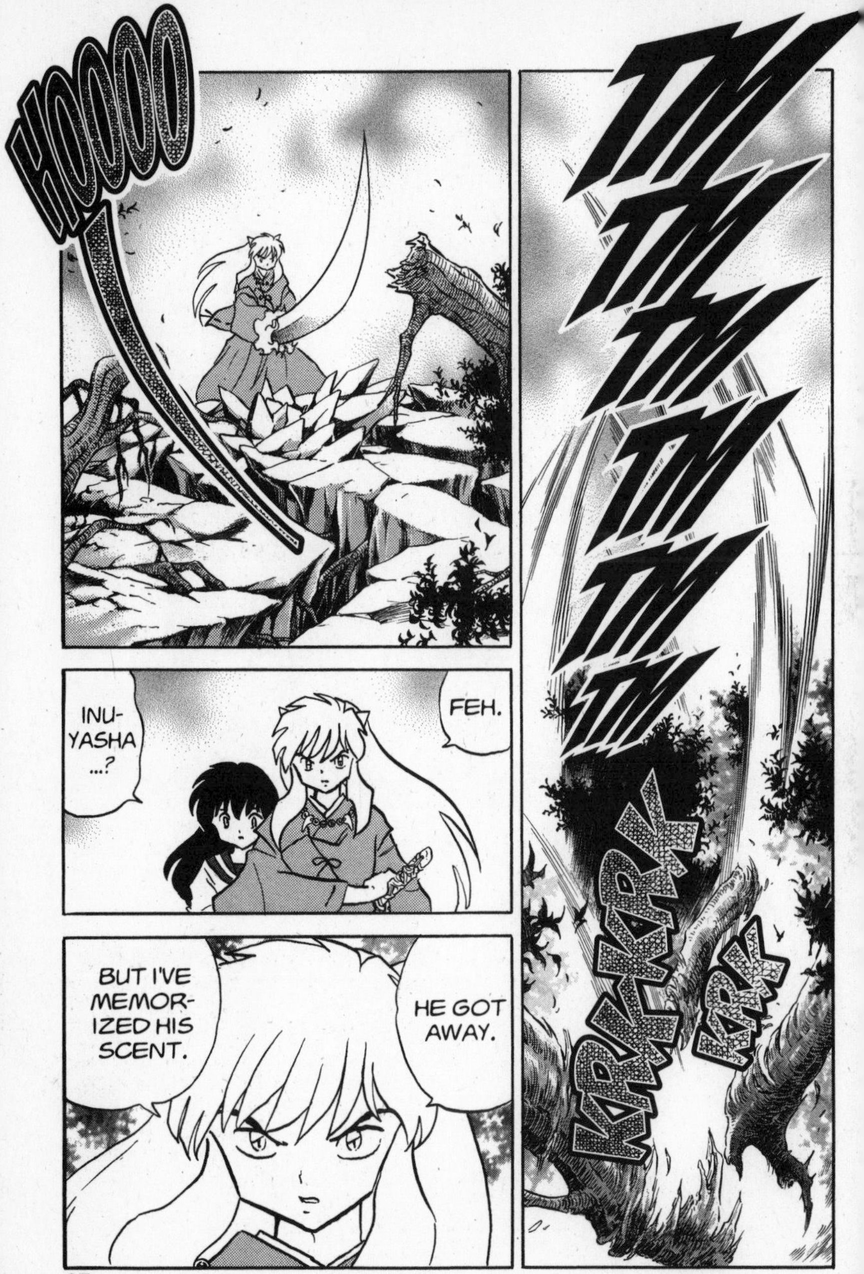
TMTMTMTMTMTM
KRAKKRAK
KRAK
HOOOO
FEH.
INU-YASHA...?
HE GOT AWAY.
BUT I'VE MEMORIZED HIS SCENT.

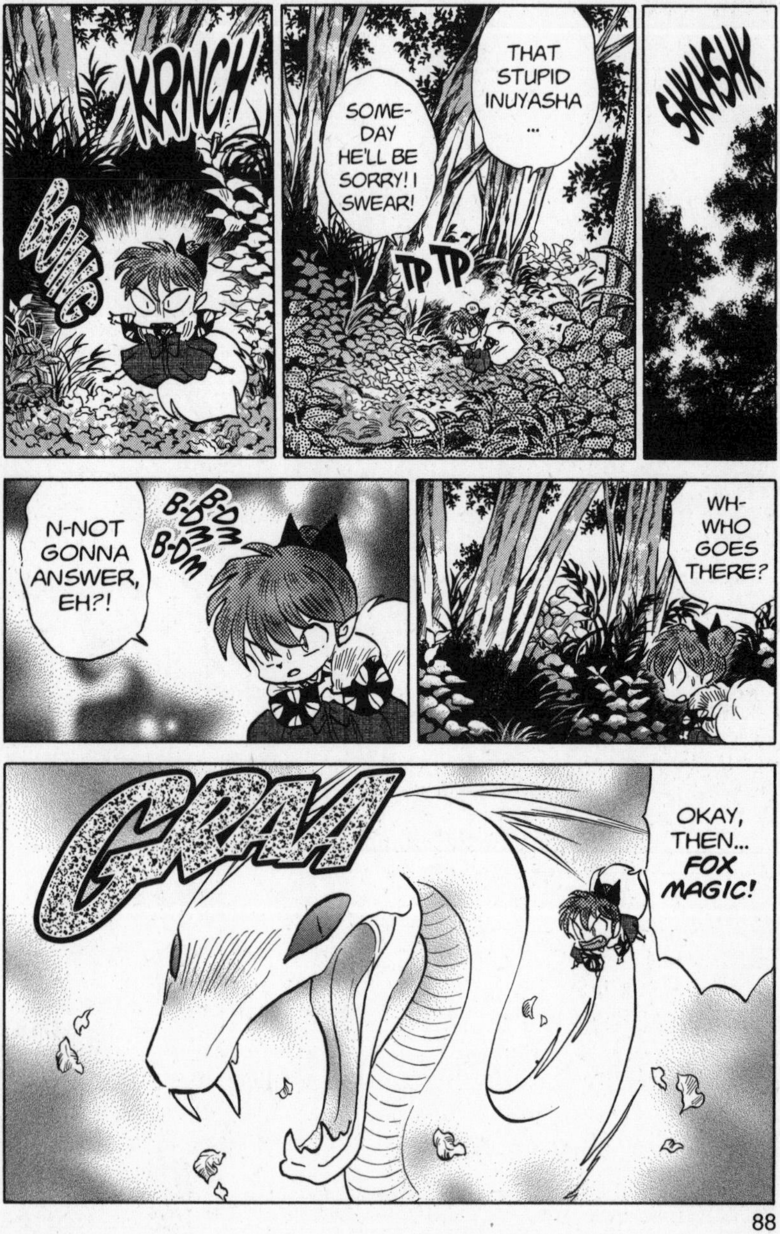
SHKSHK
THAT STUPID INUYASHA...
SOMEDAY HE'LL BE SORRY! I SWEAR!
TP TP
KRNCH
BOING
WH-WHO GOES THERE?
B-DM B-DM B-DM
N-NOT GONNA ANSWER, EH?!
OKAY, THEN... ***FOX MAGIC!***
GRAA

MY SPELL WAS NULLIFIED?!

WHA...?

CRACK

SCHWNG

EH?!

BLZT BLZT BLZT

THEN TAKE THIS!

GRRP

WOOSH

SMASHING TOP!

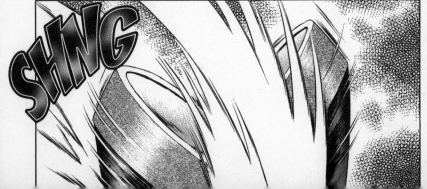

SHNG

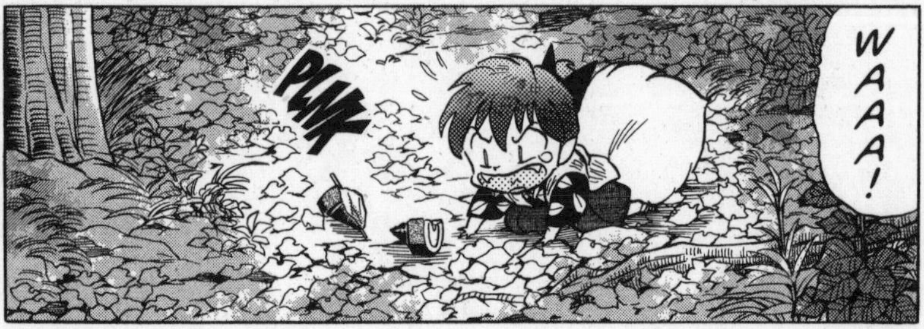
WAAAA!
PLINK
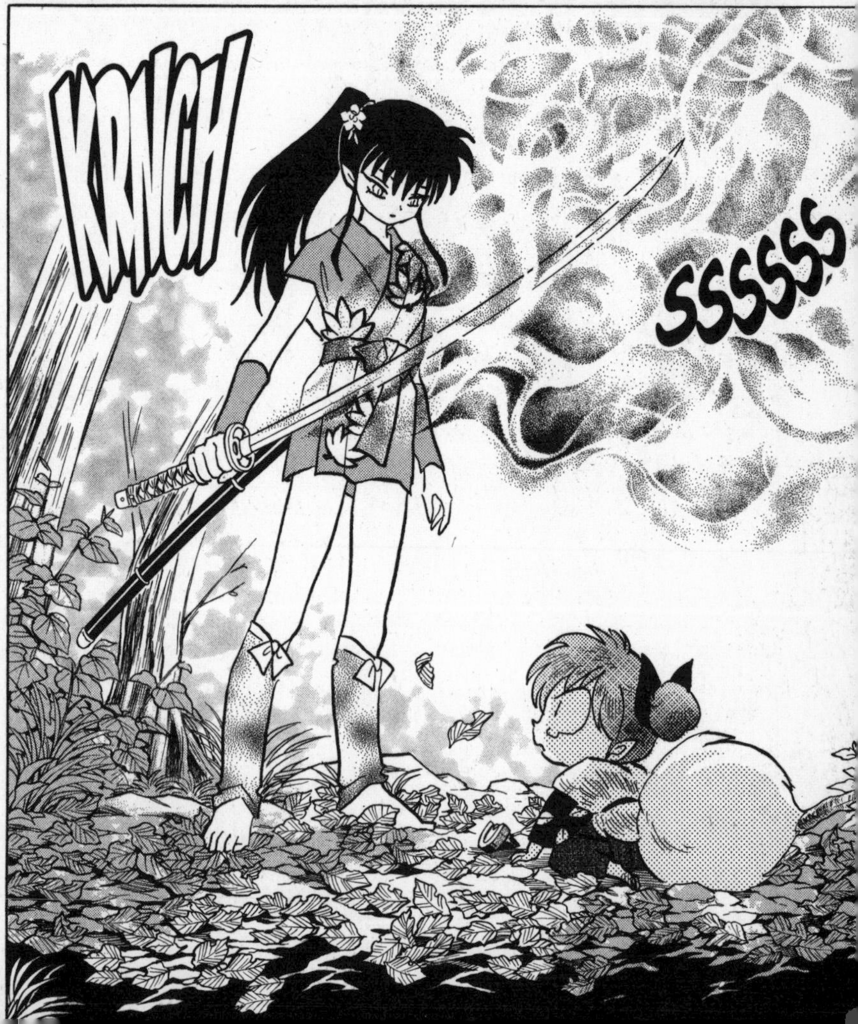
SSSSSS
KRNCH

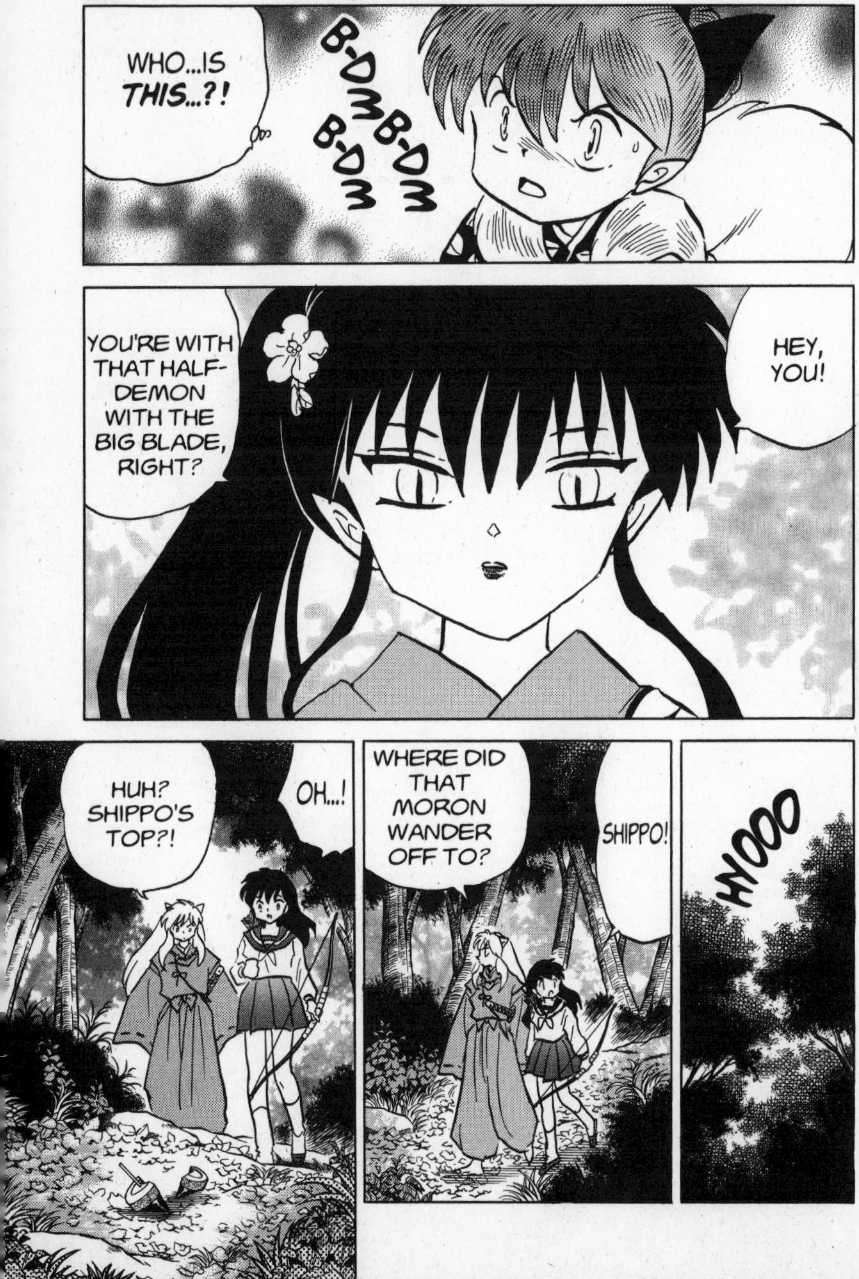
WHO...IS THIS...?!
B-DMB-DM B-DM
HEY, YOU!
YOU'RE WITH THAT HALF-DEMON WITH THE BIG BLADE, RIGHT?
HYOOO
SHIPPO!
WHERE DID THAT MORON WANDER OFF TO?
OH...!
HUH? SHIPPO'S TOP?!

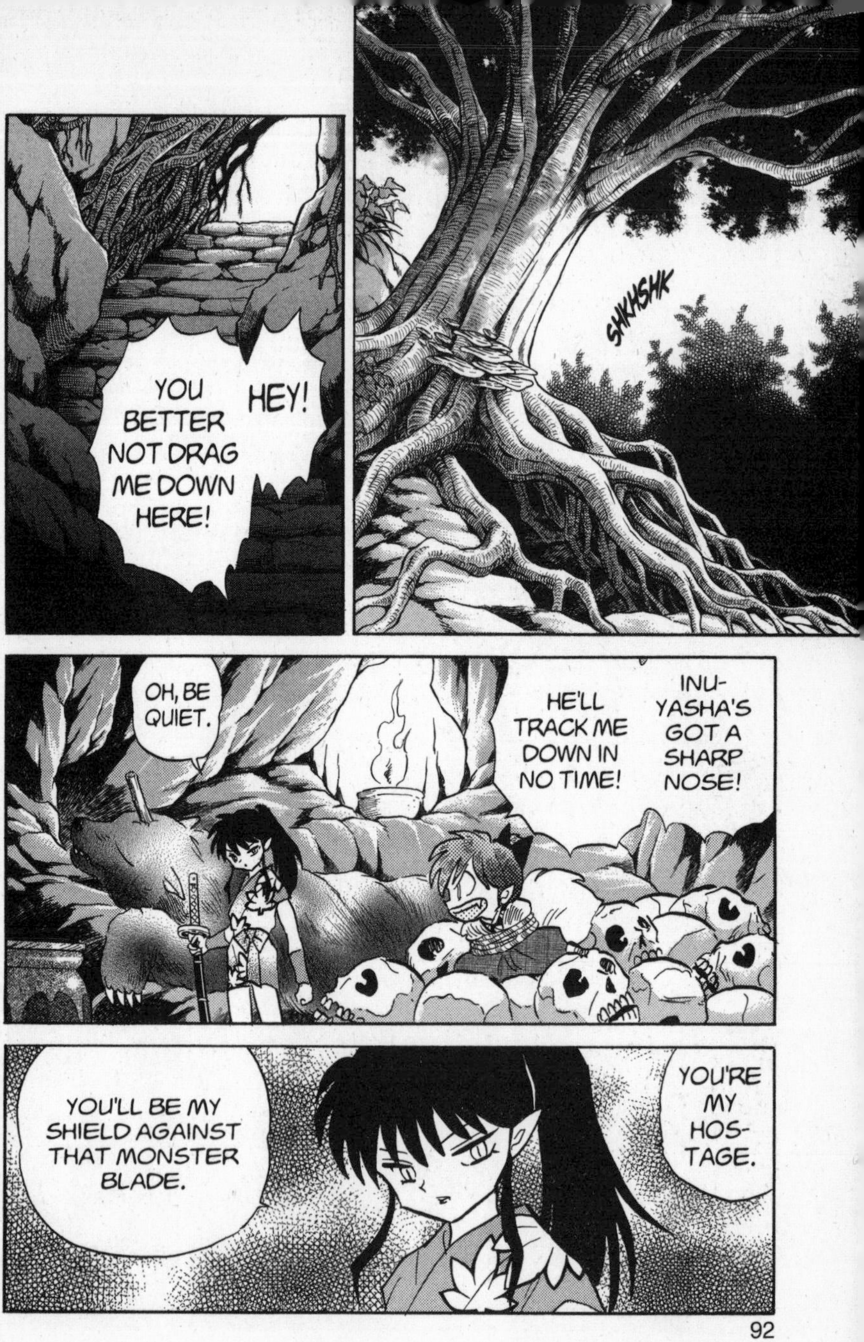
SHKHSHK
HEY!
YOU BETTER NOT DRAG ME DOWN HERE!
INU-YASHA'S GOT A SHARP NOSE!
HE'LL TRACK ME DOWN IN NO TIME!
OH, BE QUIET.
YOU'RE MY HOS-TAGE.
YOU'LL BE MY SHIELD AGAINST THAT MONSTER BLADE.

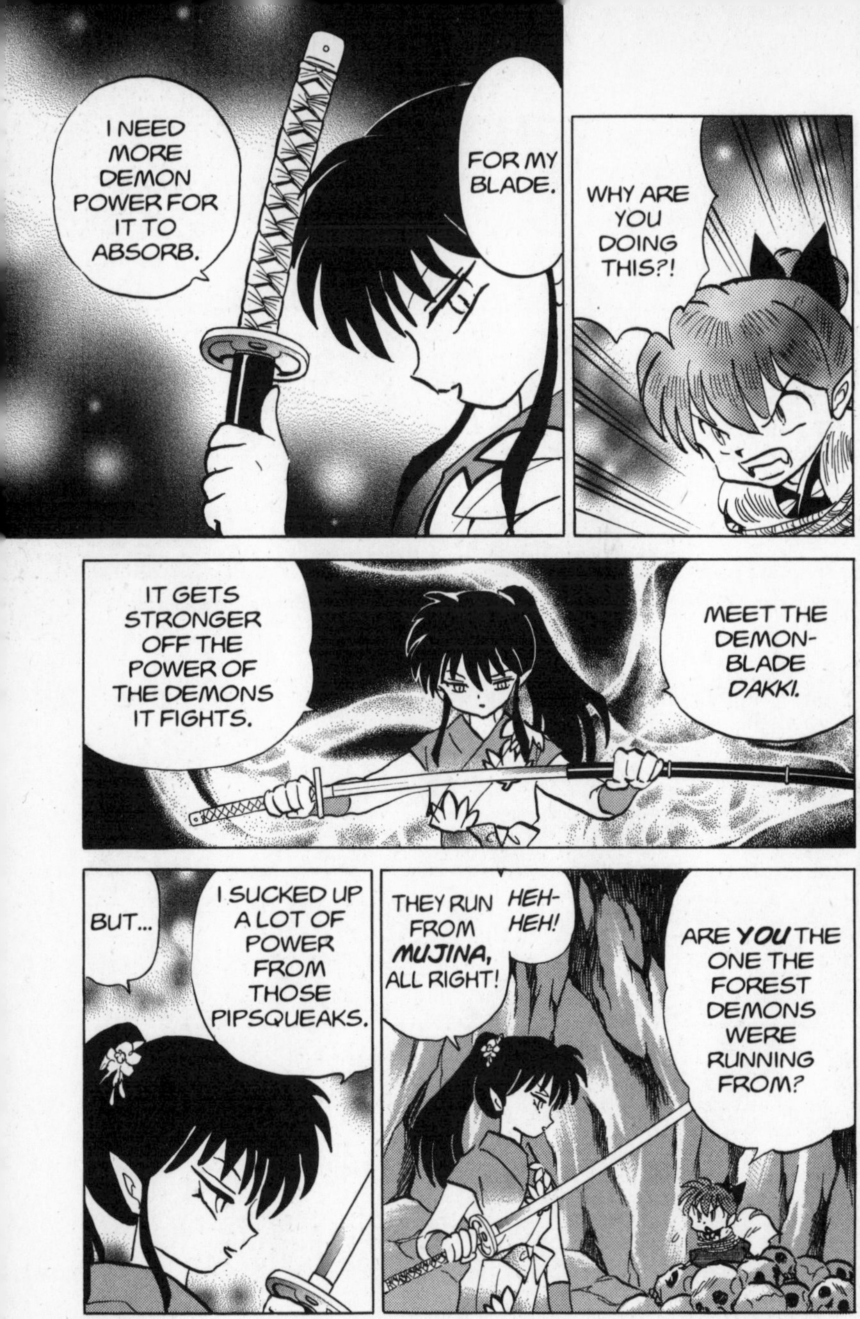
WHY ARE YOU DOING THIS?!
FOR MY BLADE.
I NEED MORE DEMON POWER FOR IT TO ABSORB.
MEET THE DEMON-BLADE DAKKI.
IT GETS STRONGER OFF THE POWER OF THE DEMONS IT FIGHTS.
ARE YOU THE ONE THE FOREST DEMONS WERE RUNNING FROM?
HEH-HEH!
THEY RUN FROM MUJINA, ALL RIGHT!
I SUCKED UP A LOT OF POWER FROM THOSE PIPSQUEAKS.
BUT...

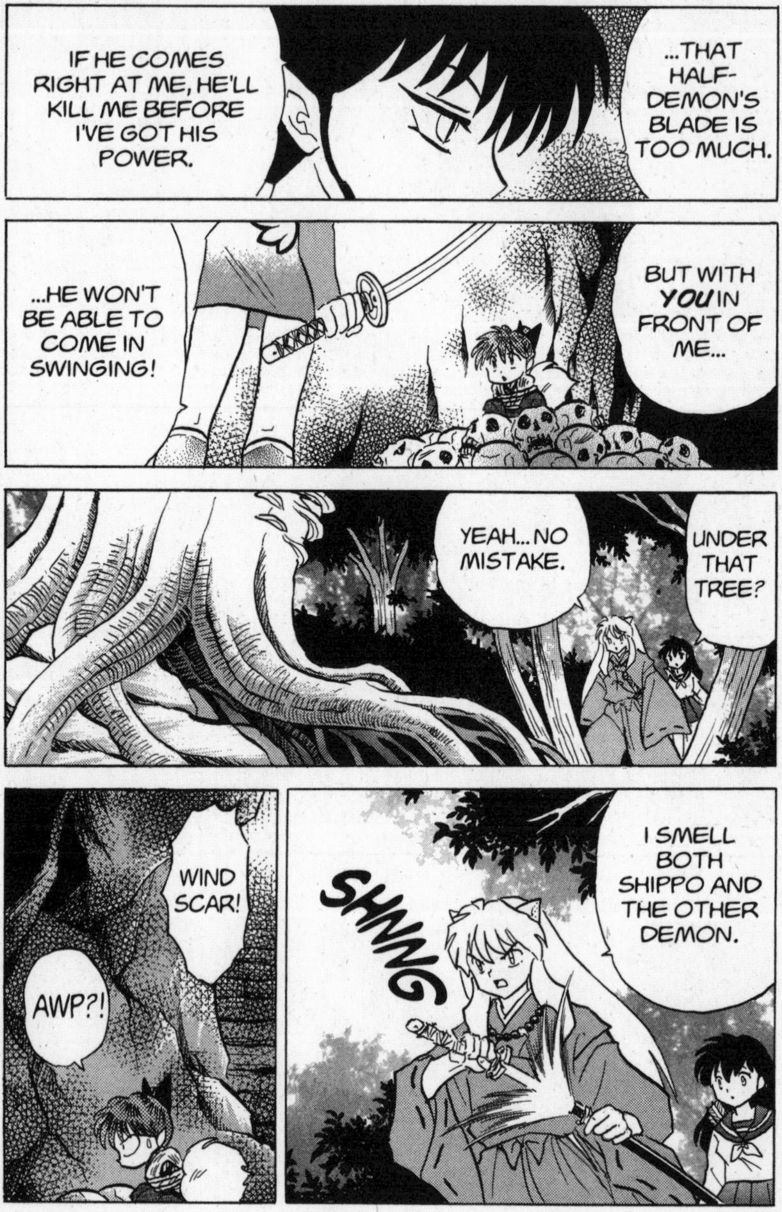
...THAT HALF-DEMON'S BLADE IS TOO MUCH.
IF HE COMES RIGHT AT ME, HE'LL KILL ME BEFORE I'VE GOT HIS POWER.
BUT WITH *YOU* IN FRONT OF ME...
...HE WON'T BE ABLE TO COME IN SWINGING!
UNDER THAT TREE?
YEAH... NO MISTAKE.
I SMELL BOTH SHIPPO AND THE OTHER DEMON.
SHNNG
WIND SCAR!
AWP?!

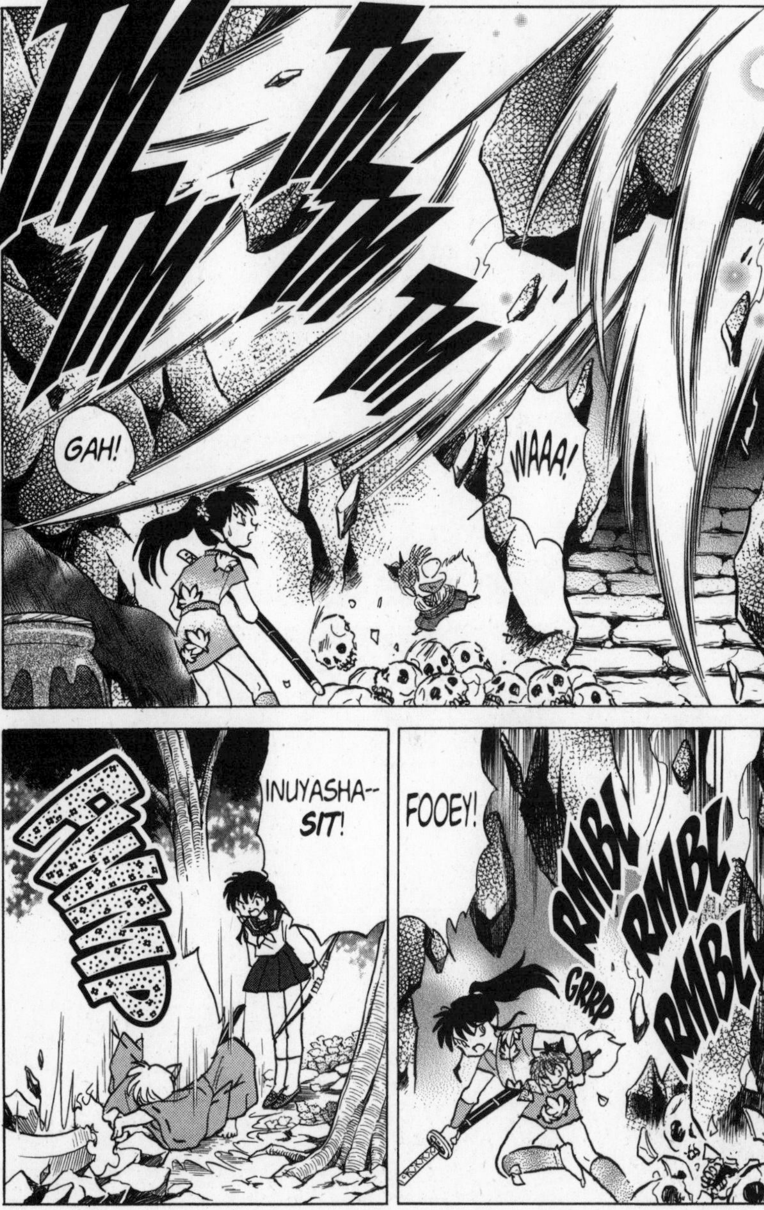
WAAA!
GAH!
FOOEY!
RMBL
RMBL
RMBL
GRRP
INUYASHA--
SIT!

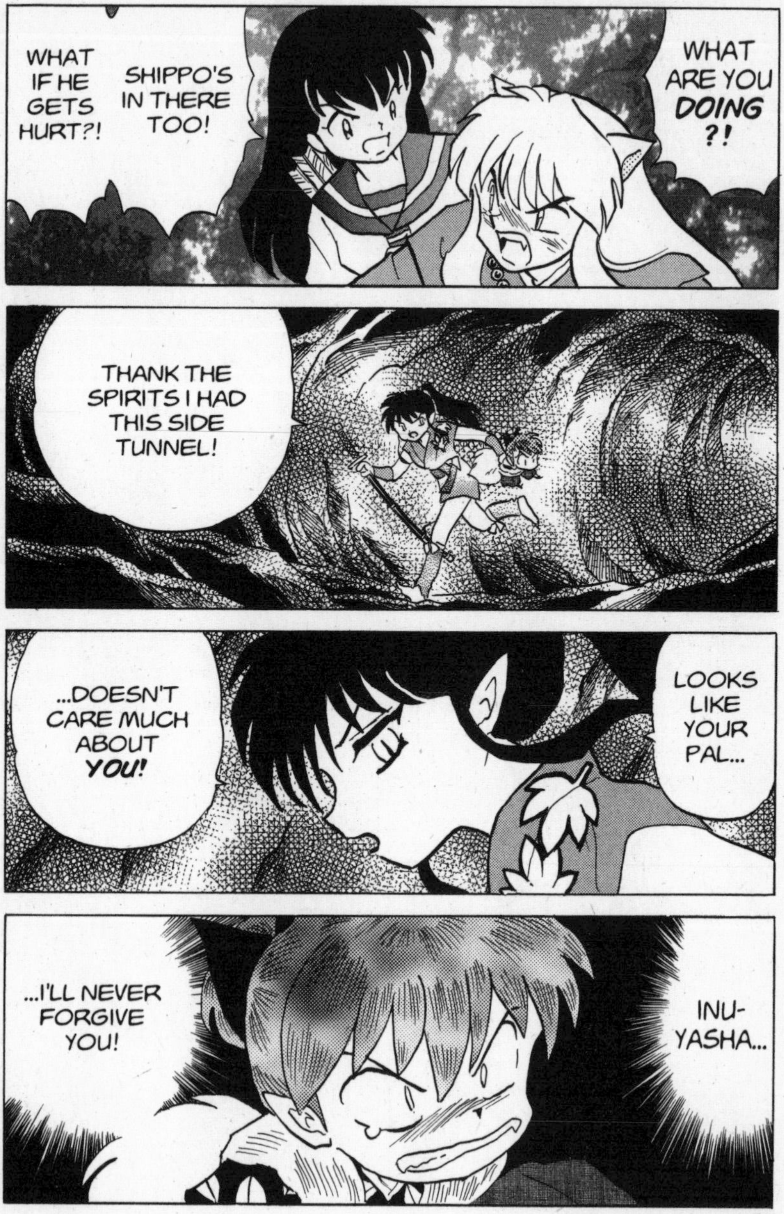
WHAT ARE YOU DOING?!
SHIPPO'S IN THERE TOO!
WHAT IF HE GETS HURT?!
THANK THE SPIRITS I HAD THIS SIDE TUNNEL!
LOOKS LIKE YOUR PAL...
...DOESN'T CARE MUCH ABOUT YOU!
INU-YASHA...
...I'LL NEVER FORGIVE YOU!

SCROLL 6
JUST CAUSES

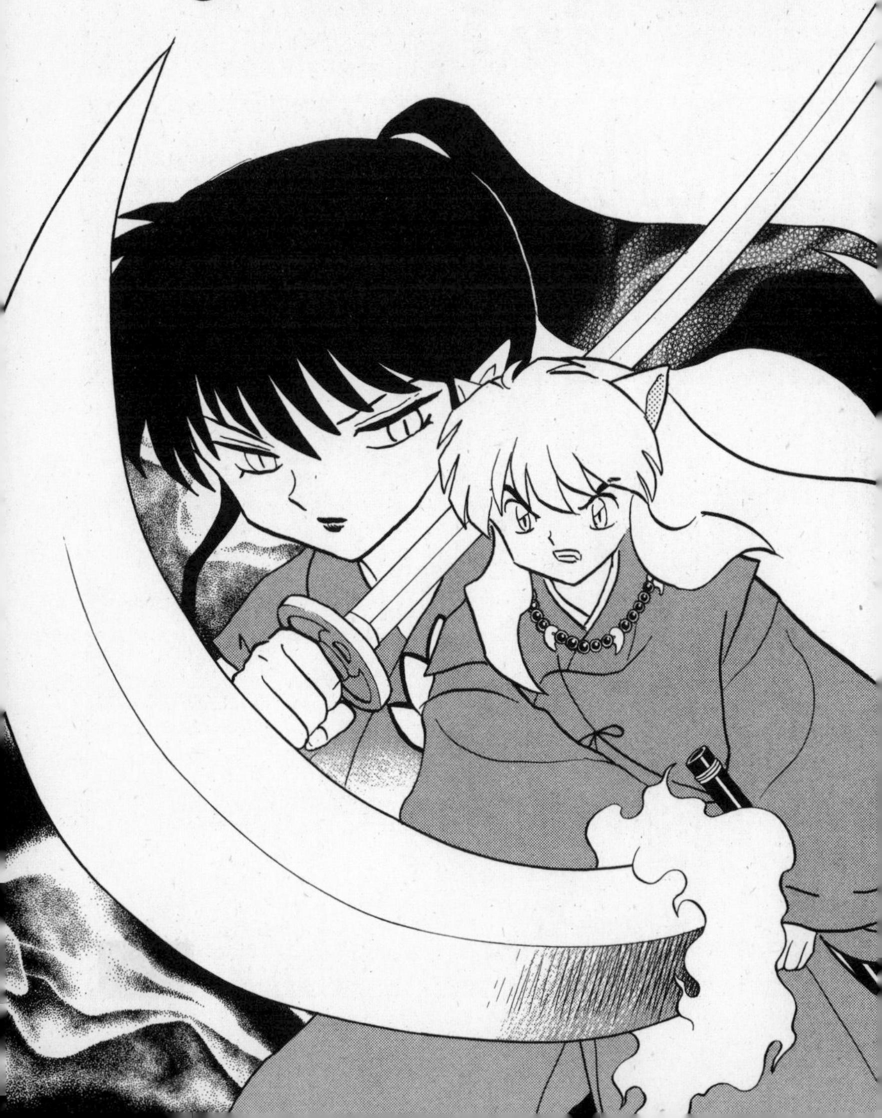

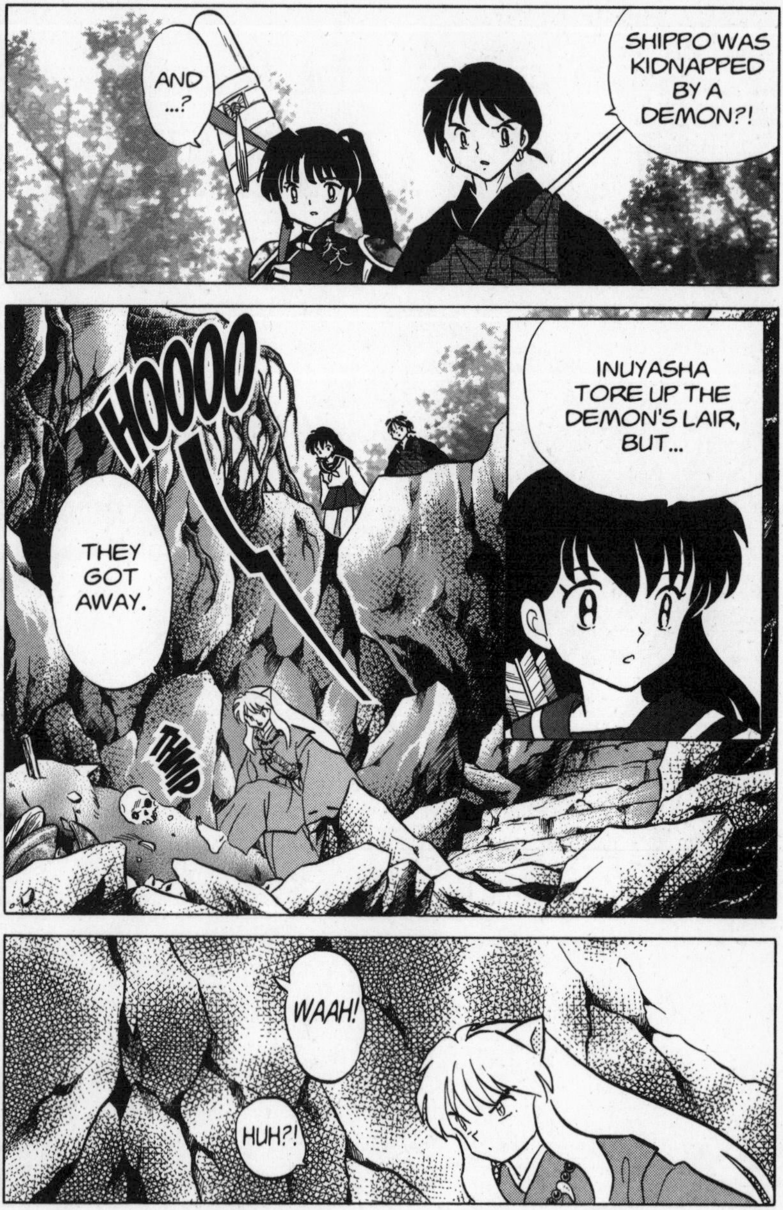
SHIPPO WAS KIDNAPPED BY A DEMON?!
AND ...?
INUYASHA TORE UP THE DEMON'S LAIR, BUT...
HOOOO
THEY GOT AWAY.
THUMP
WAAH!
HUH?!

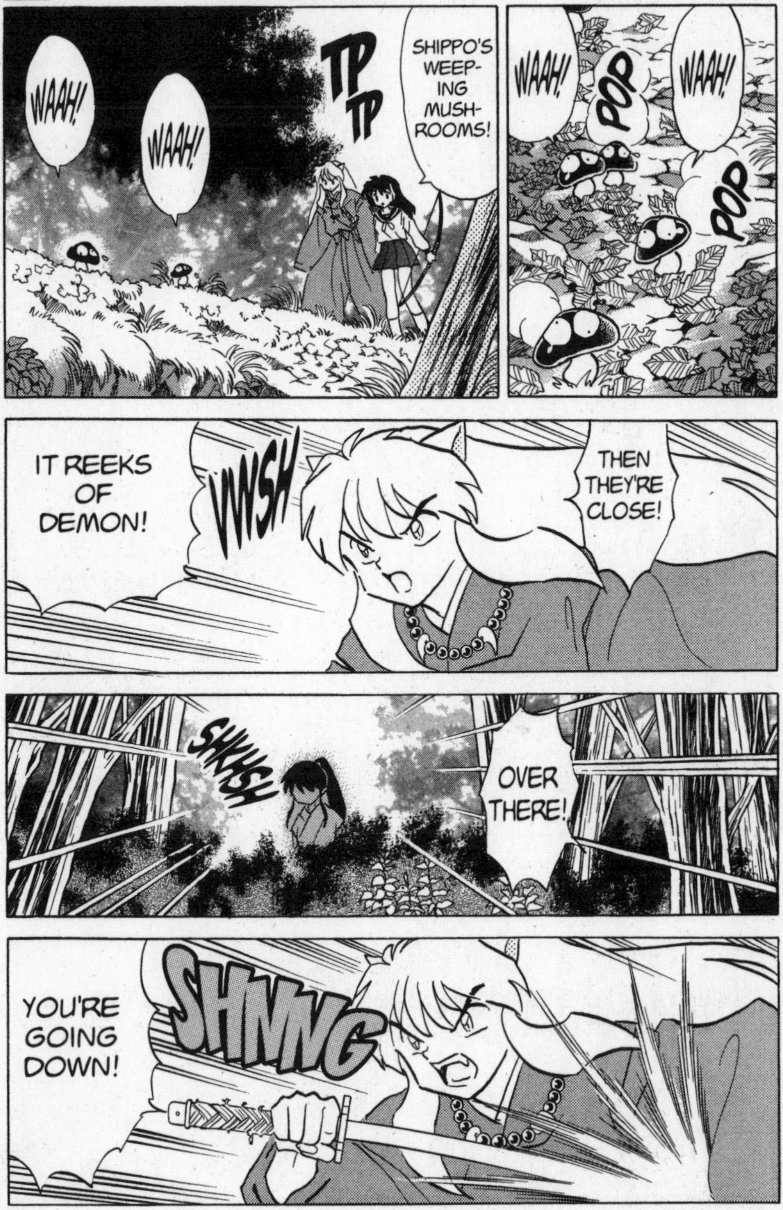
WAAH!
WAAH!
POP
POP
SHIPPO'S WEEP-ING MUSH-ROOMS!
TP TP
WAAH!
WAAH!
THEN THEY'RE CLOSE!
VWSH
IT REEKS OF DEMON!
OVER THERE!
SHKSH
SHNNG
YOU'RE GOING DOWN!

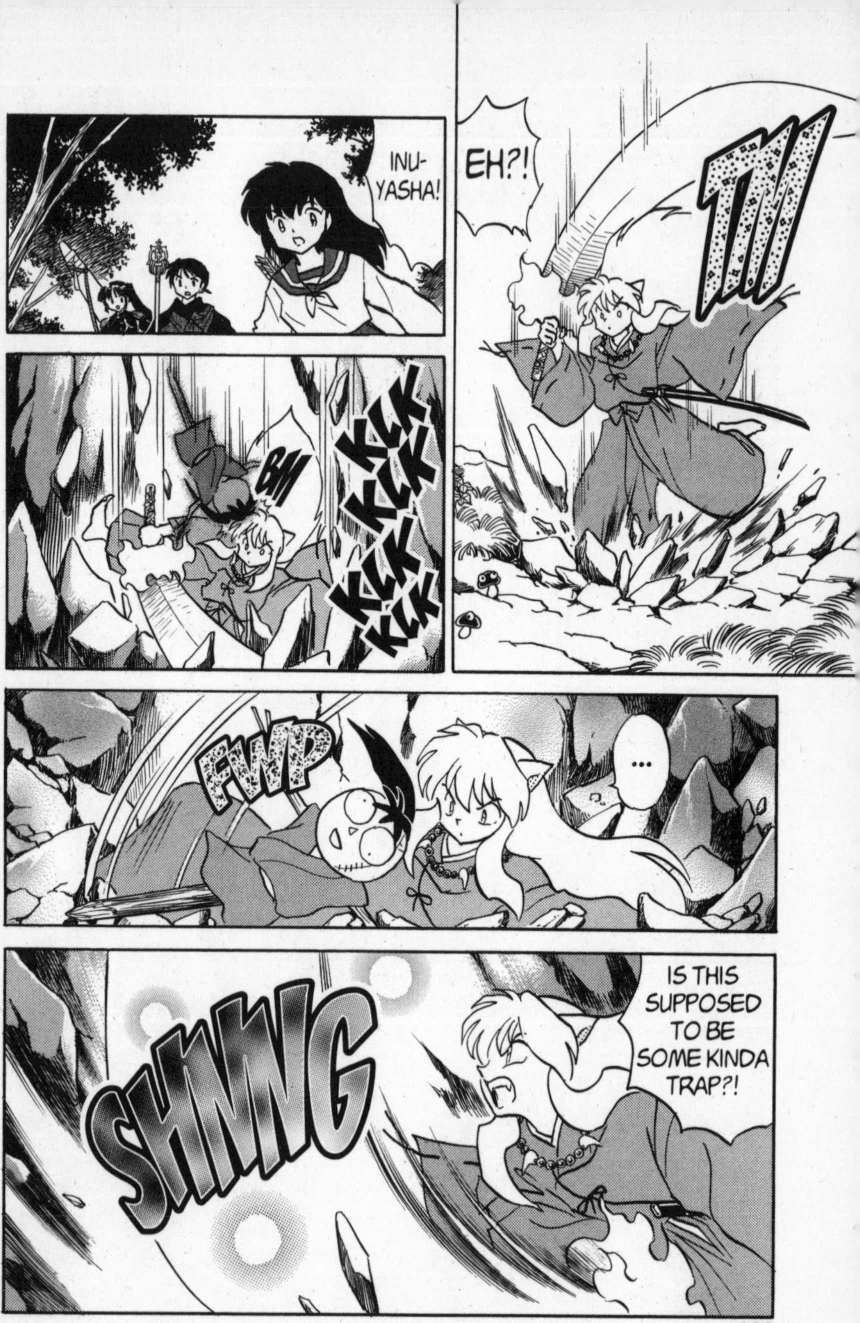
EH?!
TMP
INU-YASHA!
BM
KICK KICK KICK KICK
FWP
...
IS THIS SUPPOSED TO BE SOME KINDA TRAP?!
SHNNG

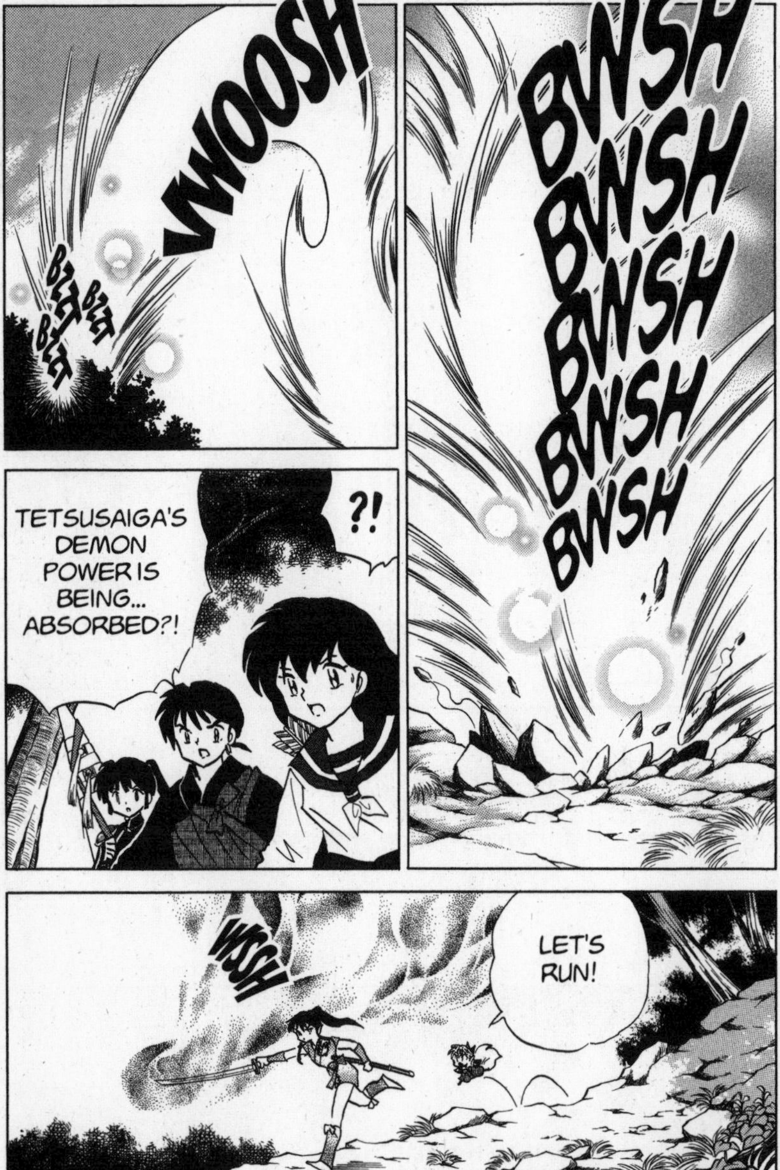
BWSH
BWSH
BWSH
BWSH
BWSH
BWSH
VWOOSH
BZZT BZZT BZZT
?!
TETSUSAIGA'S DEMON POWER IS BEING... ABSORBED?!
LET'S RUN!
WSSH

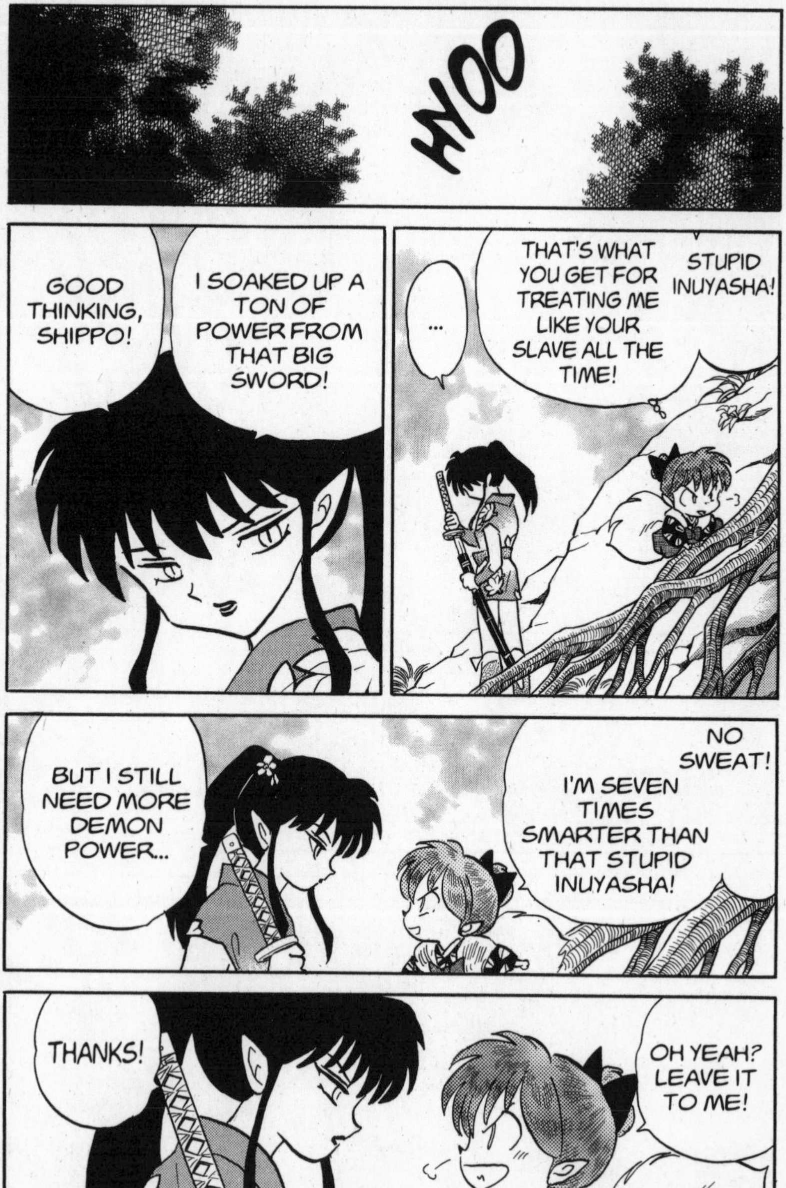
HYOO
STUPID INUYASHA!
THAT'S WHAT YOU GET FOR TREATING ME LIKE YOUR SLAVE ALL THE TIME!
...
I SOAKED UP A TON OF POWER FROM THAT BIG SWORD!
GOOD THINKING, SHIPPO!
NO SWEAT!
I'M SEVEN TIMES SMARTER THAN THAT STUPID INUYASHA!
BUT I STILL NEED MORE DEMON POWER...
OH YEAH? LEAVE IT TO ME!
THANKS!

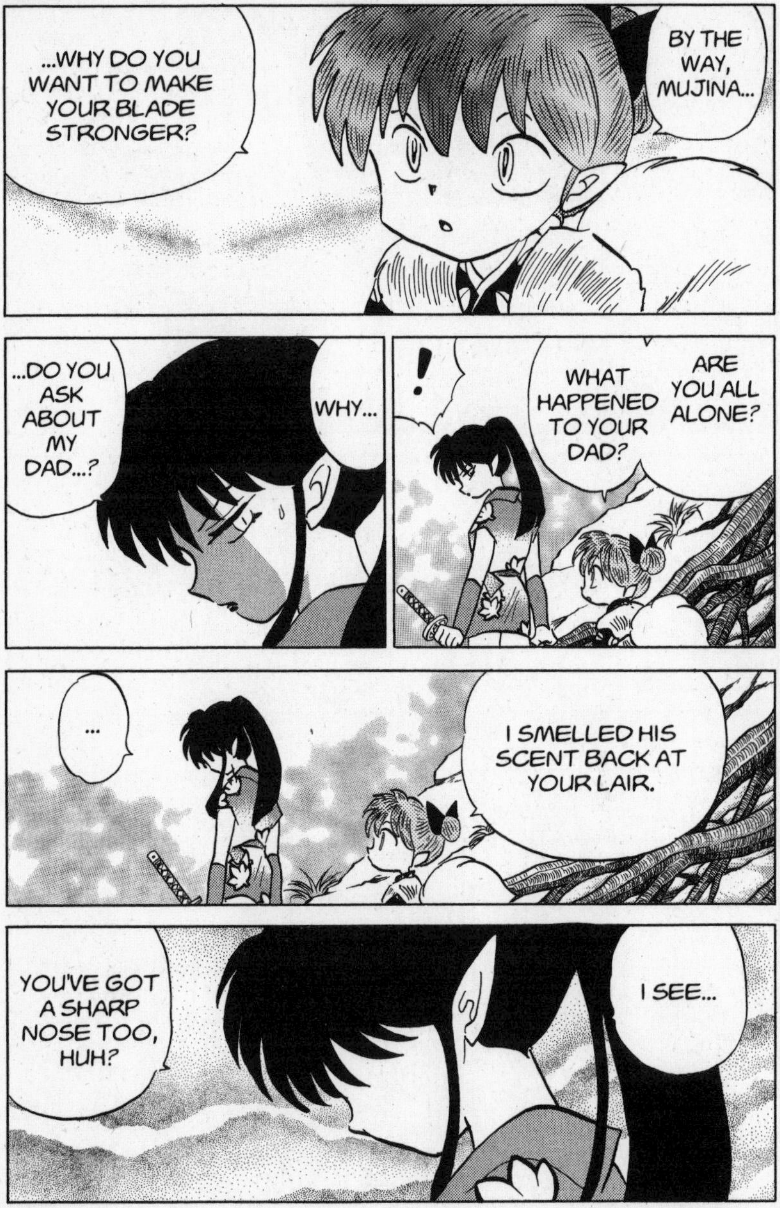
BY THE WAY, MUJINA...
...WHY DO YOU WANT TO MAKE YOUR BLADE STRONGER?
ARE YOU ALL ALONE?
WHAT HAPPENED TO YOUR DAD?
!
WHY...
...DO YOU ASK ABOUT MY DAD...?
I SMELLED HIS SCENT BACK AT YOUR LAIR.
...
I SEE...
YOU'VE GOT A SHARP NOSE TOO, HUH?

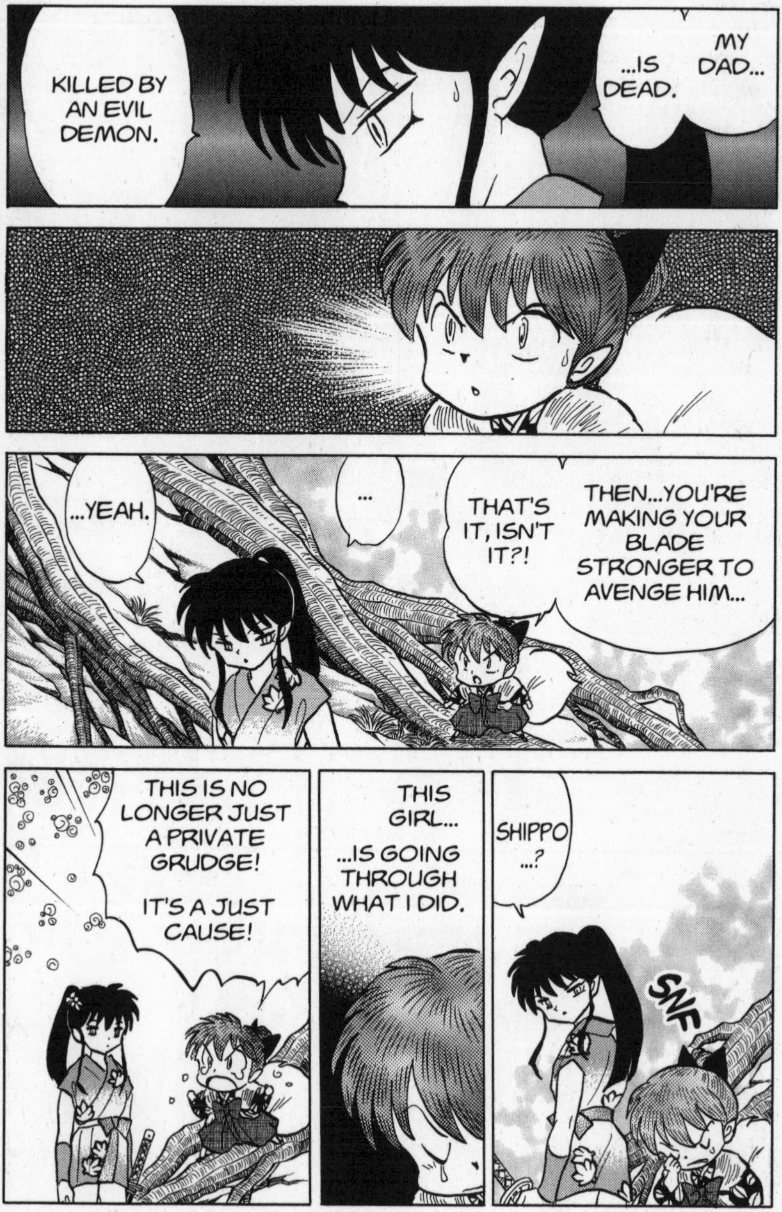
MY DAD...
...IS DEAD.
KILLED BY AN EVIL DEMON.
THEN...YOU'RE MAKING YOUR BLADE STRONGER TO AVENGE HIM...
THAT'S IT, ISN'T IT?!
...
...YEAH.
SHIPPO ...?
SNF
THIS GIRL...
...IS GOING THROUGH WHAT I DID.
THIS IS NO LONGER JUST A PRIVATE GRUDGE!
IT'S A JUST CAUSE!

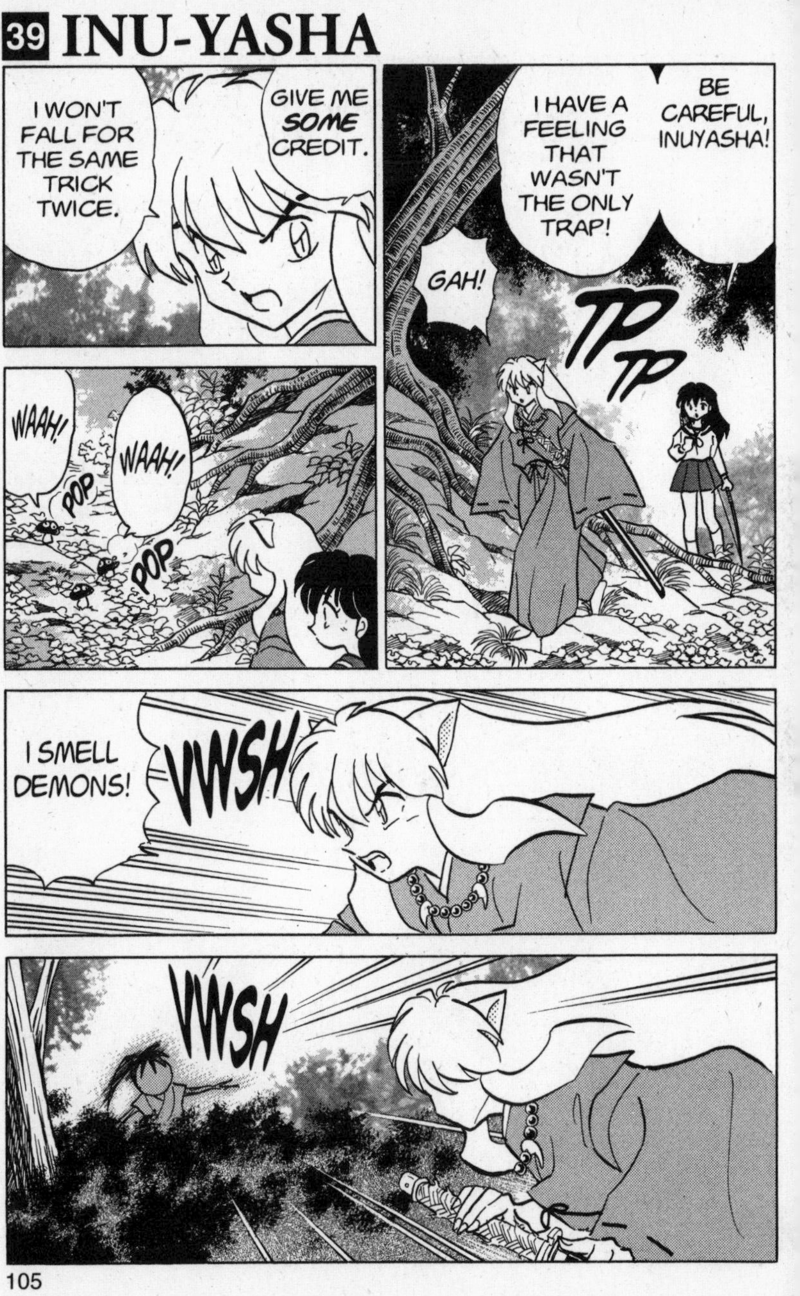
BE CAREFUL, INUYASHA!
I HAVE A FEELING THAT WASN'T THE ONLY TRAP!
GAH!
TP TP
GIVE ME SOME CREDIT.
I WON'T FALL FOR THE SAME TRICK TWICE.
WAAH!
POP
WAAH!
POP
VWSH
I SMELL DEMONS!
VWSH

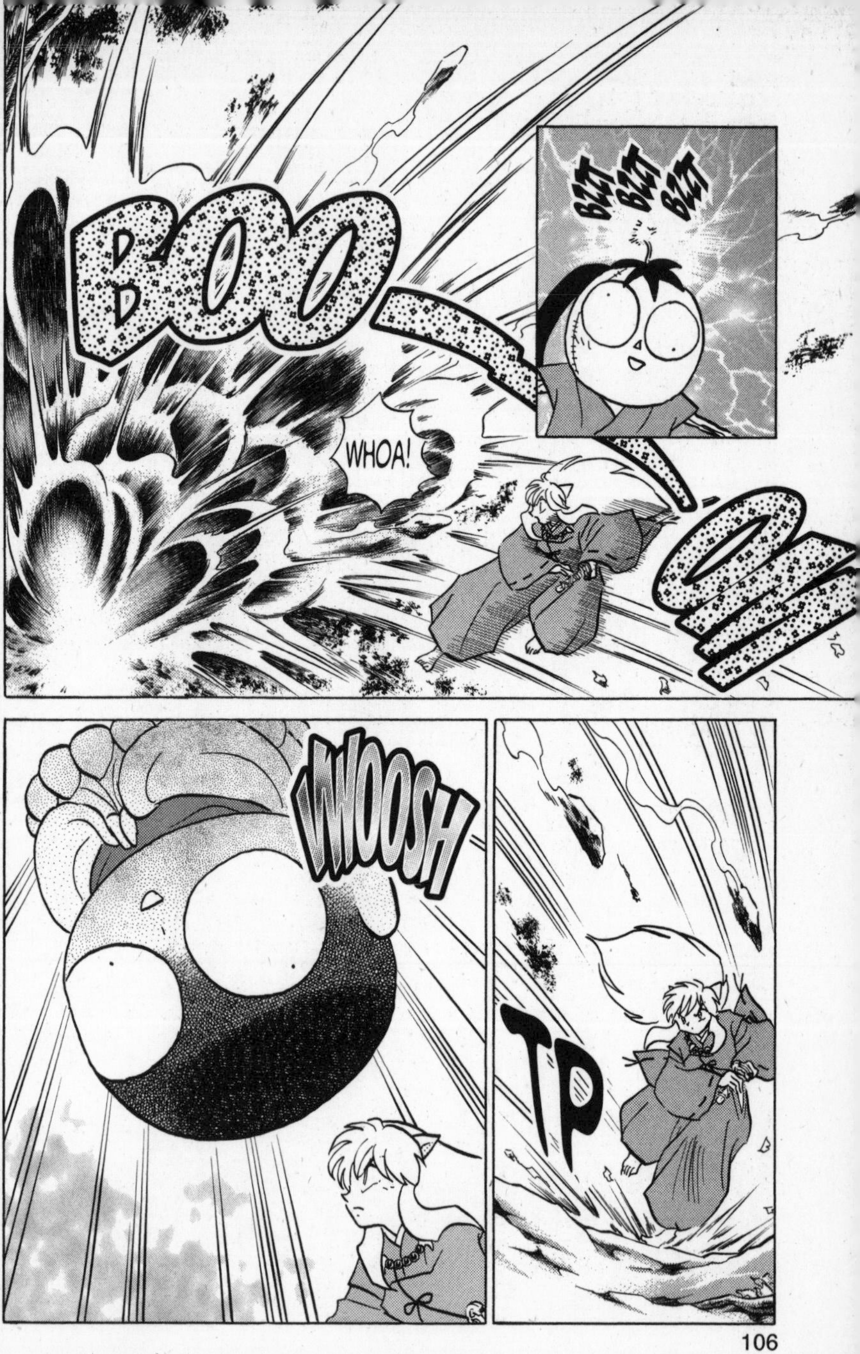
BZZT BZZT BZZT
BOO—OM
WHOA!
TP
WHOOSH

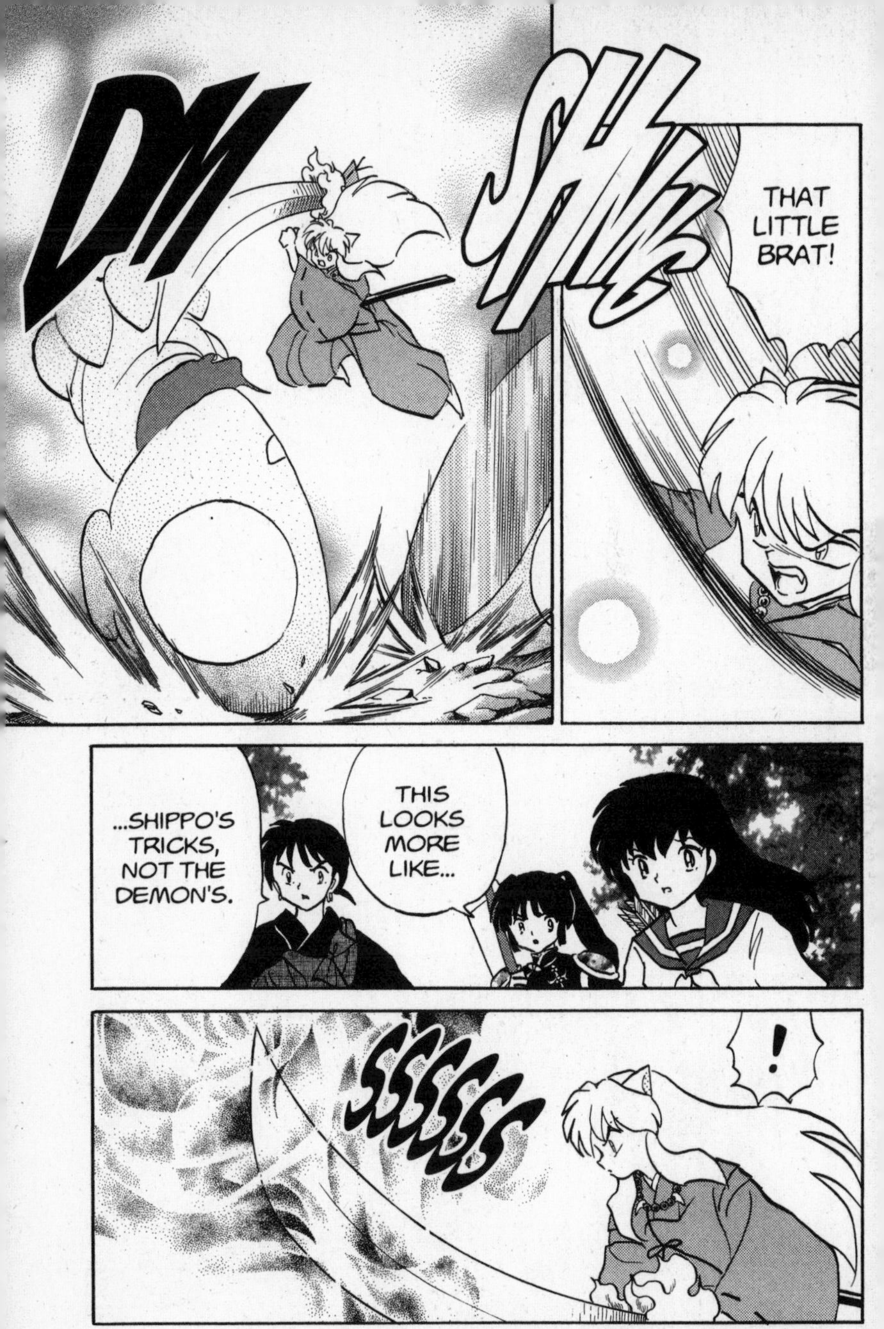
THAT LITTLE BRAT!
DM
THIS LOOKS MORE LIKE...
...SHIPPO'S TRICKS, NOT THE DEMON'S.
!

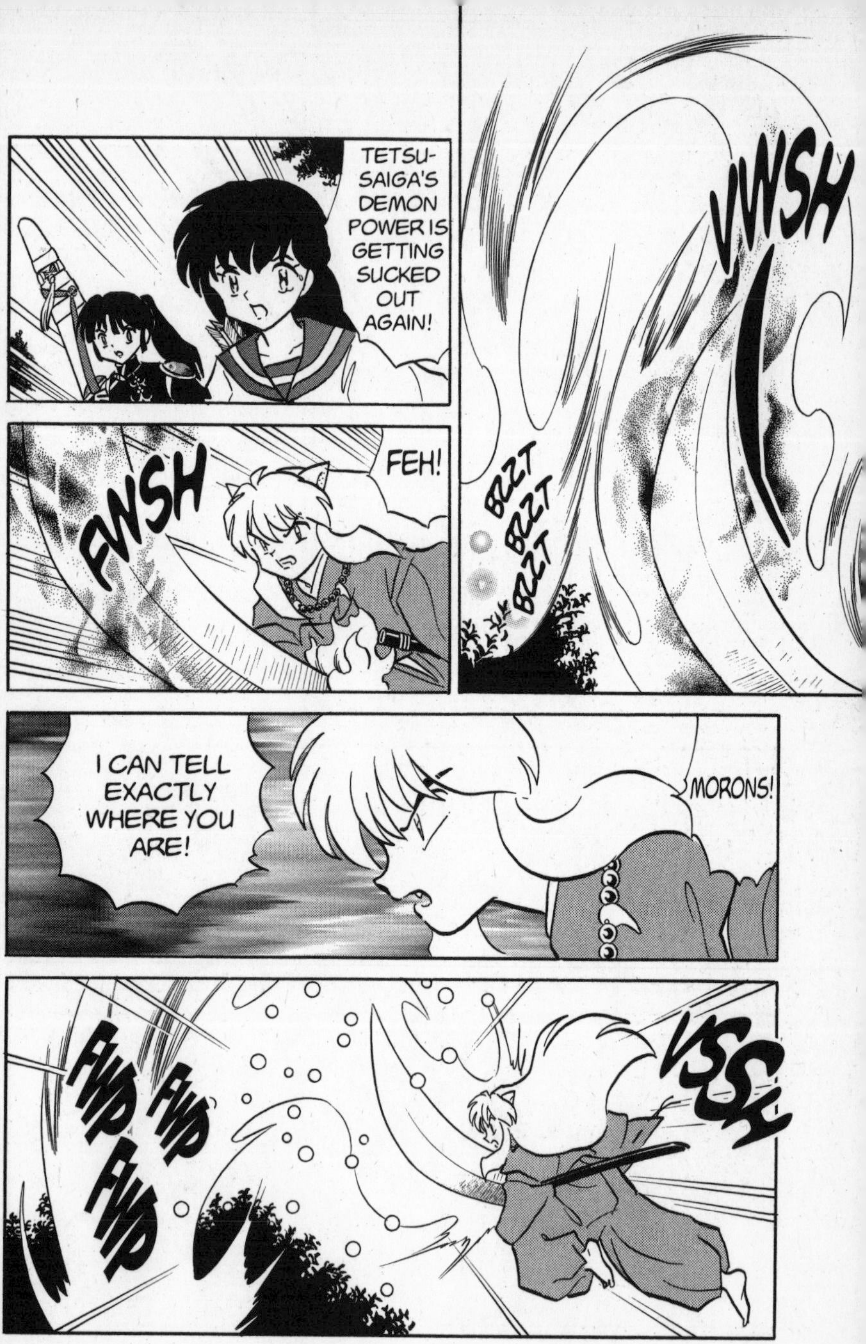
VWSH
BZZT BZZT BZZT
TETSU-SAIGA'S DEMON POWER IS GETTING SUCKED OUT AGAIN!
FEH!
FWSH
MORONS!
I CAN TELL EXACTLY WHERE YOU ARE!
VSSH
FWIP FWIP FWIP FWIP

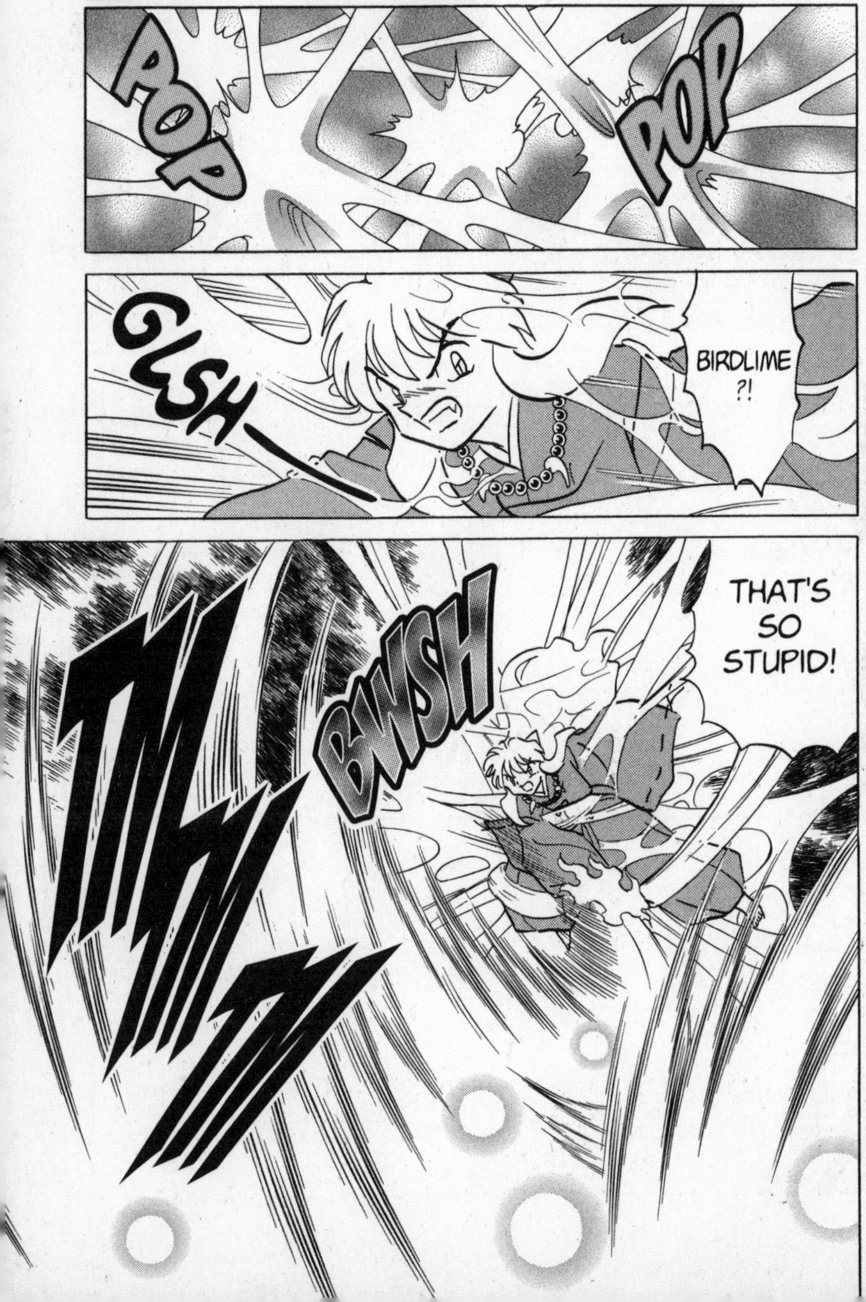
POP
POP
BIRDLIME ?!
GLSH
THAT'S SO STUPID!
BWSH

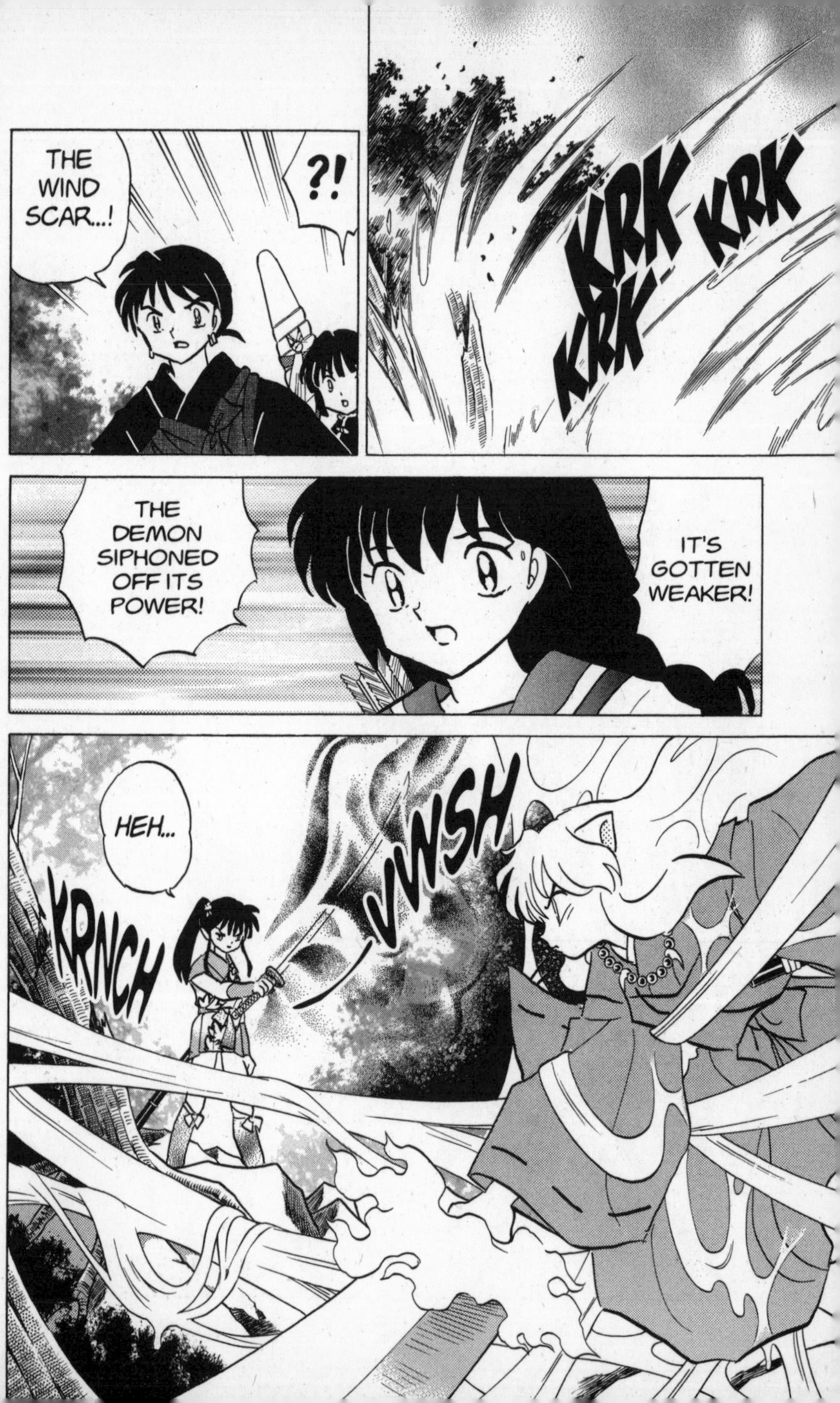
KRK KRK KRK
?!
THE WIND SCAR...!
IT'S GOTTEN WEAKER!
THE DEMON SIPHONED OFF ITS POWER!
VWSH
HEH...
KRNCH

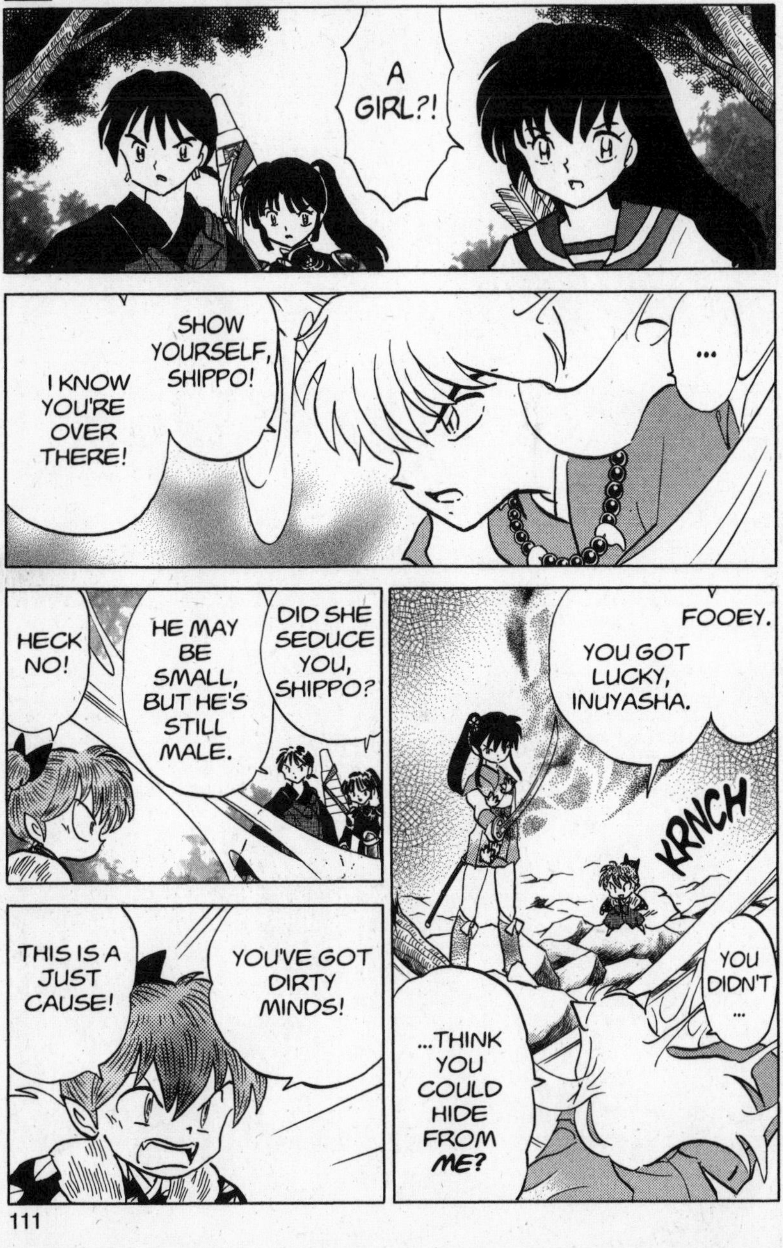
A GIRL?!
...
SHOW YOURSELF, SHIPPO!
I KNOW YOU'RE OVER THERE!
FOOEY.
YOU GOT LUCKY, INUYASHA.
KRNCH
YOU DIDN'T ...
...THINK YOU COULD HIDE FROM *ME?*
DID SHE SEDUCE YOU, SHIPPO?
HE MAY BE SMALL, BUT HE'S STILL MALE.
HECK NO!
YOU'VE GOT DIRTY MINDS!
THIS IS A JUST CAUSE!

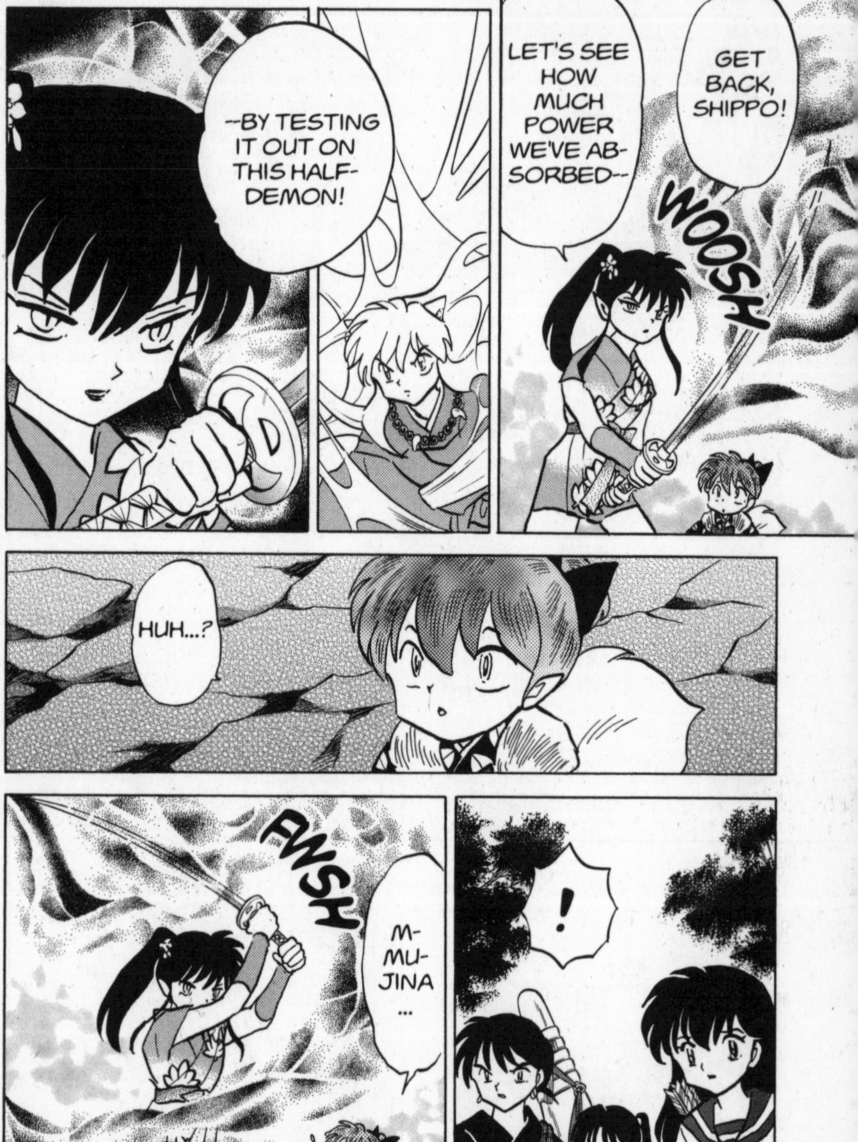
GET BACK, SHIPPO!
LET'S SEE HOW MUCH POWER WE'VE ABSORBED--
WOOSH
--BY TESTING IT OUT ON THIS HALF-DEMON!
HUH...?
!
FWSH
M-MU-JINA...

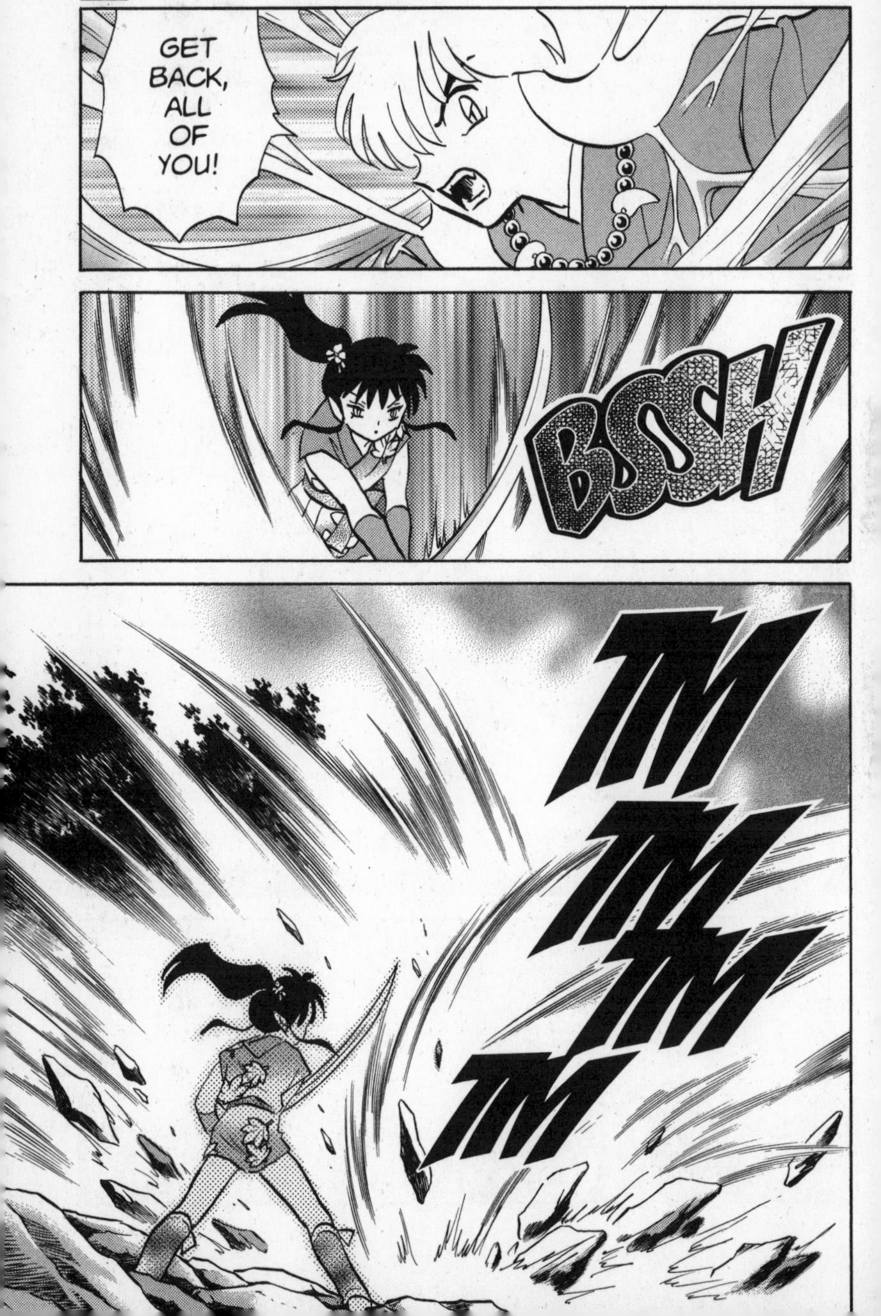
GET BACK, ALL OF YOU!
BSSH

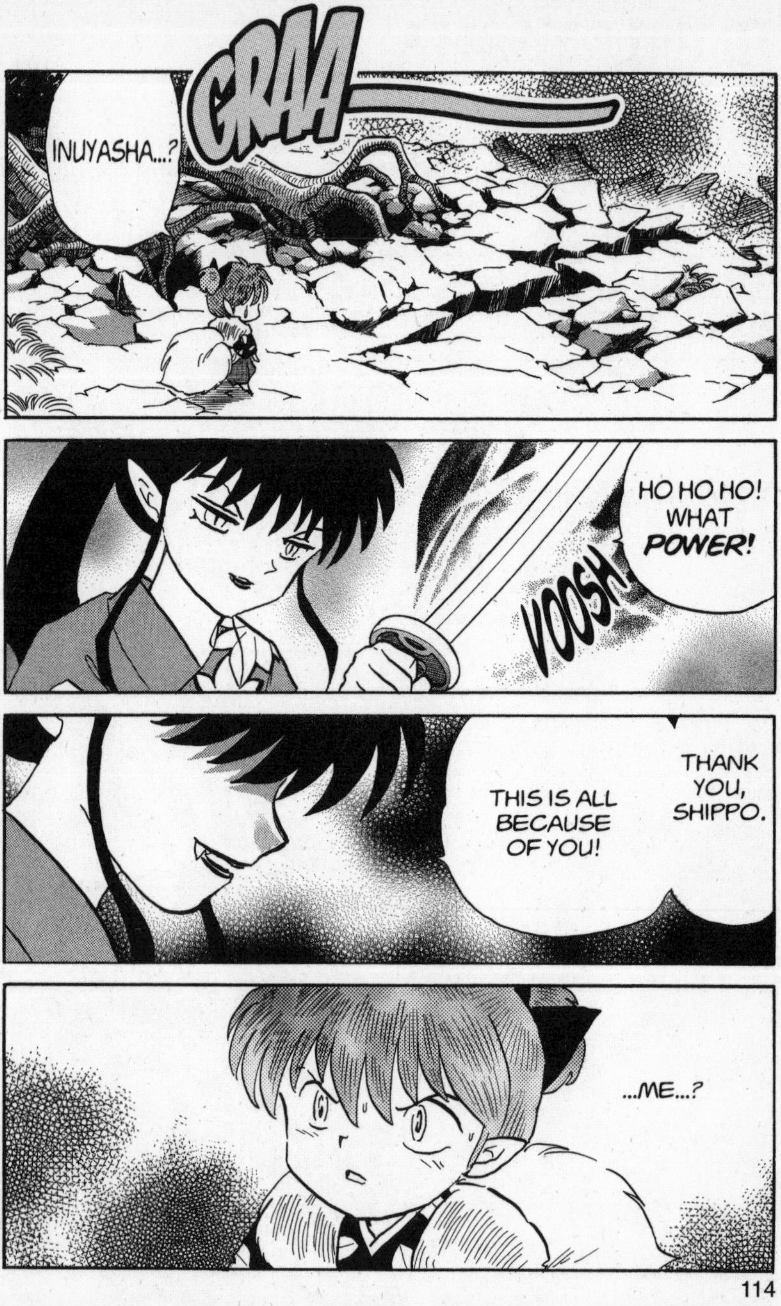
GRAA
INUYASHA...?
HO HO HO! WHAT POWER!
VOOSH
THANK YOU, SHIPPO.
THIS IS ALL BECAUSE OF YOU!
...ME...?

SCROLL 7

TRICKERY

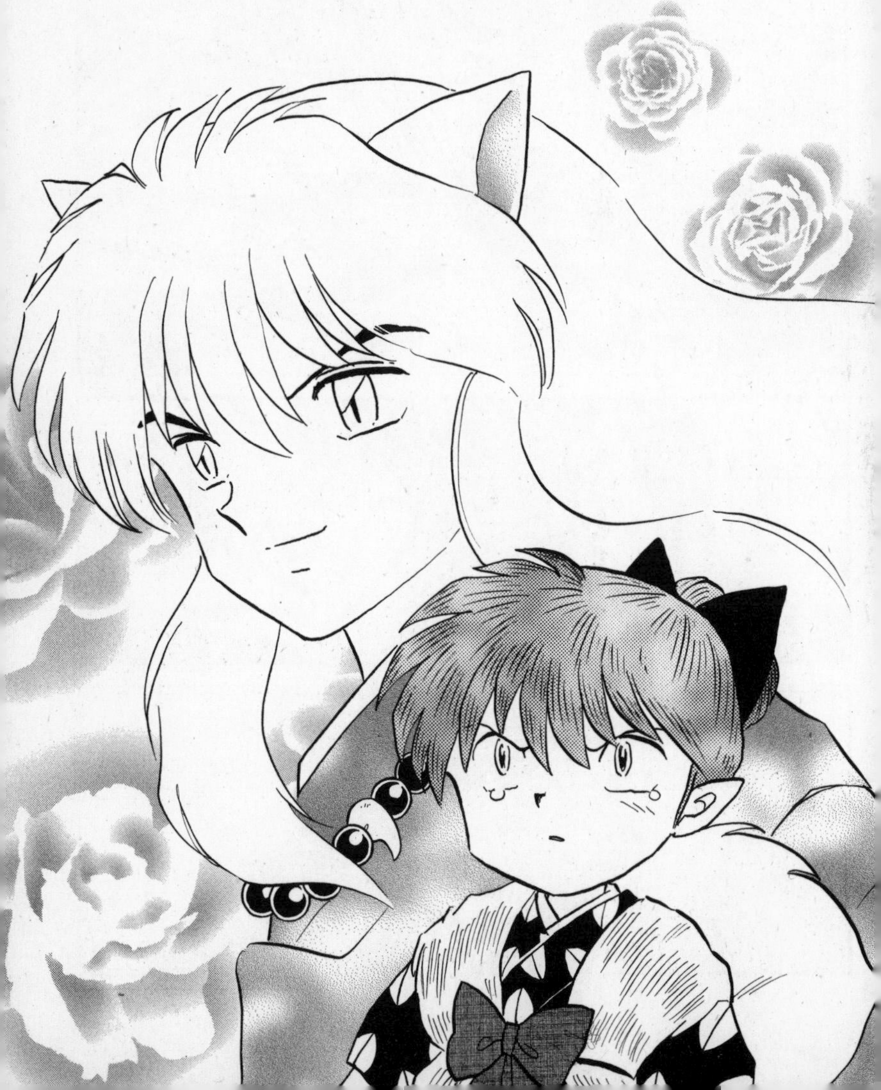

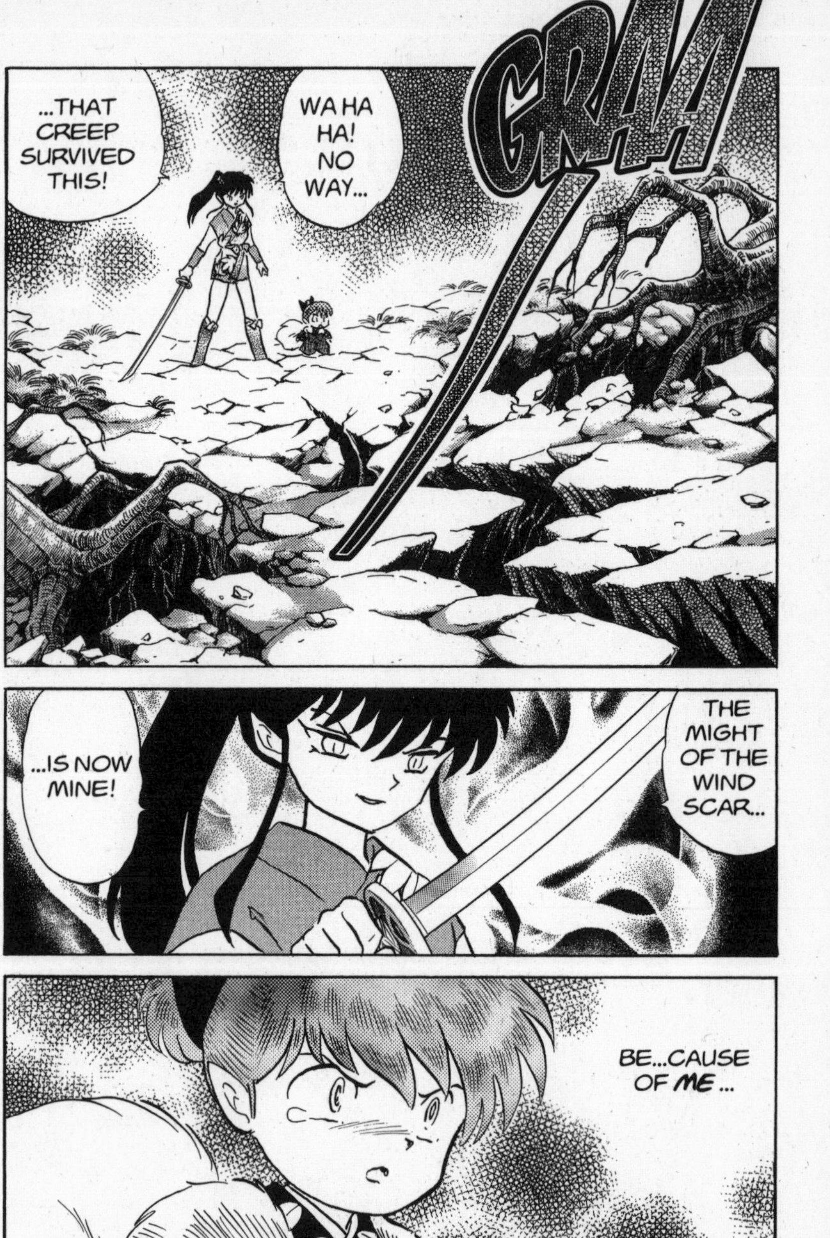
GRAM
WA HA HA! NO WAY...
...THAT CREEP SURVIVED THIS!
THE MIGHT OF THE WIND SCAR...
...IS NOW MINE!
BE...CAUSE OF *ME*...

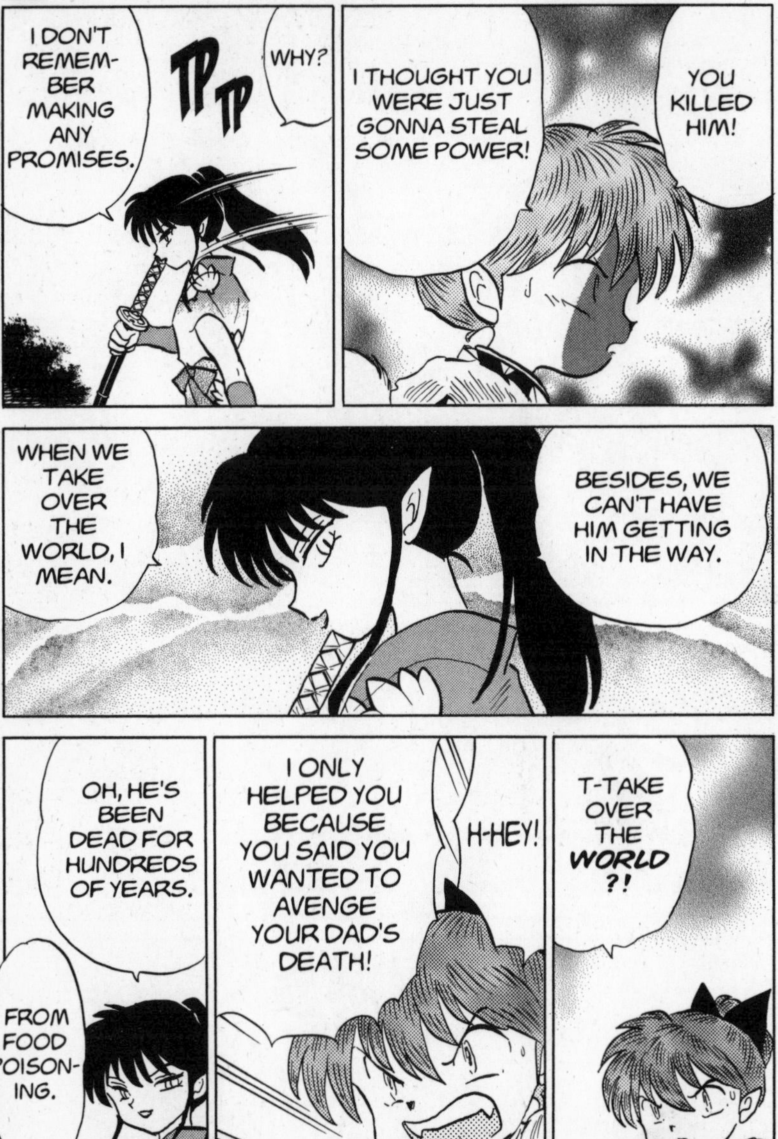
YOU KILLED HIM!
I THOUGHT YOU WERE JUST GONNA STEAL SOME POWER!
WHY?
TP TP
I DON'T REMEMBER MAKING ANY PROMISES.
BESIDES, WE CAN'T HAVE HIM GETTING IN THE WAY.
WHEN WE TAKE OVER THE WORLD, I MEAN.
T-TAKE OVER THE WORLD?!
H-HEY!
I ONLY HELPED YOU BECAUSE YOU SAID YOU WANTED TO AVENGE YOUR DAD'S DEATH!
OH, HE'S BEEN DEAD FOR HUNDREDS OF YEARS.
FROM FOOD POISONING.

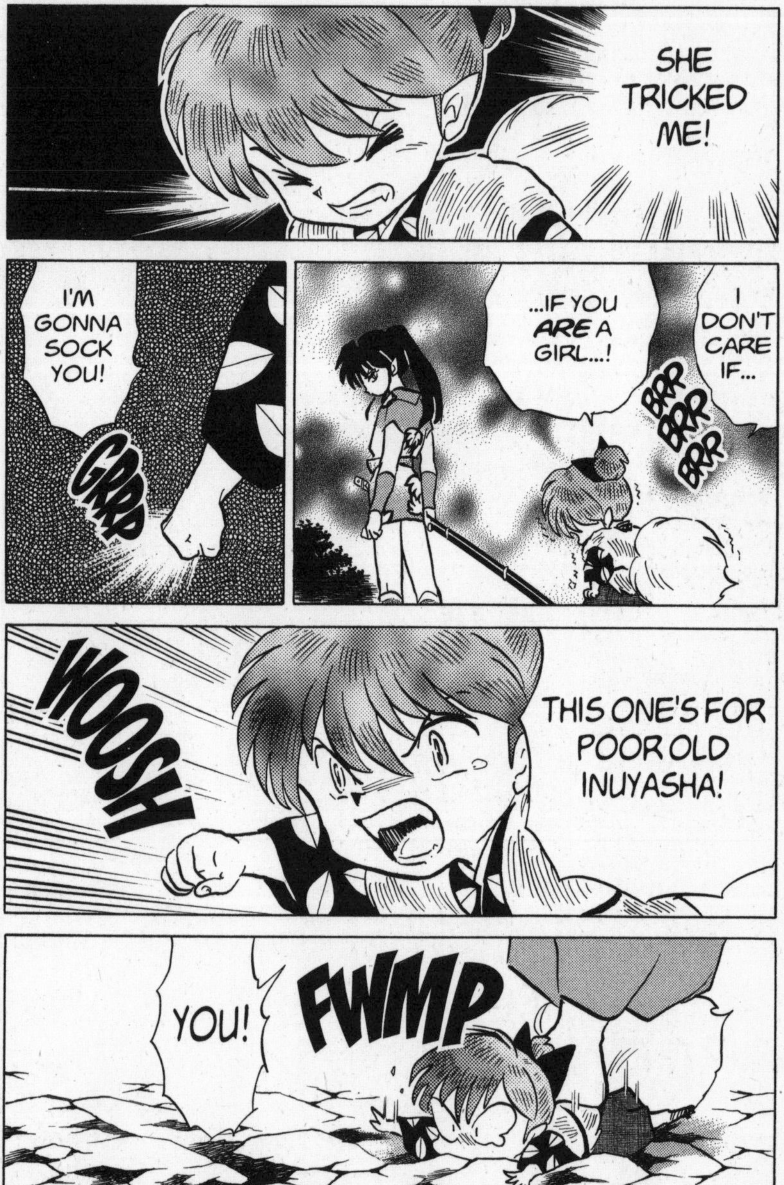
SHE TRICKED ME!
I DON'T CARE IF...
...IF YOU ARE A GIRL...!
BRR BRR BRR
I'M GONNA SOCK YOU!
GRRP
THIS ONE'S FOR POOR OLD INUYASHA!
WOOSH
FWMP
YOU!

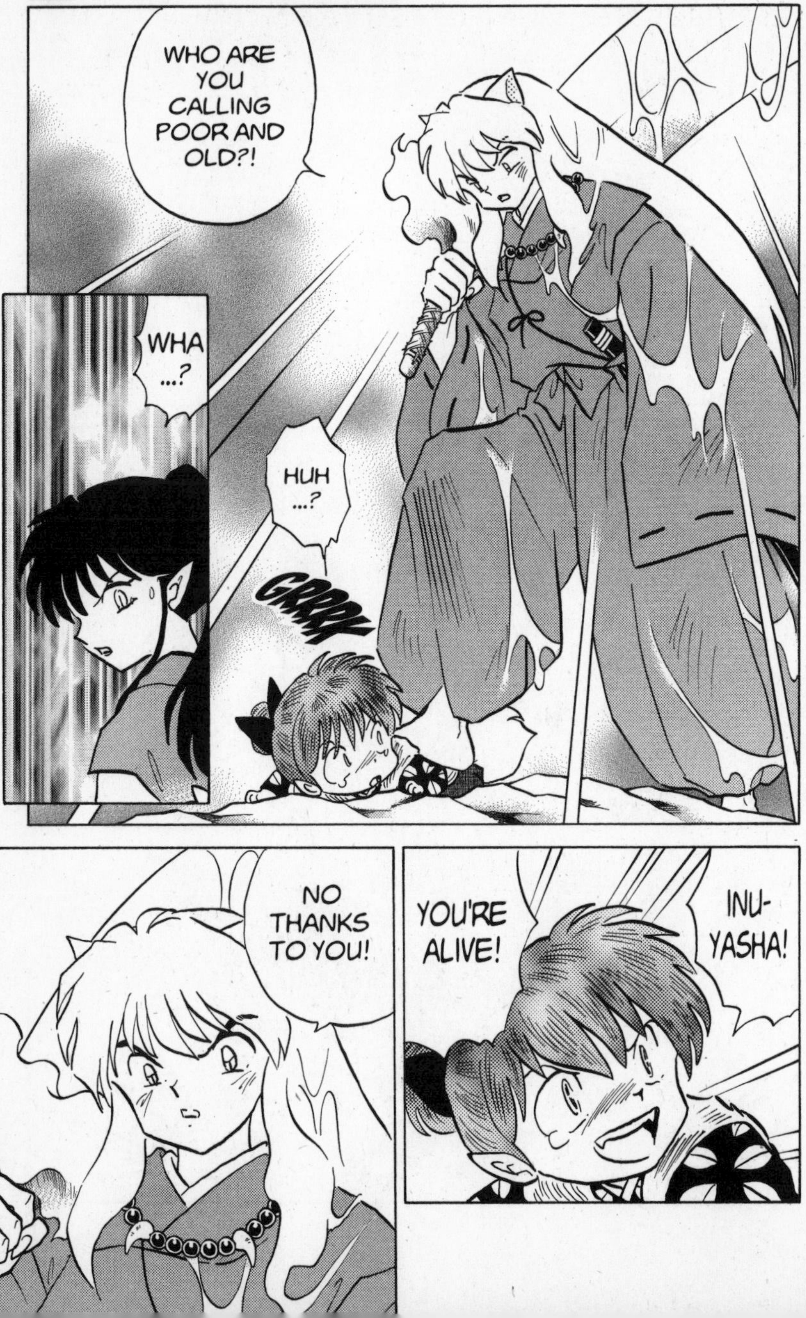
WHO ARE YOU CALLING POOR AND OLD?!
HUH ...?
GRRRK
WHA ...?
INU-YASHA!
YOU'RE ALIVE!
NO THANKS TO YOU!

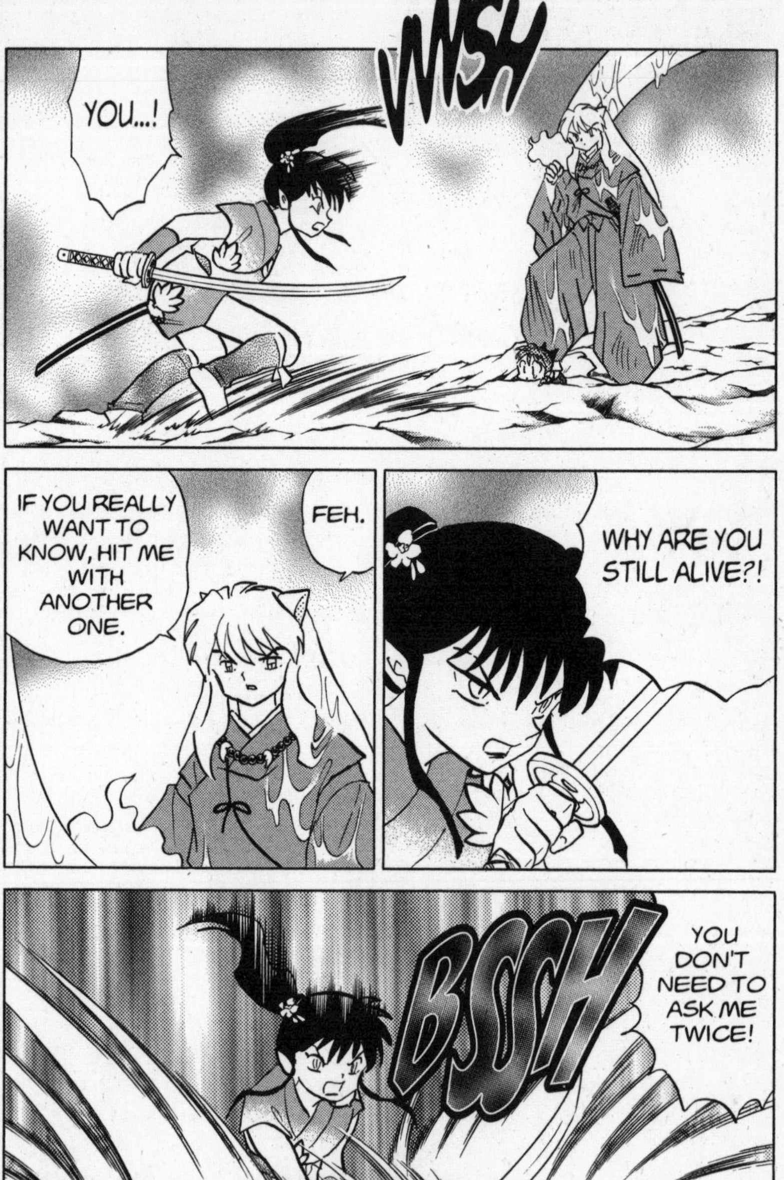
WHSH
YOU...!
WHY ARE YOU STILL ALIVE?!
FEH.
IF YOU REALLY WANT TO KNOW, HIT ME WITH ANOTHER ONE.
YOU DON'T NEED TO ASK ME TWICE!
BSCH

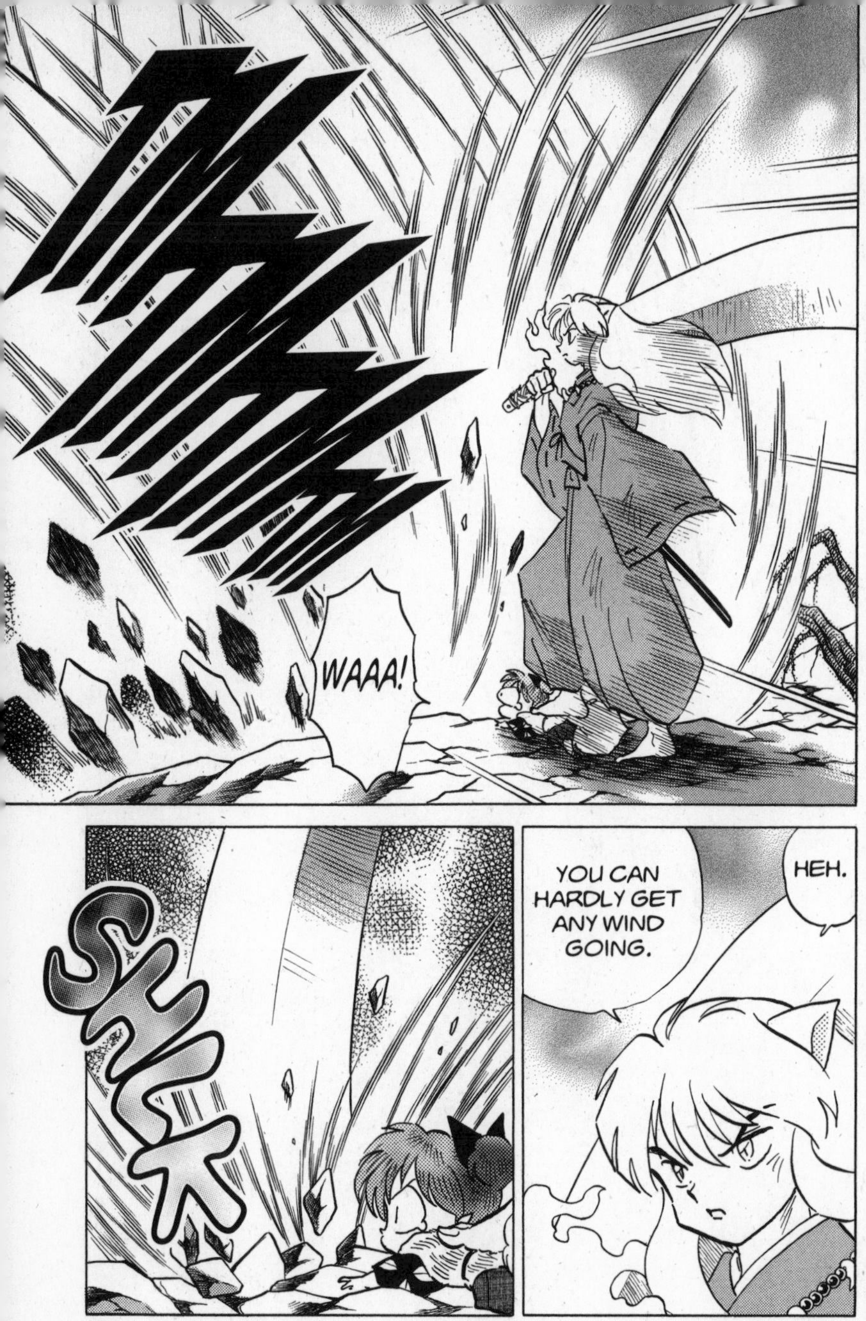
WAAA!
HEH.
YOU CAN HARDLY GET ANY WIND GOING.
SHUK

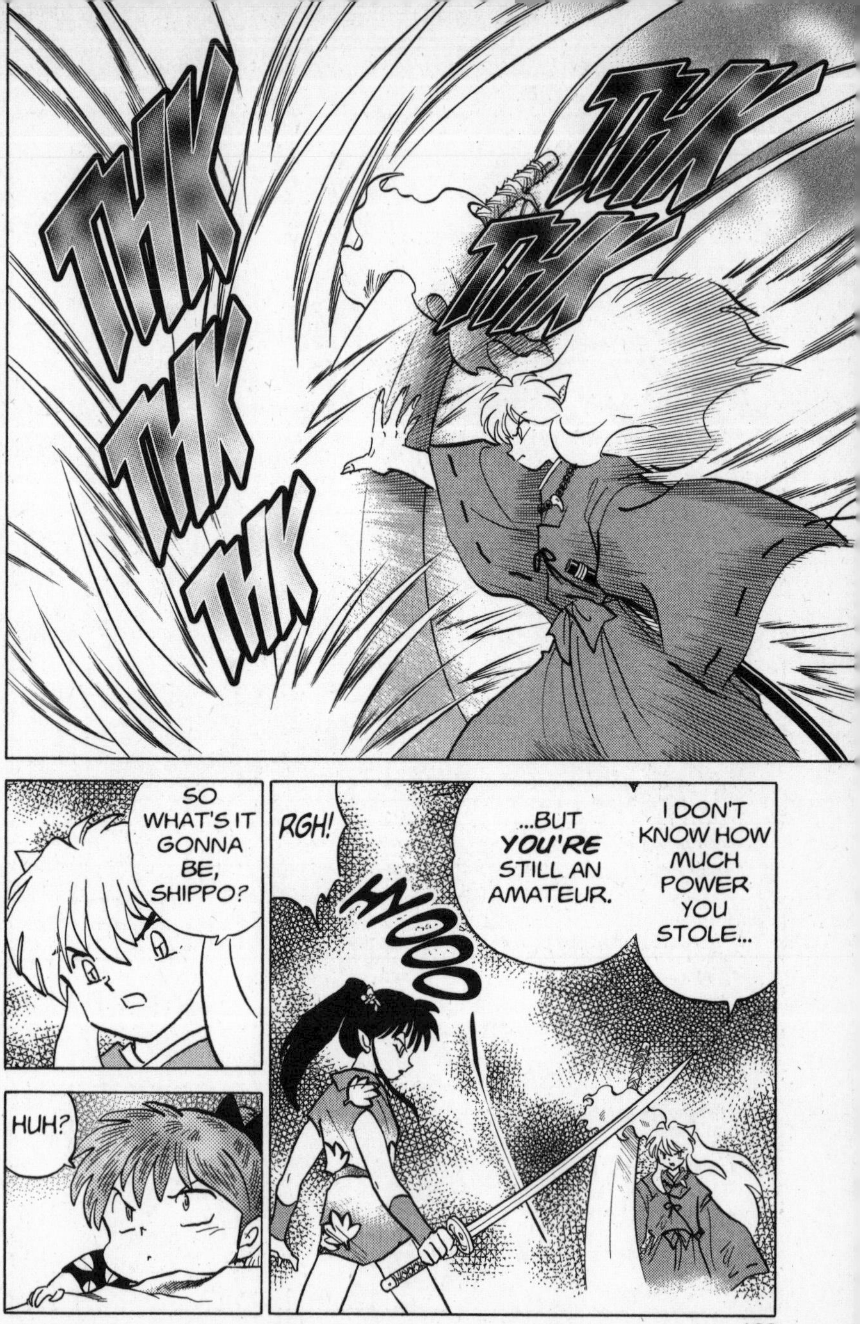
THK
THK
THK
THK
THK
I DON'T KNOW HOW MUCH POWER YOU STOLE...
...BUT **YOU'RE** STILL AN AMATEUR.
HYOOO
RGH!
SO WHAT'S IT GONNA BE, SHIPPO?
HUH?

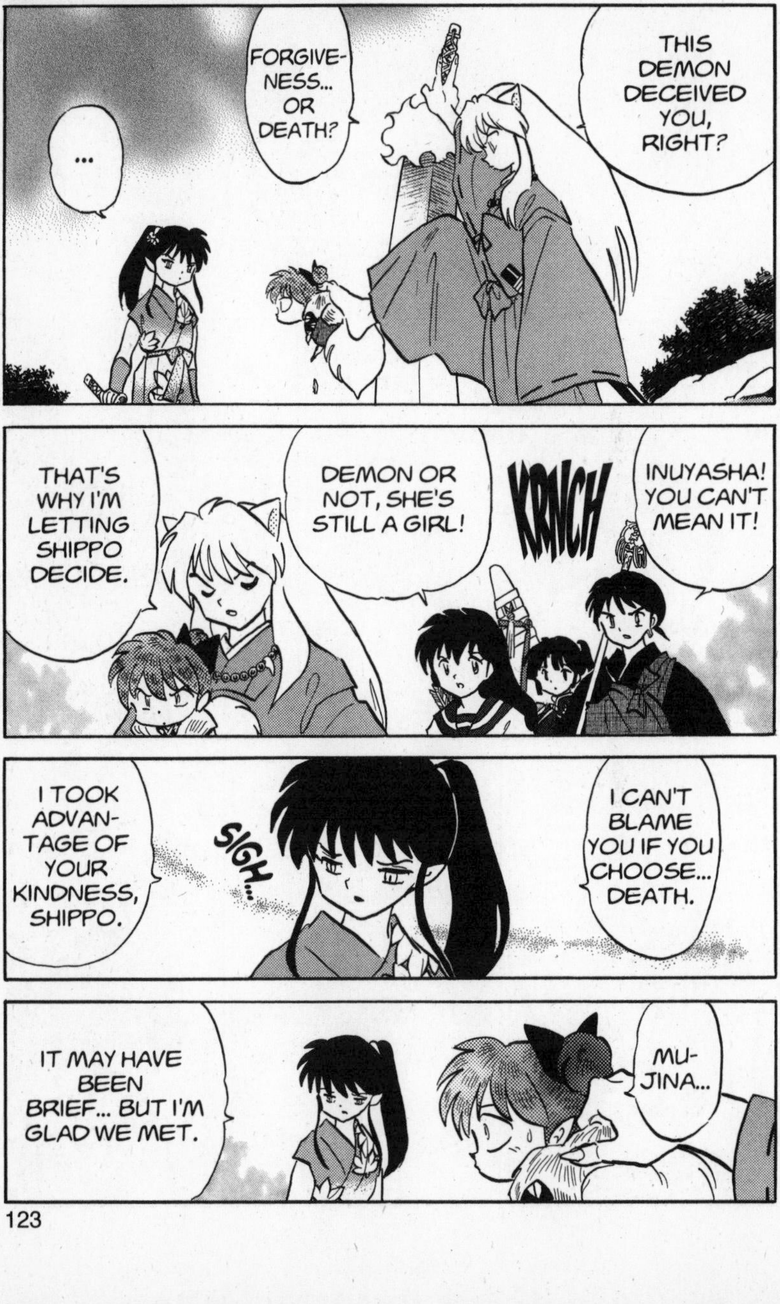
THIS DEMON DECEIVED YOU, RIGHT?
FORGIVENESS... OR DEATH?
...
INUYASHA! YOU CAN'T MEAN IT!
KRNCH
DEMON OR NOT, SHE'S STILL A GIRL!
THAT'S WHY I'M LETTING SHIPPO DECIDE.
I CAN'T BLAME YOU IF YOU CHOOSE... DEATH.
SIGH...
I TOOK ADVANTAGE OF YOUR KINDNESS, SHIPPO.
MUJINA...
IT MAY HAVE BEEN BRIEF... BUT I'M GLAD WE MET.

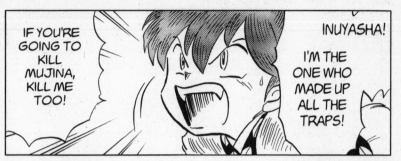

INUYASHA!
I'M THE ONE WHO MADE UP ALL THE TRAPS!
IF YOU'RE GOING TO KILL MUJINA, KILL ME TOO!
YEAH?
RUN, MUJINA!
I'LL DELAY 'EM!
SHIPPO ...
... THANK YOU.
SNF
FOR THOSE TEARS...
...I FORGIVE YOU EVERYTHING.
NOW GO, MUJINA!
...

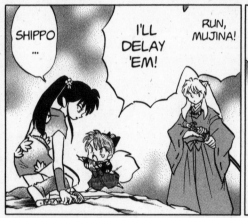

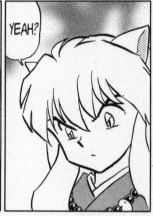

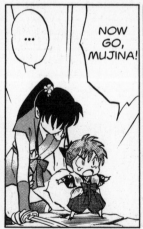

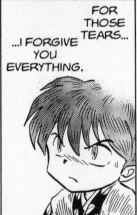

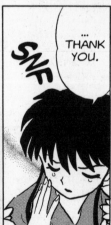

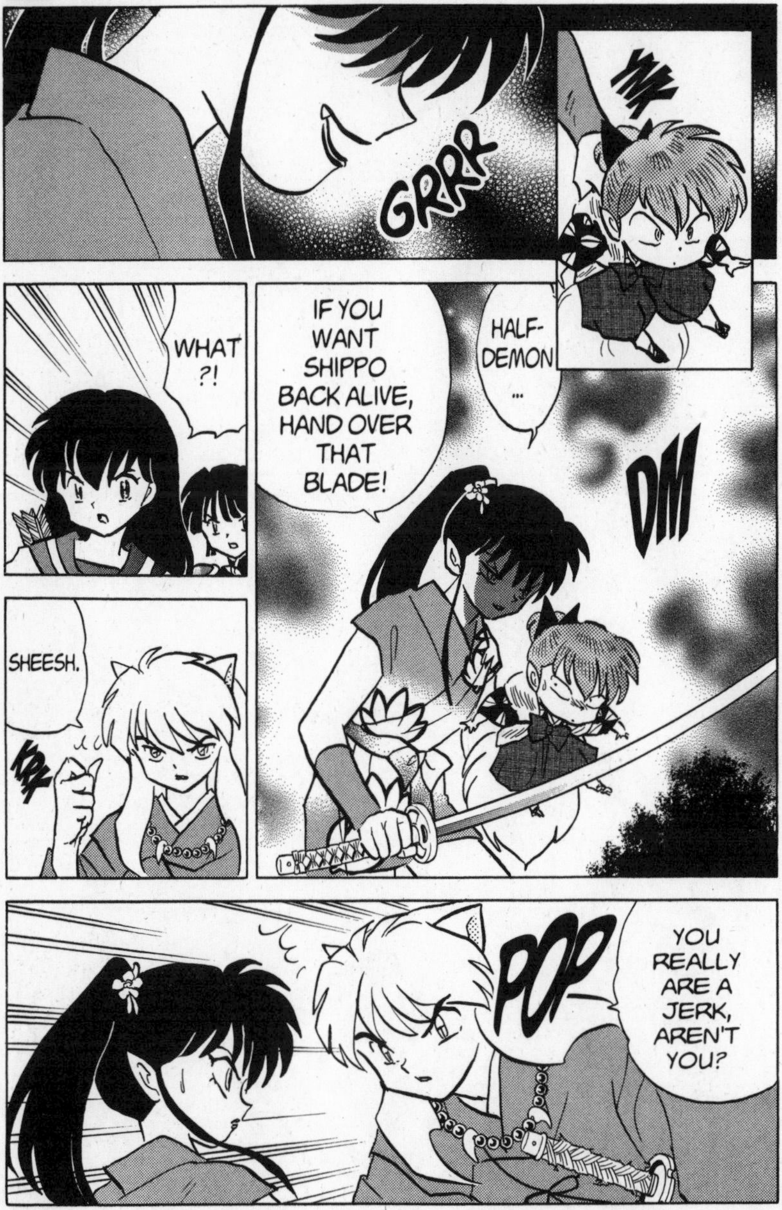
GRRR
HALF-DEMON...
IF YOU WANT SHIPPO BACK ALIVE, HAND OVER THAT BLADE!
DM
WHAT?!
SHEESH.
KRK
YOU REALLY ARE A JERK, AREN'T YOU?
POP

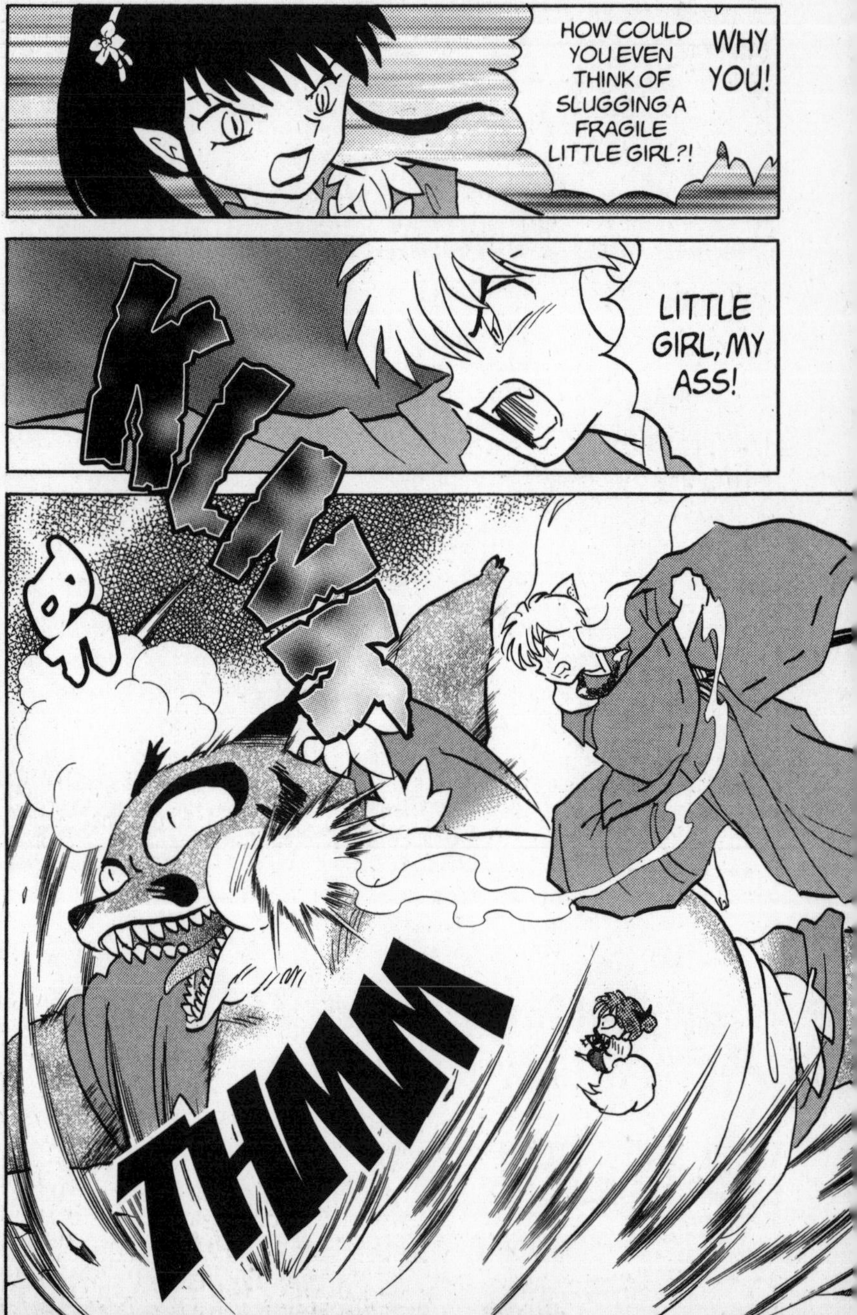
WHY YOU!
HOW COULD YOU EVEN THINK OF SLUGGING A FRAGILE LITTLE GIRL?!
LITTLE GIRL, MY ASS!
BF
THMM

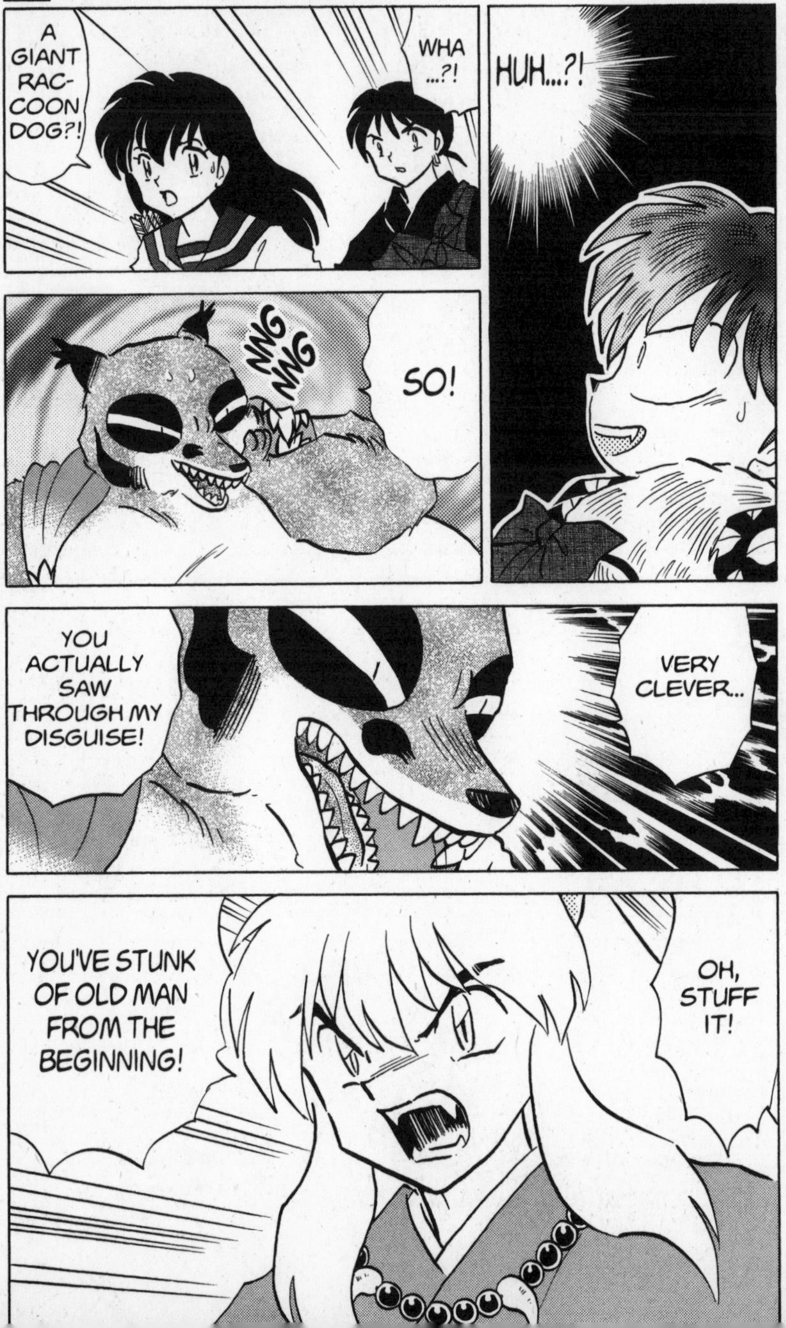
HUH...?!
WHA ...?!
A GIANT RAC-COON DOG?!
SO!
NNG NNG
VERY CLEVER...
YOU ACTUALLY SAW THROUGH MY DISGUISE!
OH, STUFF IT!
YOU'VE STUNK OF OLD MAN FROM THE BEGINNING!

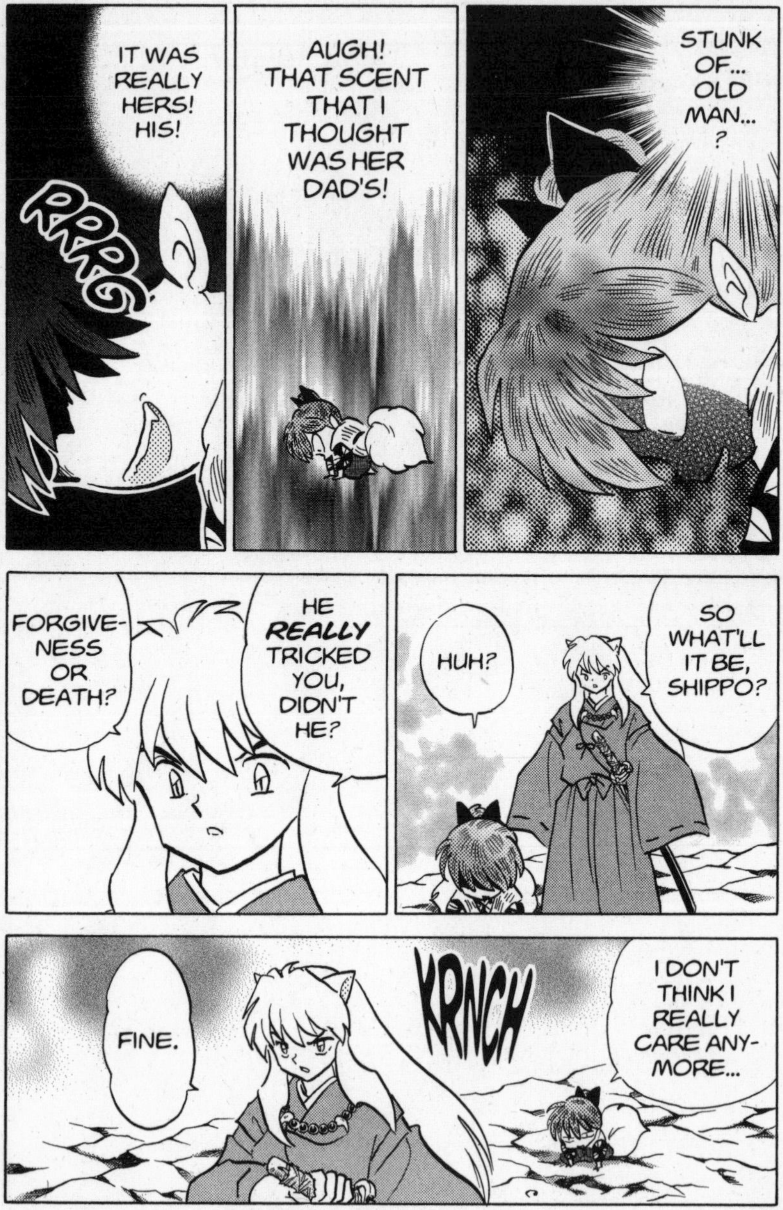
STUNK OF... OLD MAN...?
AUGH! THAT SCENT THAT I THOUGHT WAS HER DAD'S!
IT WAS REALLY HERS! HIS!
RRRG
SO WHAT'LL IT BE, SHIPPO?
HUH?
HE **REALLY** TRICKED YOU, DIDN'T HE?
FORGIVE-NESS OR DEATH?
I DON'T THINK I REALLY CARE ANY-MORE...
KRNCH
FINE.

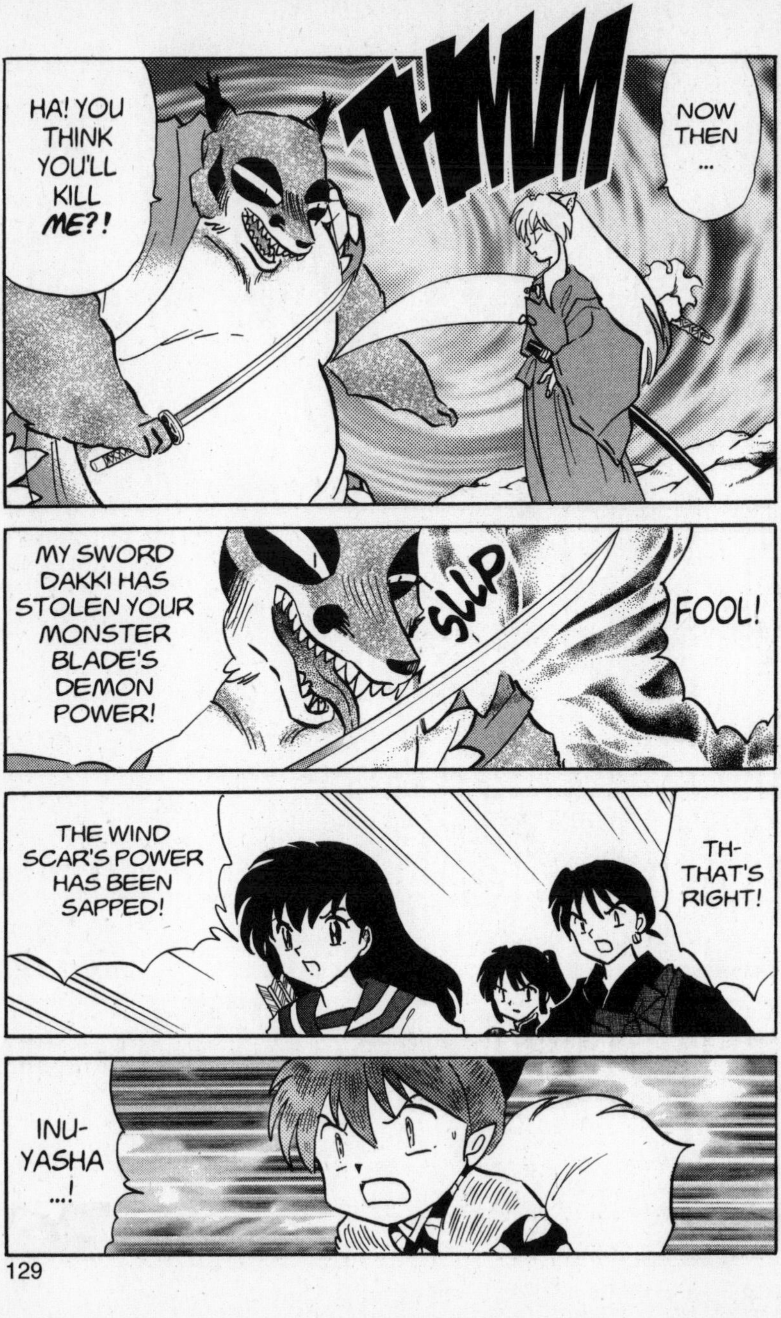
NOW THEN ...
THMM
HA! YOU THINK YOU'LL KILL ME?!
FOOL!
SLIP
MY SWORD DAKKI HAS STOLEN YOUR MONSTER BLADE'S DEMON POWER!
TH- THAT'S RIGHT!
THE WIND SCAR'S POWER HAS BEEN SAPPED!
INU-YASHA ...!

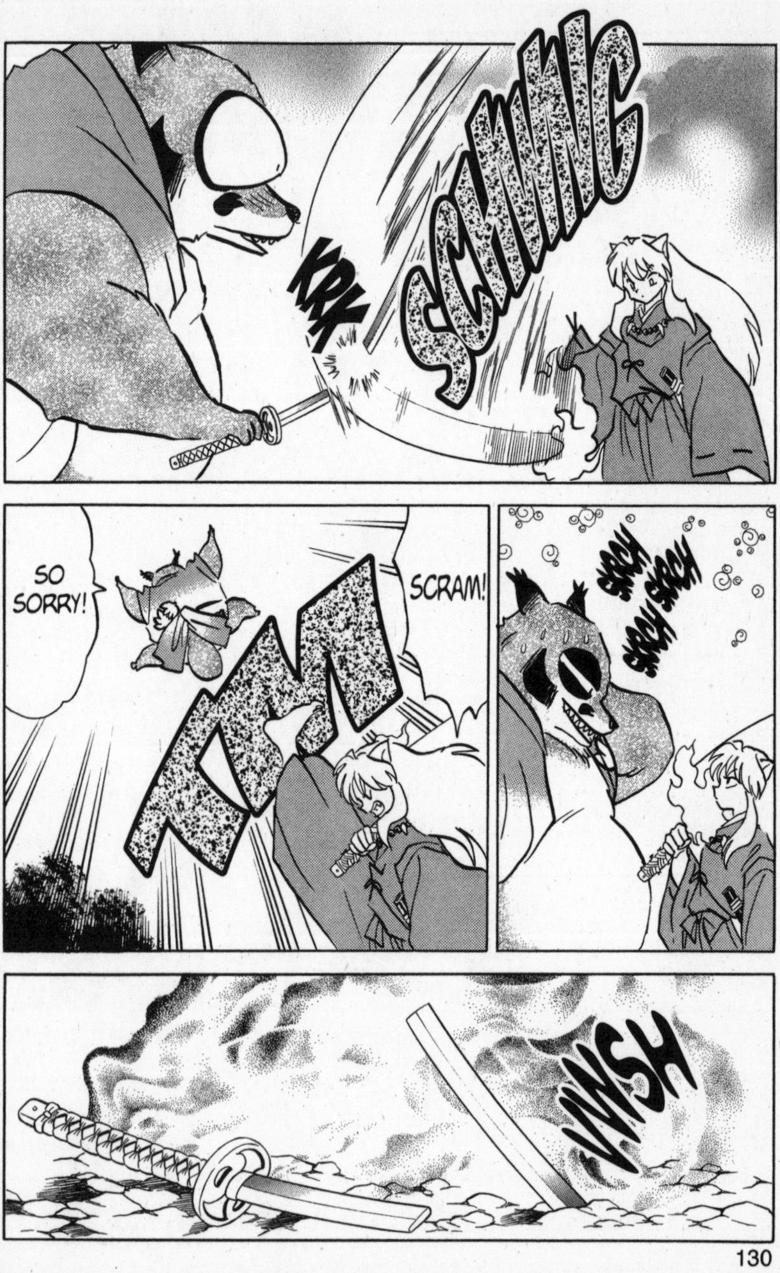
SCHWING
KRK
SRCH SRCH
SRCH SRCH
SCRAM!
TMP
SO SORRY!
VWSH

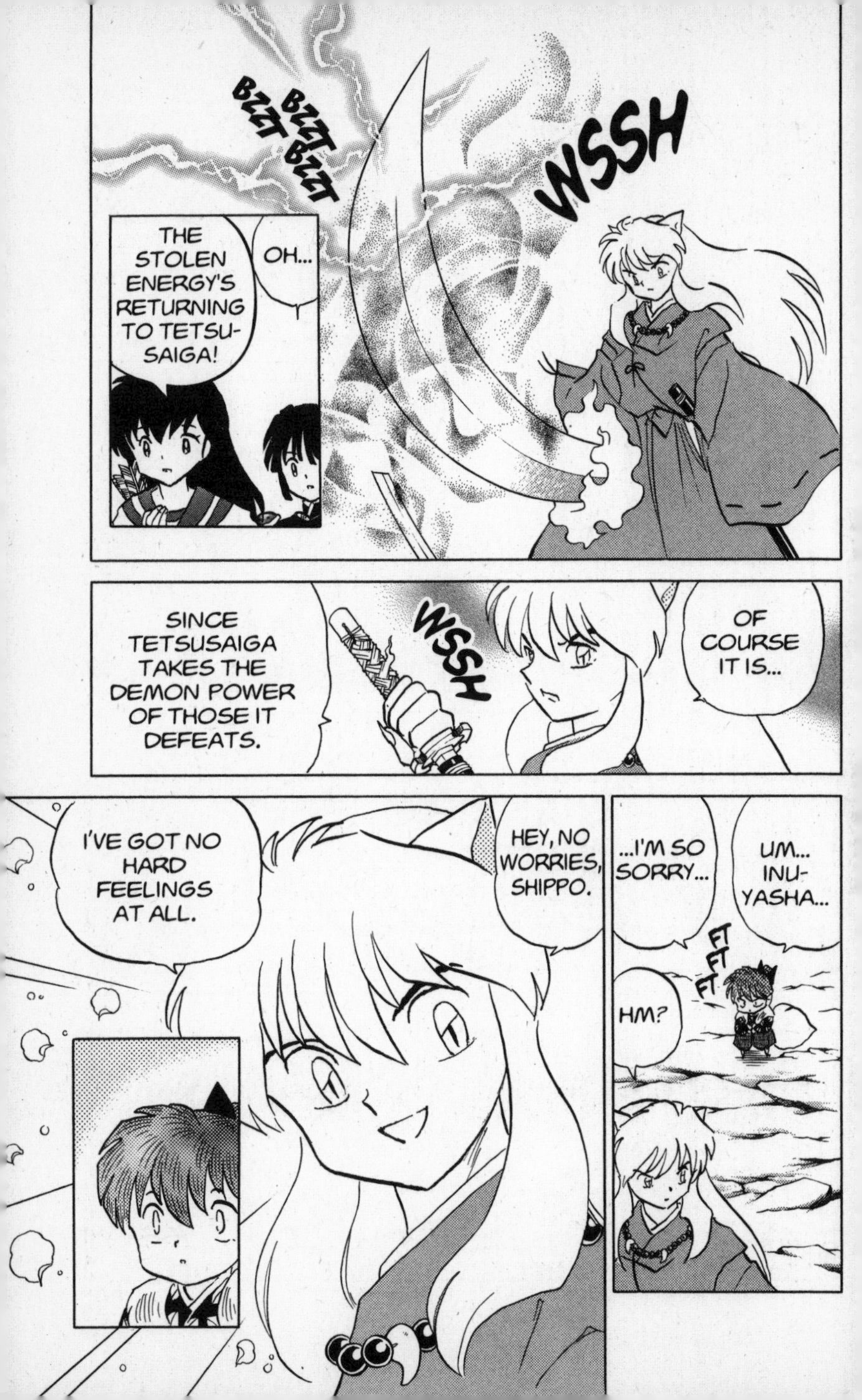
WSSH
BZZT BZZT
OH...
THE STOLEN ENERGY'S RETURNING TO TETSU-SAIGA!
OF COURSE IT IS...
WSSH
SINCE TETSUSAIGA TAKES THE DEMON POWER OF THOSE IT DEFEATS.
UM... INU-YASHA...
...I'M SO SORRY...
FT FT FT
HM?
HEY, NO WORRIES, SHIPPO.
I'VE GOT NO HARD FEELINGS AT ALL.

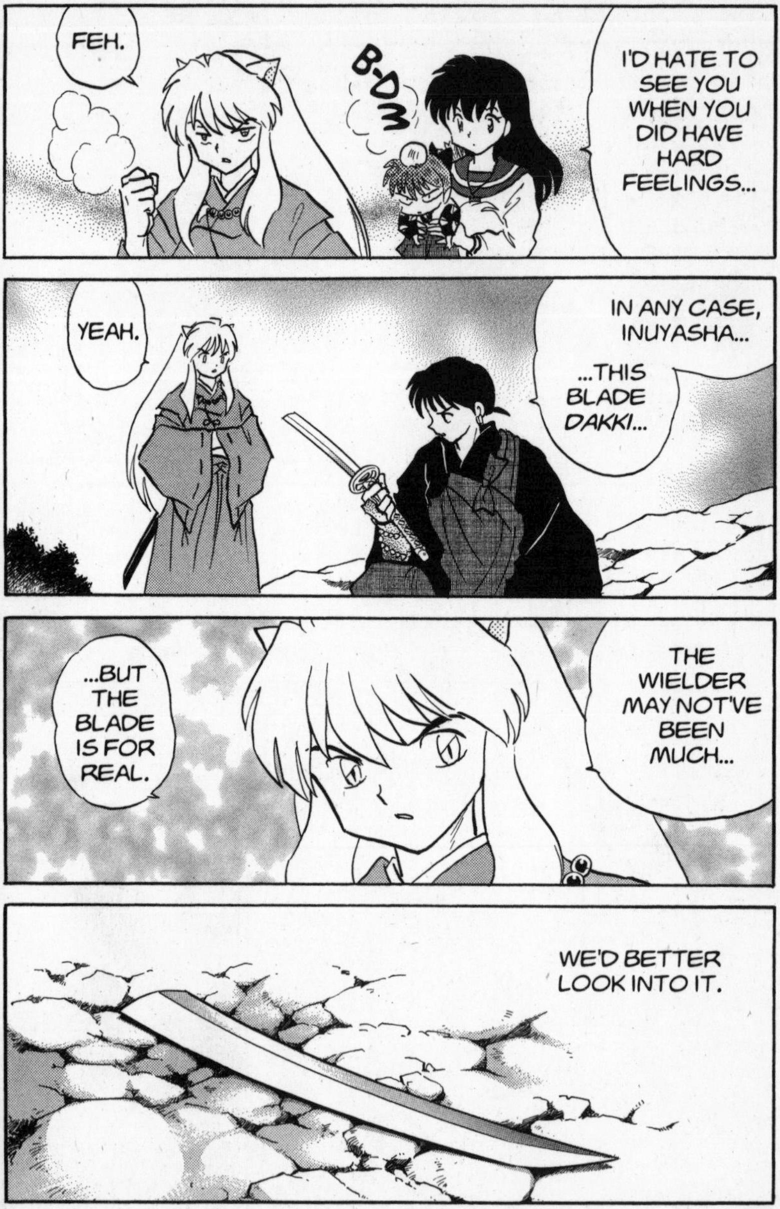
I'D HATE TO SEE YOU WHEN YOU DID HAVE HARD FEELINGS...
B-DM
FEH.
IN ANY CASE, INUYASHA...
...THIS BLADE DAKKI...
YEAH.
THE WIELDER MAY NOT'VE BEEN MUCH...
...BUT THE BLADE IS FOR REAL.
WE'D BETTER LOOK INTO IT.

SCROLL 8

TOSHU

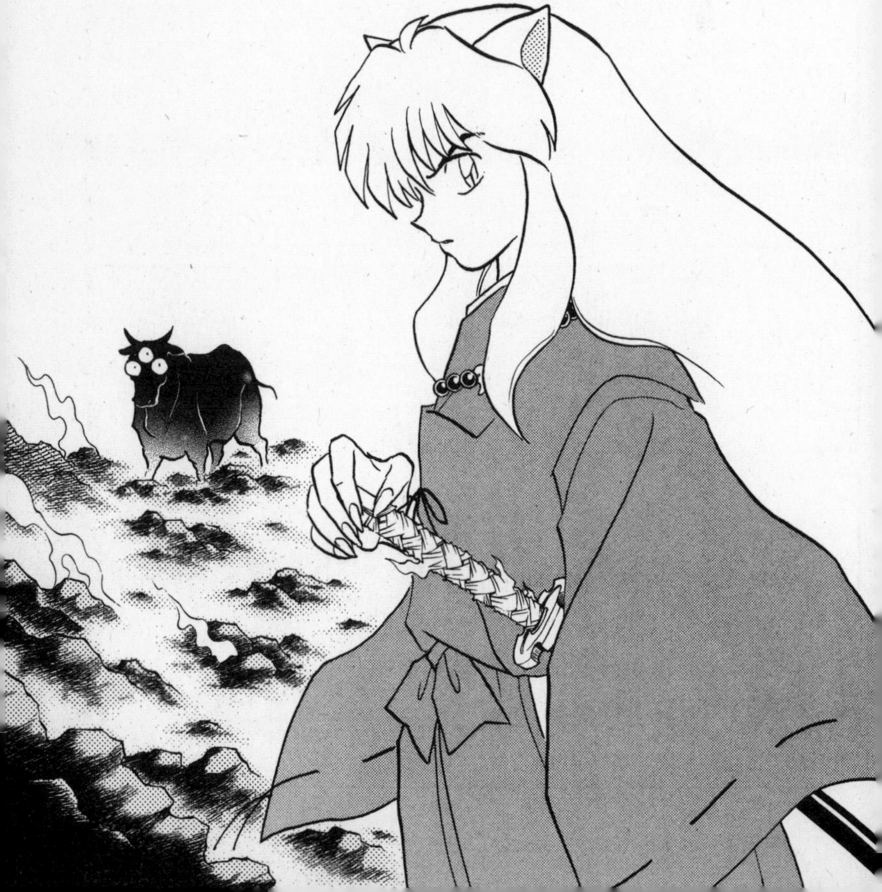

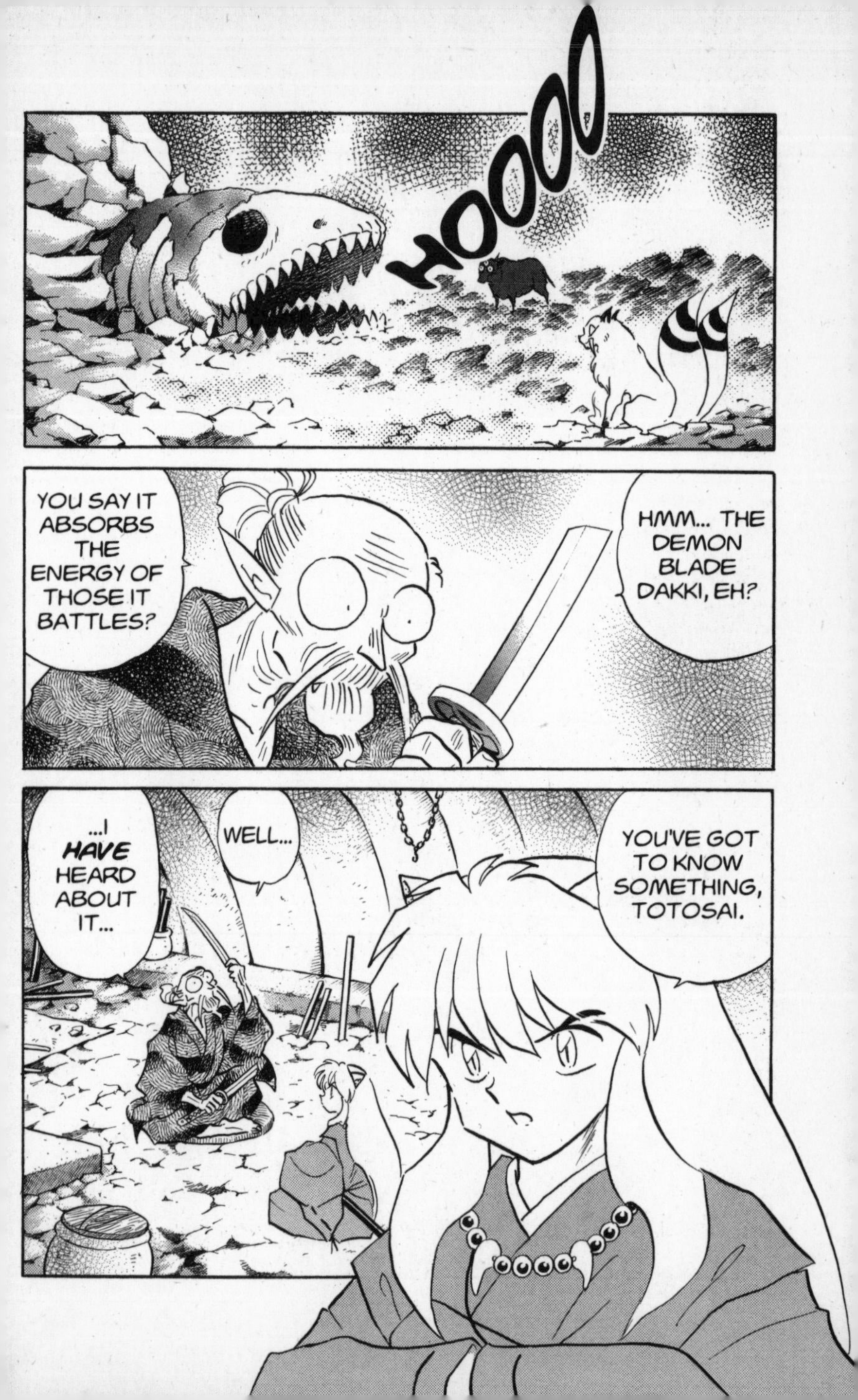
HOOOOO
HMM... THE DEMON BLADE DAKKI, EH?
YOU SAY IT ABSORBS THE ENERGY OF THOSE IT BATTLES?
YOU'VE GOT TO KNOW SOMETHING, TOTOSAI.
WELL...
...I *HAVE* HEARD ABOUT IT...

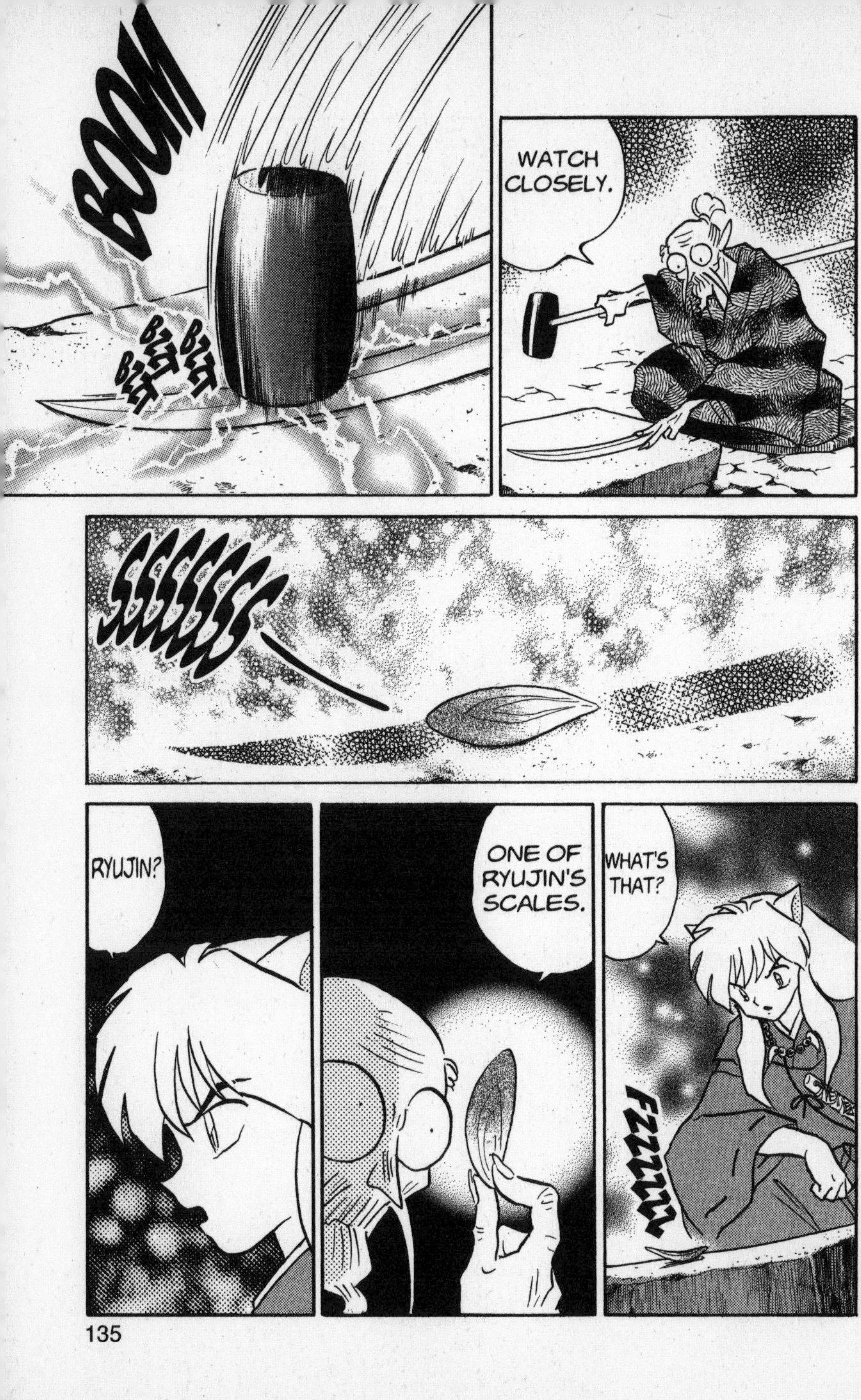
WATCH CLOSELY.
BOOM
BZZT BZZT BZZT
SSSSSSS
WHAT'S THAT?
FZZZZZ
ONE OF RYUJIN'S SCALES.
RYUJIN?

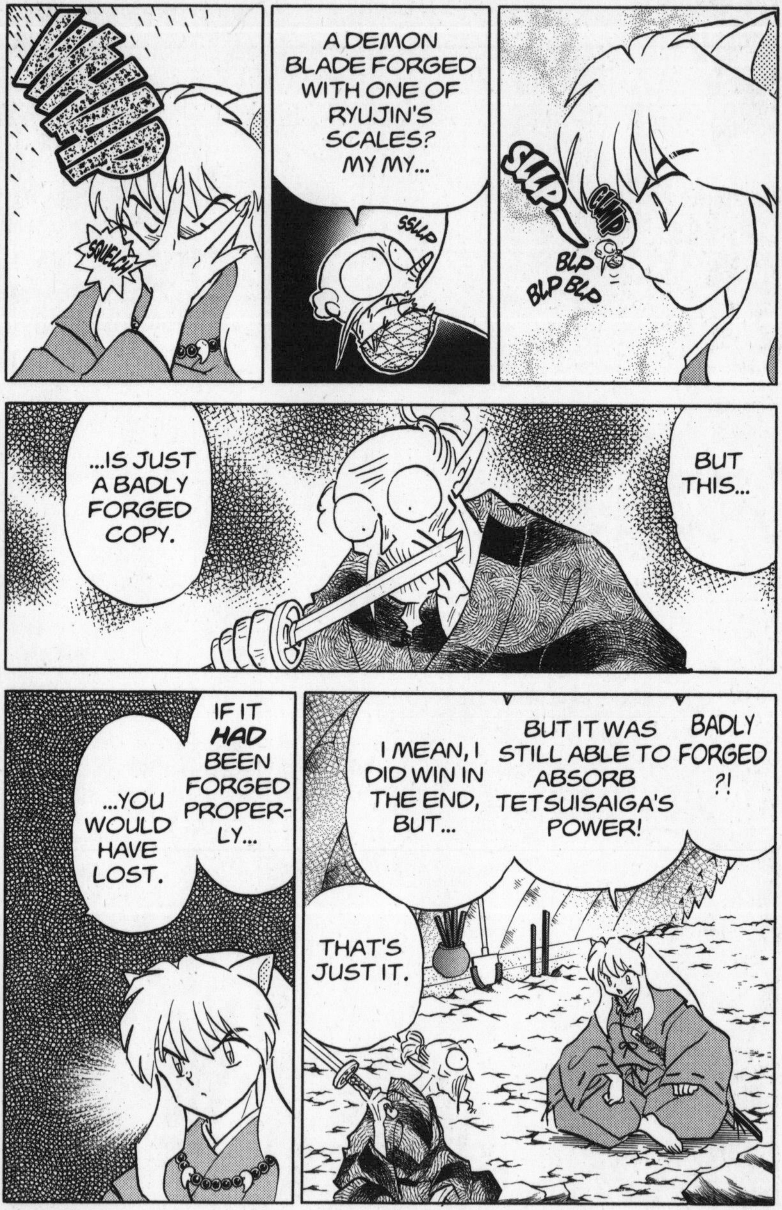
SLIP
GLMP
BLP
BLP BLP
A DEMON BLADE FORGED WITH ONE OF RYUJIN'S SCALES? MY MY...
SSLLP
WHIP
SQUELCH
BUT THIS...
...IS JUST A BADLY FORGED COPY.
BADLY FORGED ?!
BUT IT WAS STILL ABLE TO ABSORB TETSUSAIGA'S POWER!
I MEAN, I DID WIN IN THE END, BUT...
THAT'S JUST IT.
IF IT *HAD* BEEN FORGED PROPER-LY...
...YOU WOULD HAVE LOST.

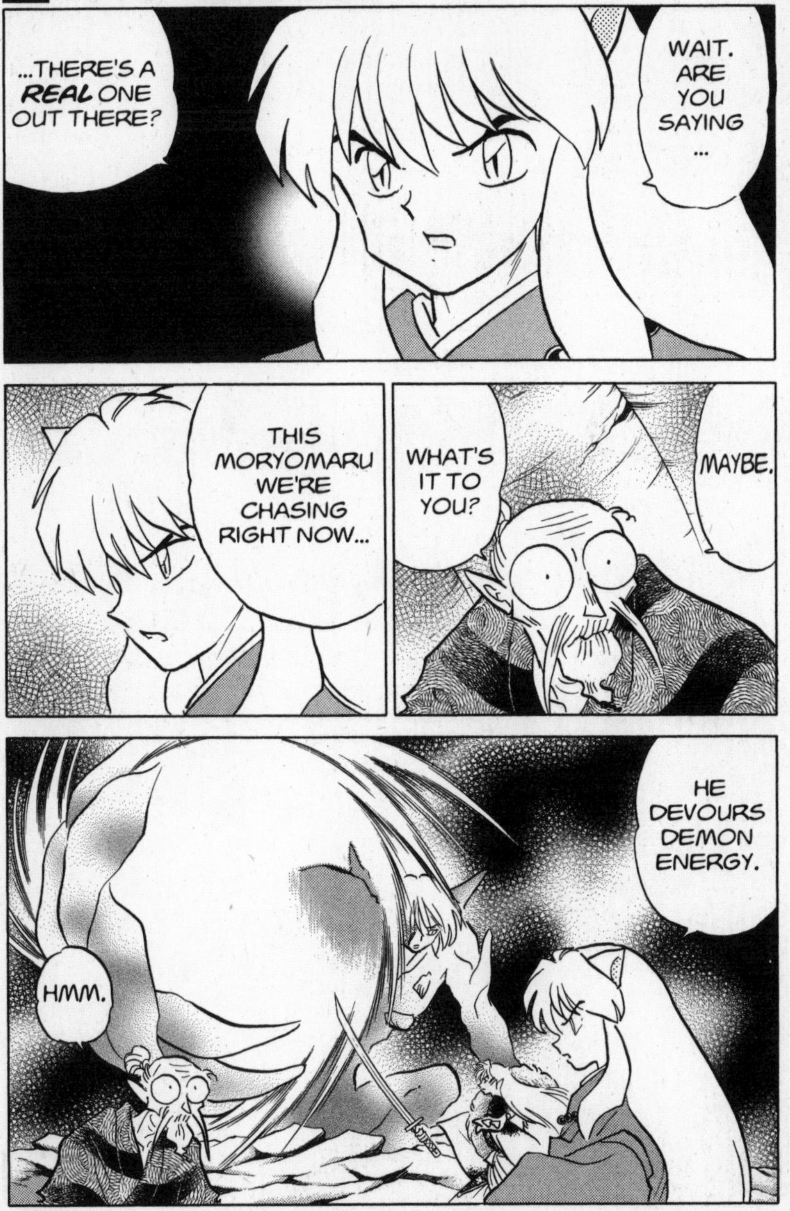
WAIT. ARE YOU SAYING ...
...THERE'S A *REAL* ONE OUT THERE?
MAYBE.
WHAT'S IT TO YOU?
THIS MORYOMARU WE'RE CHASING RIGHT NOW...
HE DEVOURS DEMON ENERGY.
HMM.

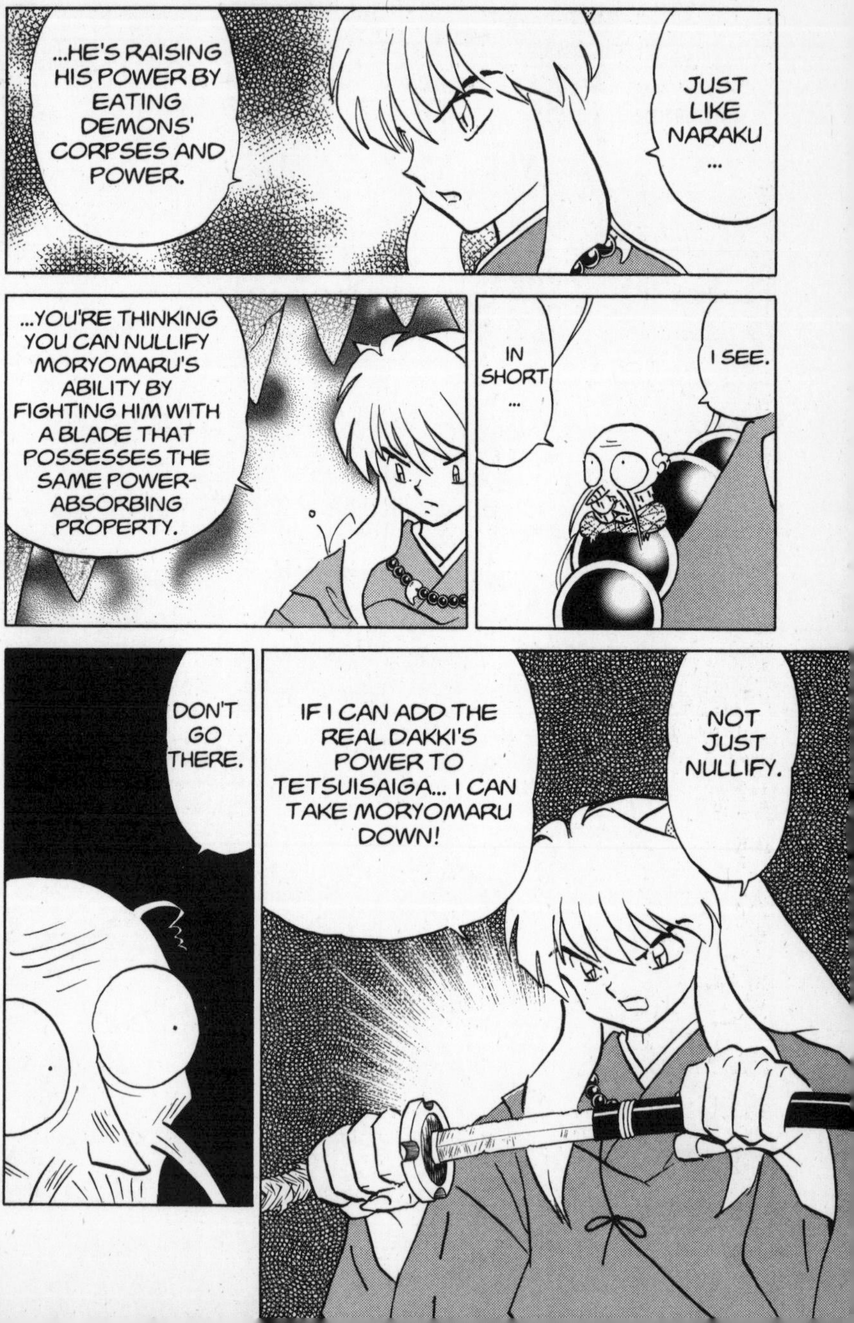
JUST LIKE NARAKU...
...HE'S RAISING HIS POWER BY EATING DEMONS' CORPSES AND POWER.
I SEE.
IN SHORT...
...YOU'RE THINKING YOU CAN NULLIFY MORYOMARU'S ABILITY BY FIGHTING HIM WITH A BLADE THAT POSSESSES THE SAME POWER-ABSORBING PROPERTY.
NOT JUST NULLIFY.
IF I CAN ADD THE REAL DAKKI'S POWER TO TETSUISAIGA... I CAN TAKE MORYOMARU DOWN!
DON'T GO THERE.

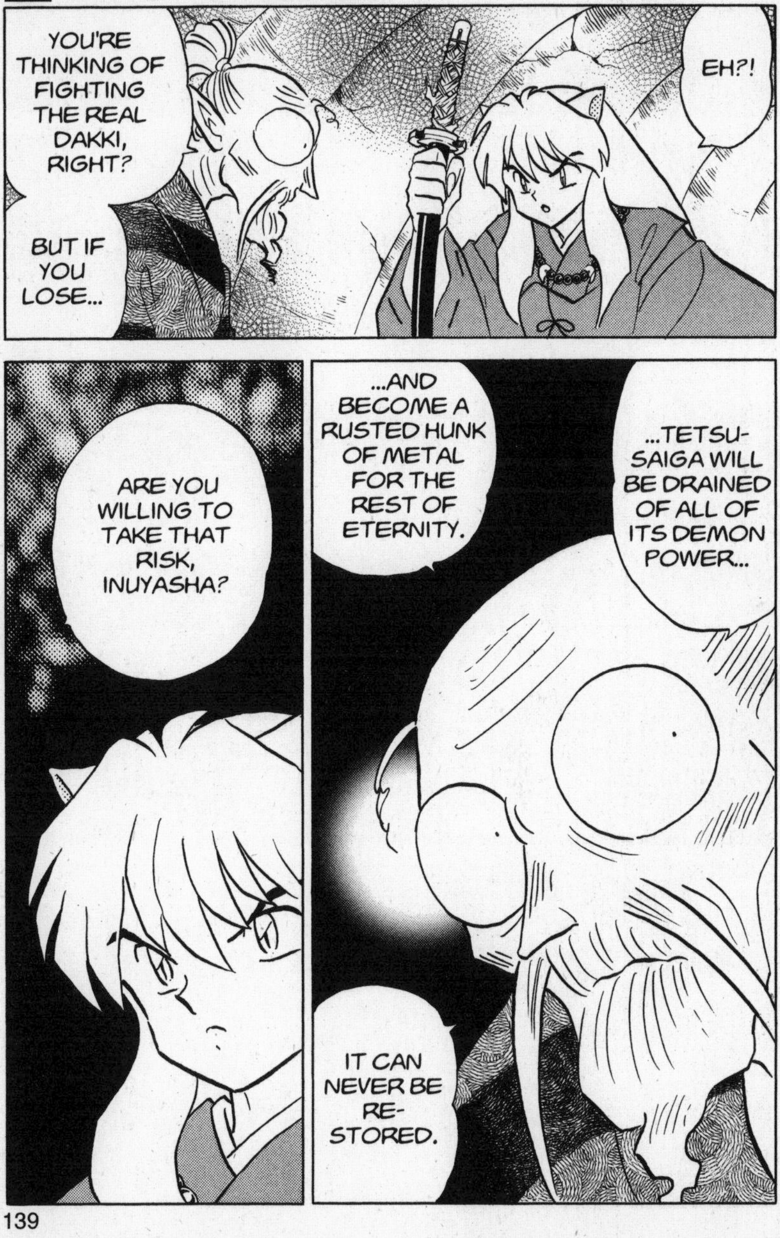
EH?!
YOU'RE THINKING OF FIGHTING THE REAL DAKKI, RIGHT?
BUT IF YOU LOSE...
...TETSU-SAIGA WILL BE DRAINED OF ALL OF ITS DEMON POWER...
...AND BECOME A RUSTED HUNK OF METAL FOR THE REST OF ETERNITY.
IT CAN NEVER BE RE-STORED.
ARE YOU WILLING TO TAKE THAT RISK, INUYASHA?

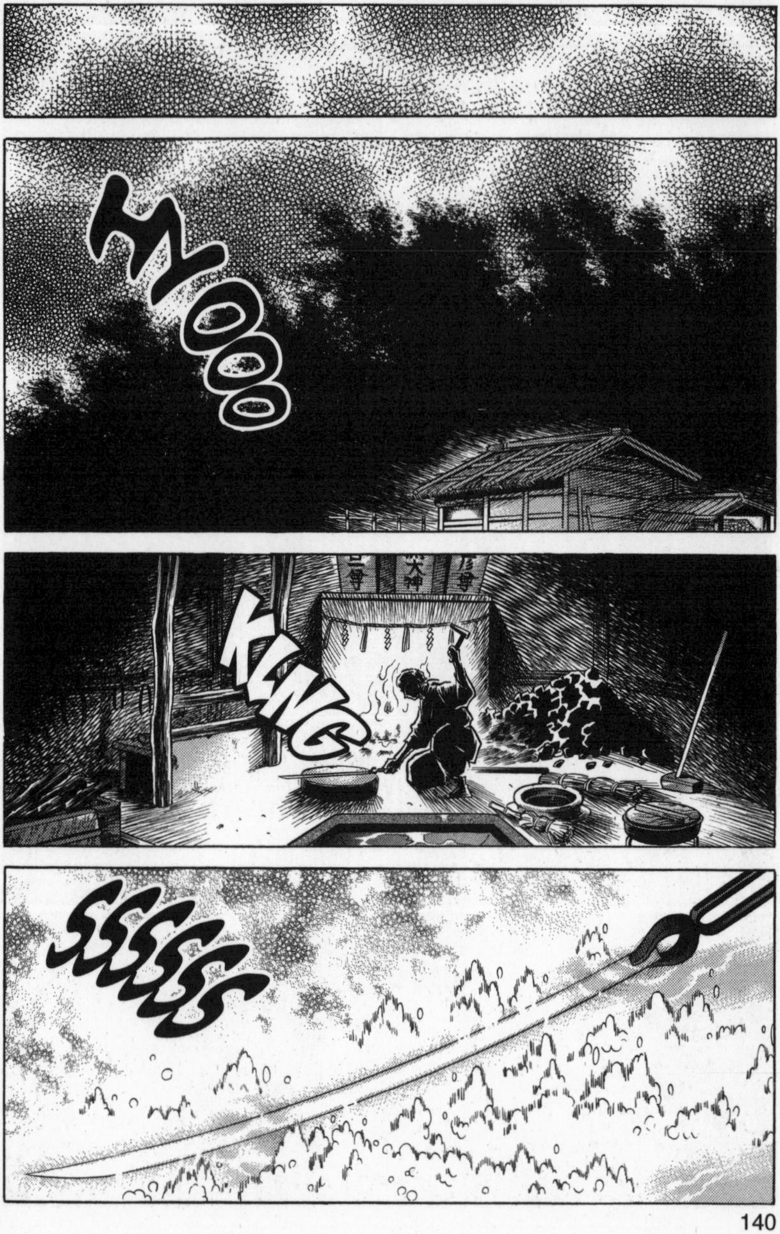
HYOOO
KLNG
SSSSS

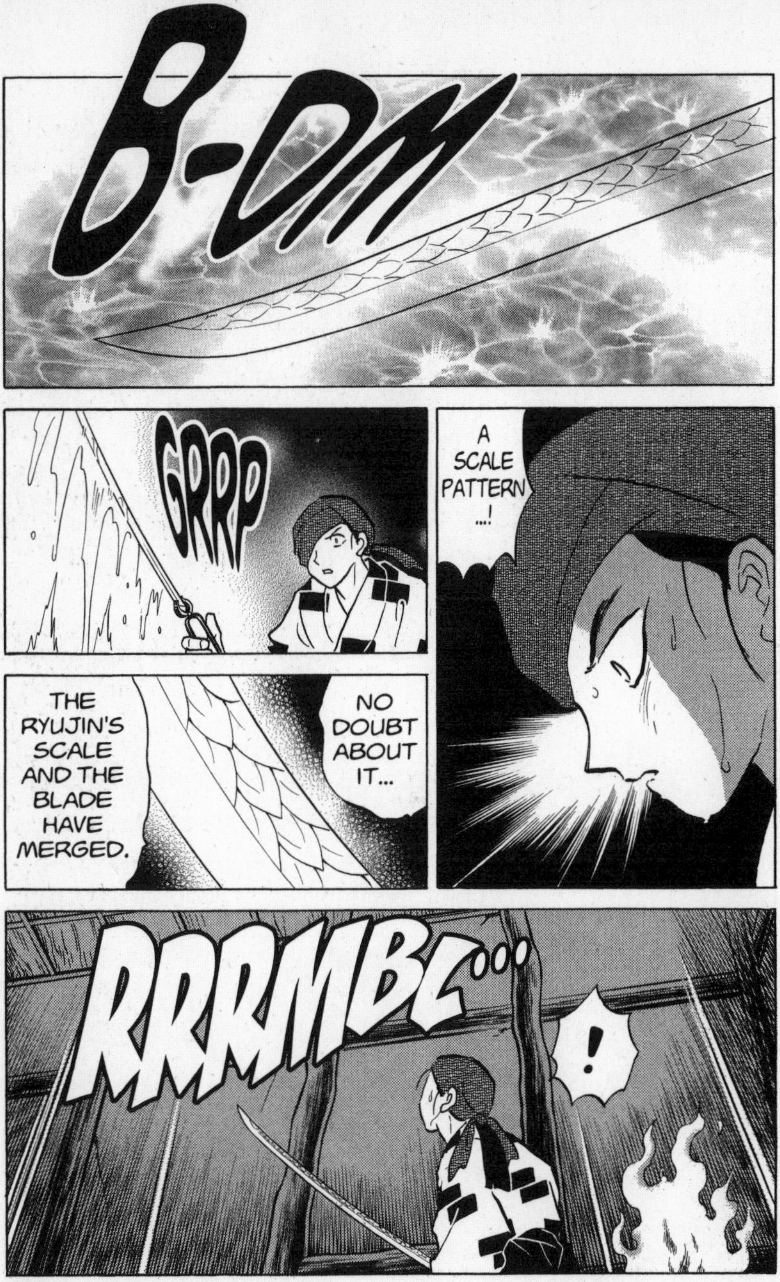
B-OM
A SCALE PATTERN ...!
GRRP
NO DOUBT ABOUT IT...
THE RYUJIN'S SCALE AND THE BLADE HAVE MERGED.
RRRMBL...
!

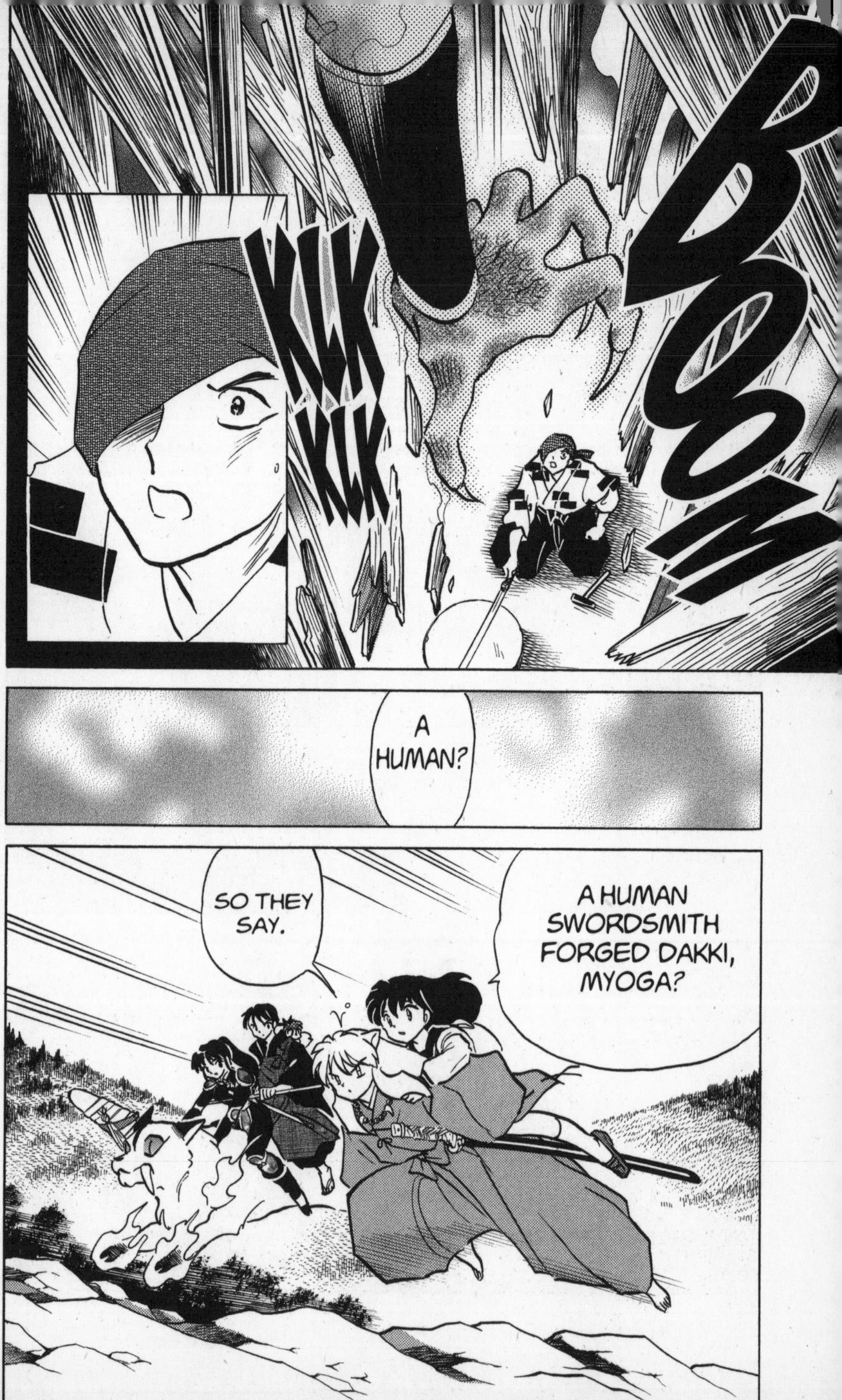
BOOM!!
KLK KLK
A HUMAN?
A HUMAN SWORDSMITH FORGED DAKKI, MYOGA?
SO THEY SAY.

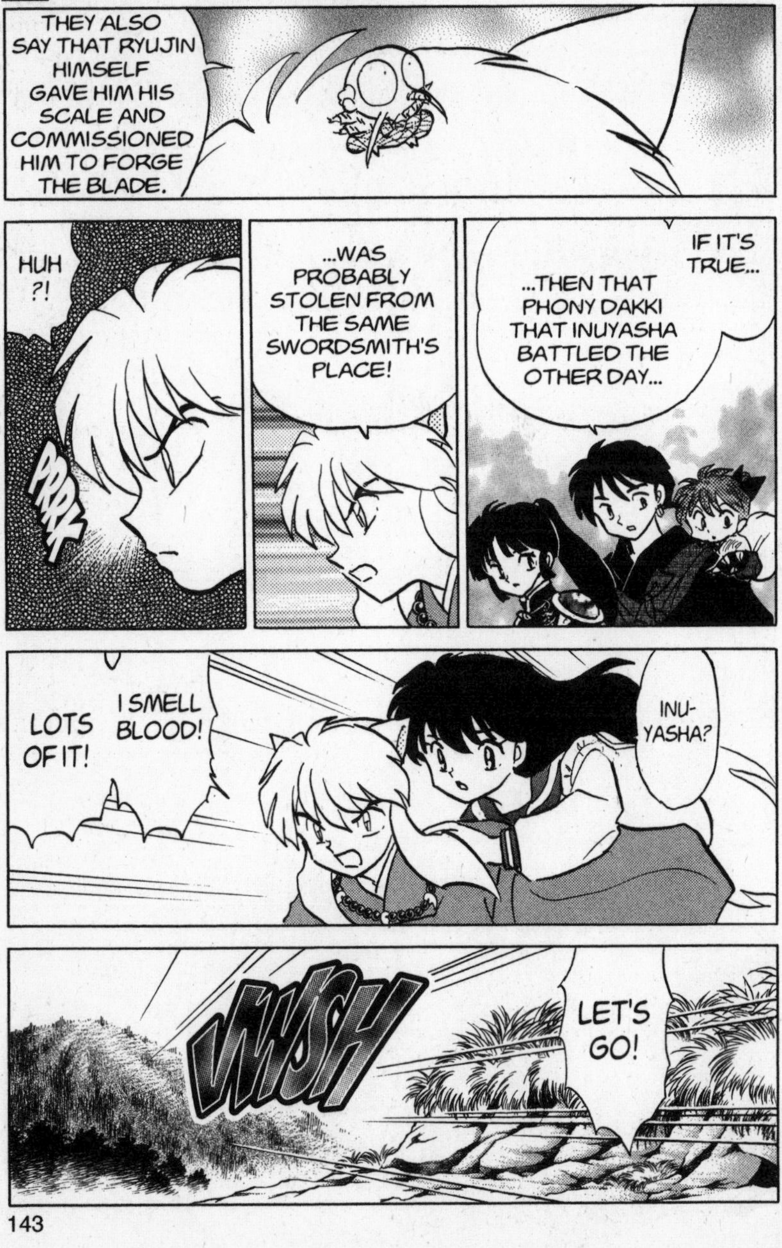
THEY ALSO SAY THAT RYUJIN HIMSELF GAVE HIM HIS SCALE AND COMMISSIONED HIM TO FORGE THE BLADE.
IF IT'S TRUE...
...THEN THAT PHONY DAKKI THAT INUYASHA BATTLED THE OTHER DAY...
...WAS PROBABLY STOLEN FROM THE SAME SWORDSMITH'S PLACE!
HUH ?!
PRRK
INU-YASHA?
I SMELL BLOOD!
LOTS OF IT!
LET'S GO!
WHSH

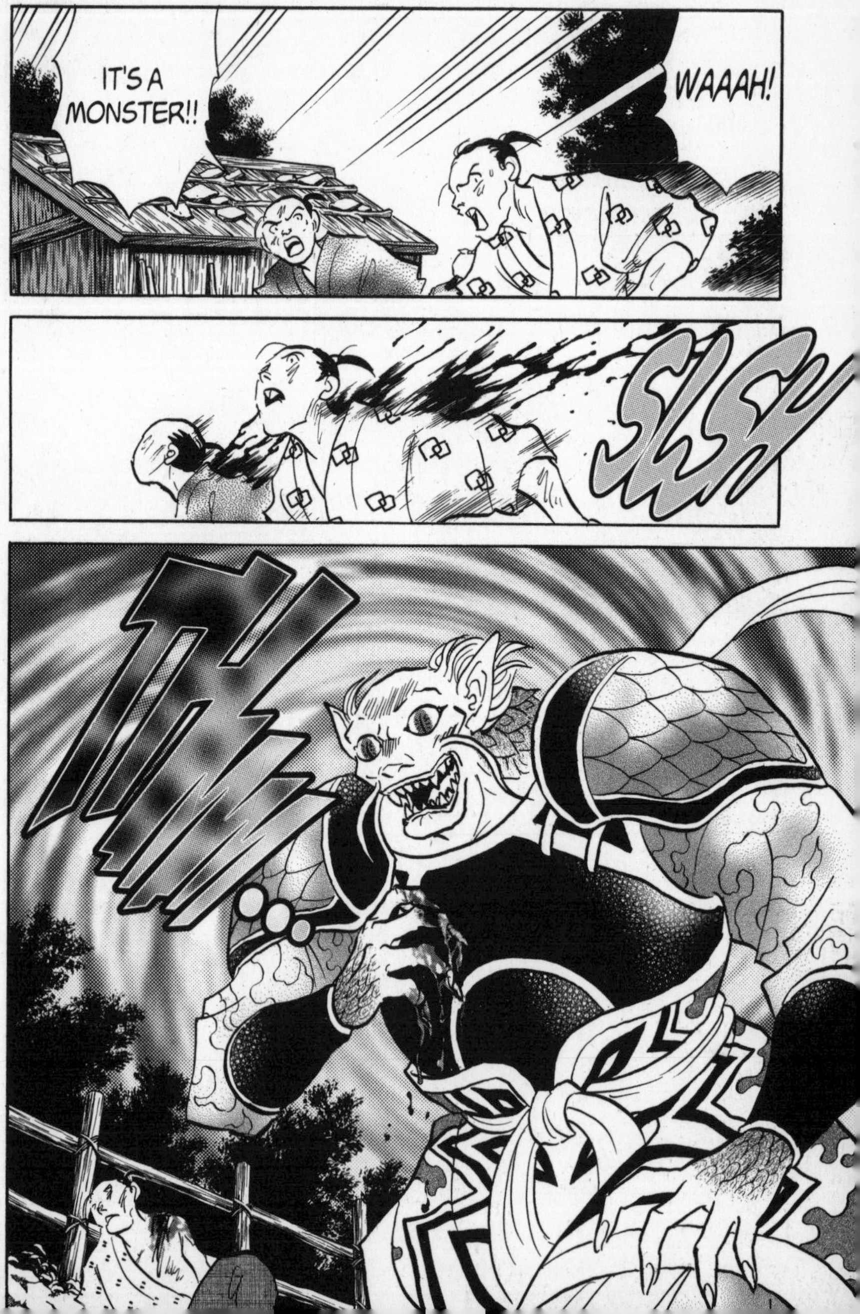
WAAAH!
IT'S A MONSTER!!
SLSH

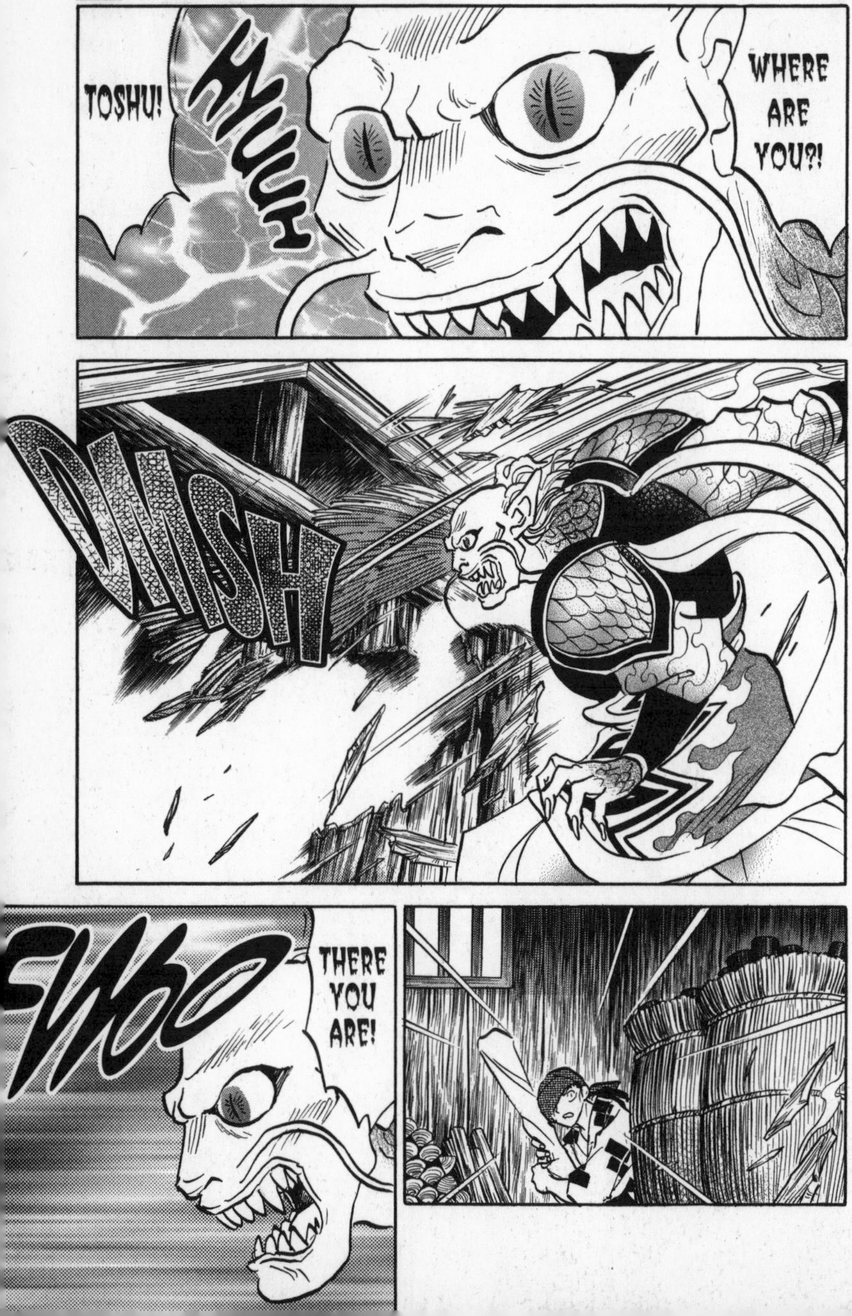
WHERE ARE YOU?!
HNUUH
TOSHU!
CHMISH
THERE YOU ARE!
FWOO

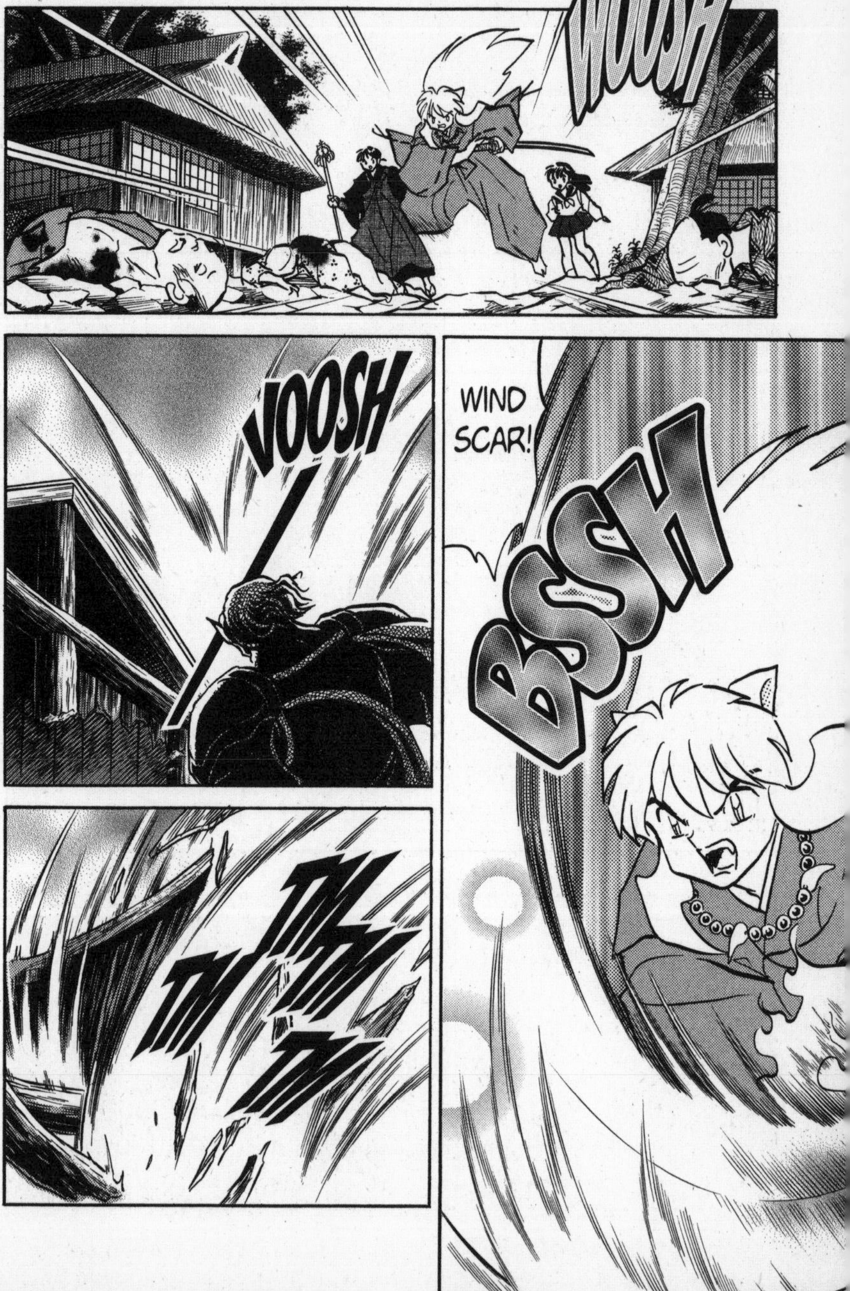
WOOSH
WIND SCAR!
BSSH
VOOSH

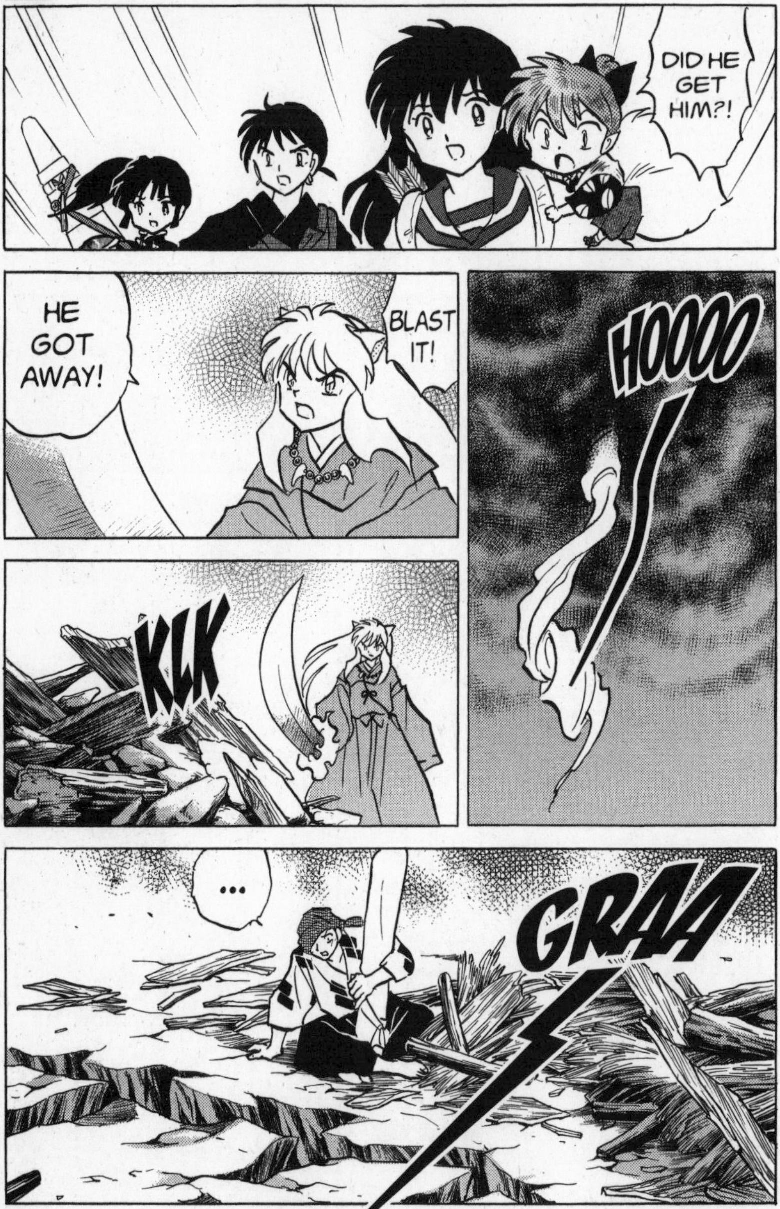
DID HE GET HIM?!
HOOOO
BLAST IT!
HE GOT AWAY!
KLK
GRAA
...

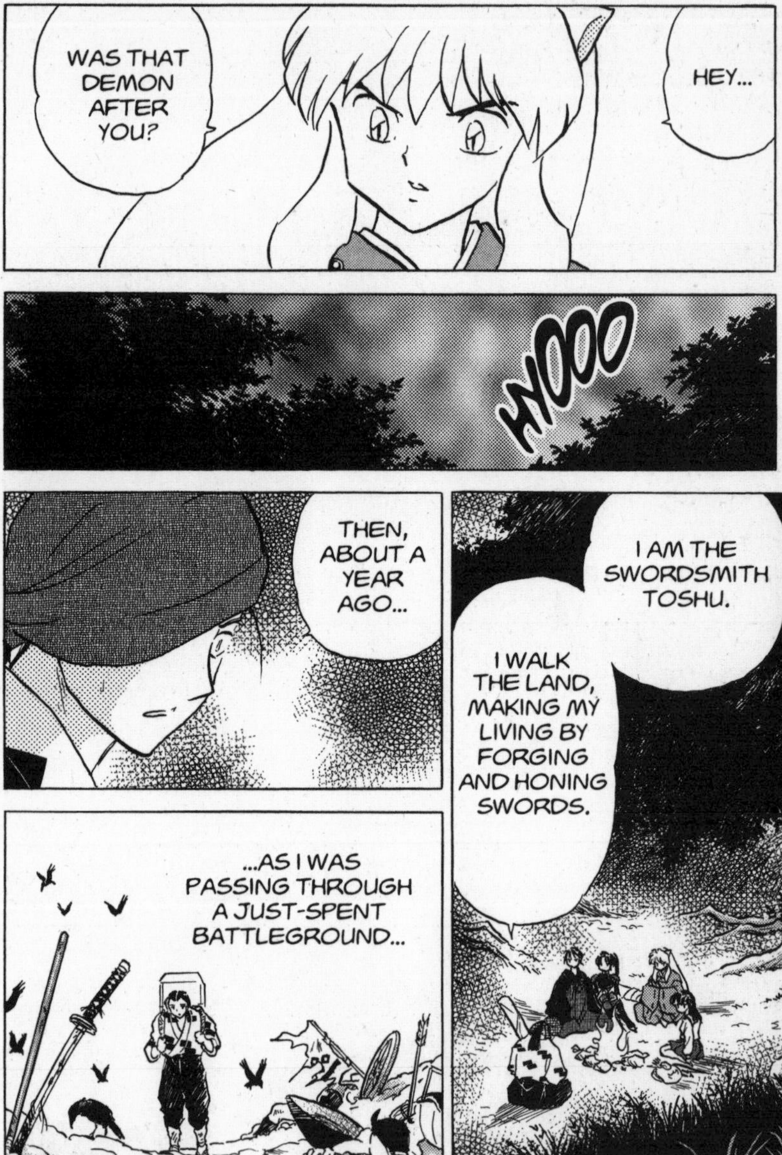
HEY...
WAS THAT DEMON AFTER YOU?
HYOOO
I AM THE SWORDSMITH TOSHU.
I WALK THE LAND, MAKING MY LIVING BY FORGING AND HONING SWORDS.
THEN, ABOUT A YEAR AGO...
...AS I WAS PASSING THROUGH A JUST-SPENT BATTLEGROUND...

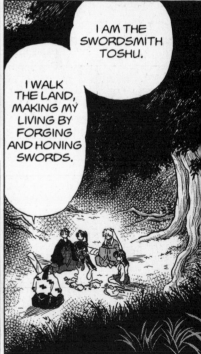

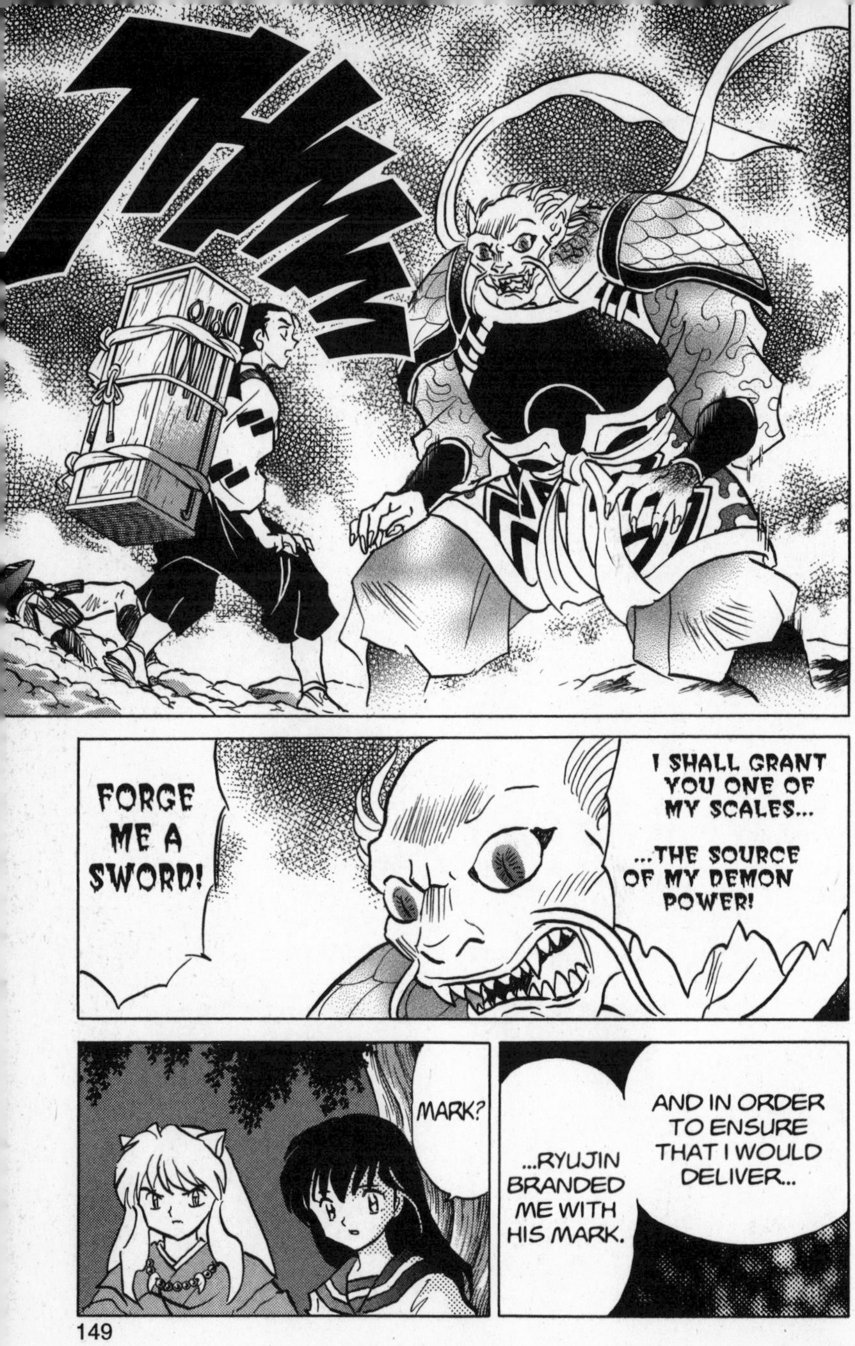
I SHALL GRANT YOU ONE OF MY SCALES...
...THE SOURCE OF MY DEMON POWER!
FORGE ME A SWORD!
AND IN ORDER TO ENSURE THAT I WOULD DELIVER...
...RYUJIN BRANDED ME WITH HIS MARK.
MARK?

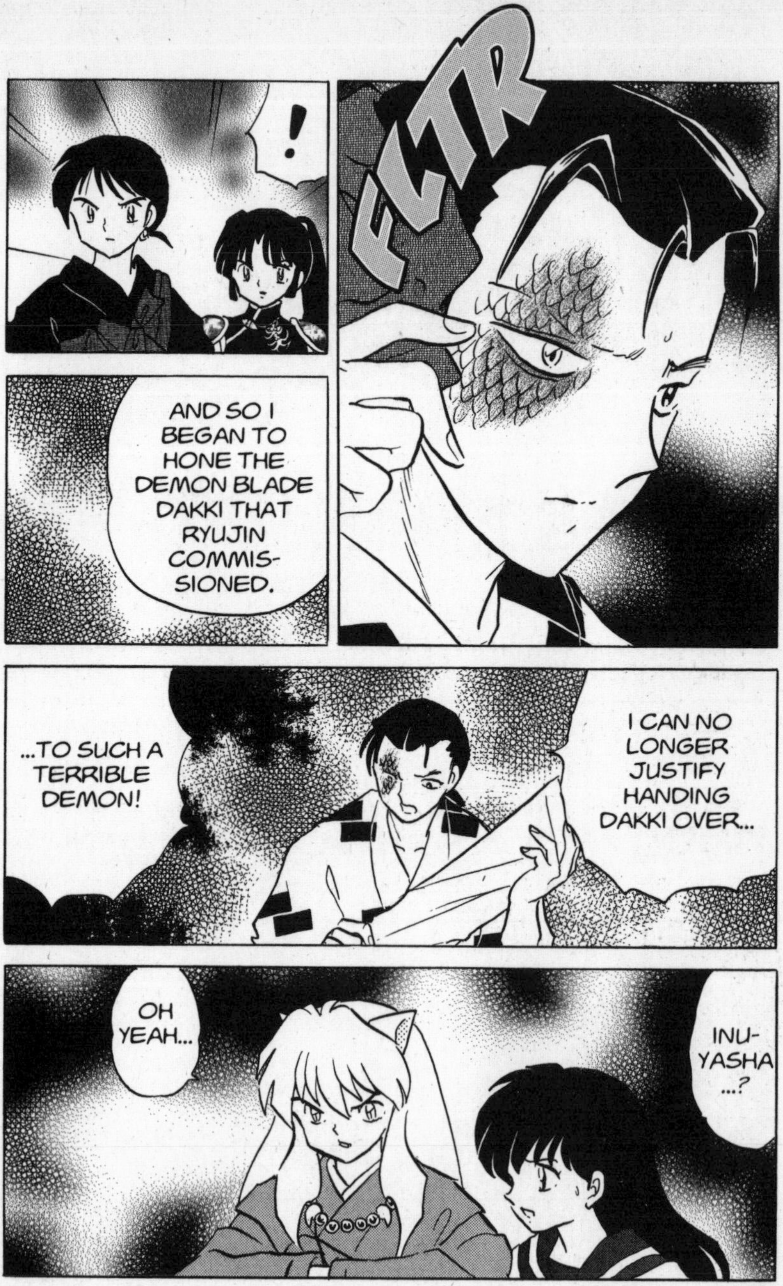
FLTR
!
AND SO I BEGAN TO HONE THE DEMON BLADE DAKKI THAT RYUJIN COMMISSIONED.
I CAN NO LONGER JUSTIFY HANDING DAKKI OVER...
...TO SUCH A TERRIBLE DEMON!
INU-YASHA ...?
OH YEAH...

SCROLL 9

RYUJIN'S SHIELD

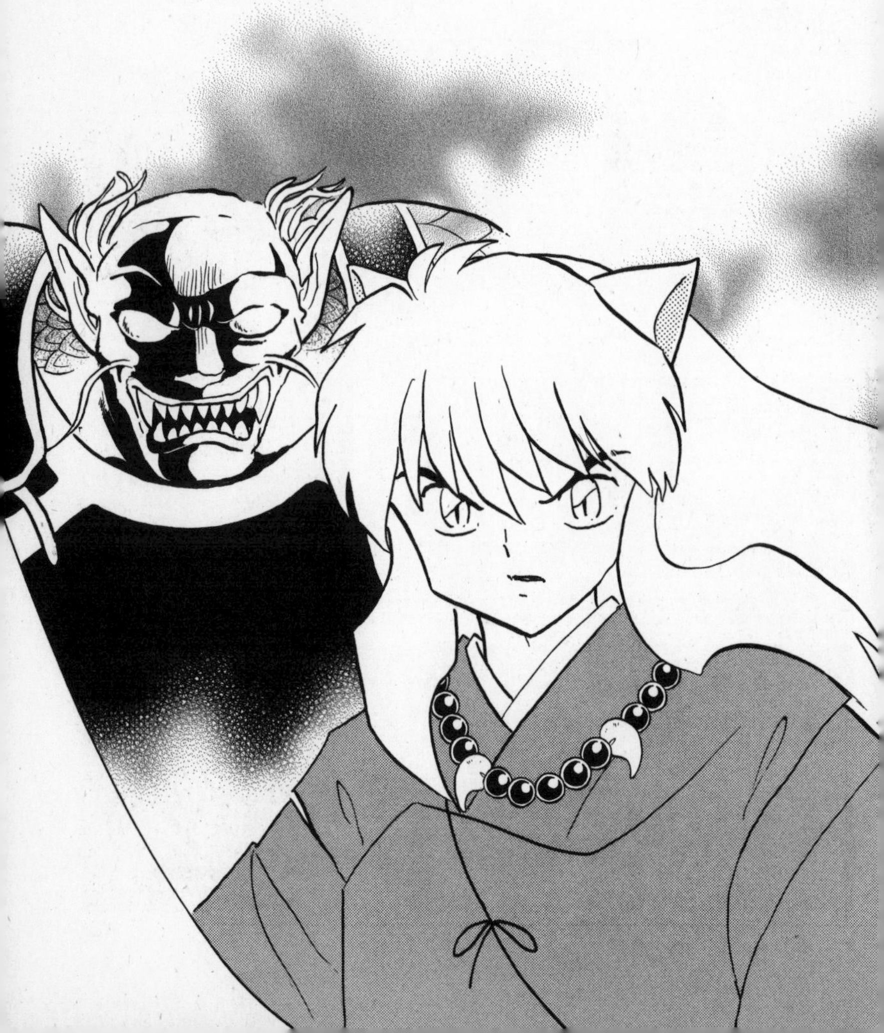

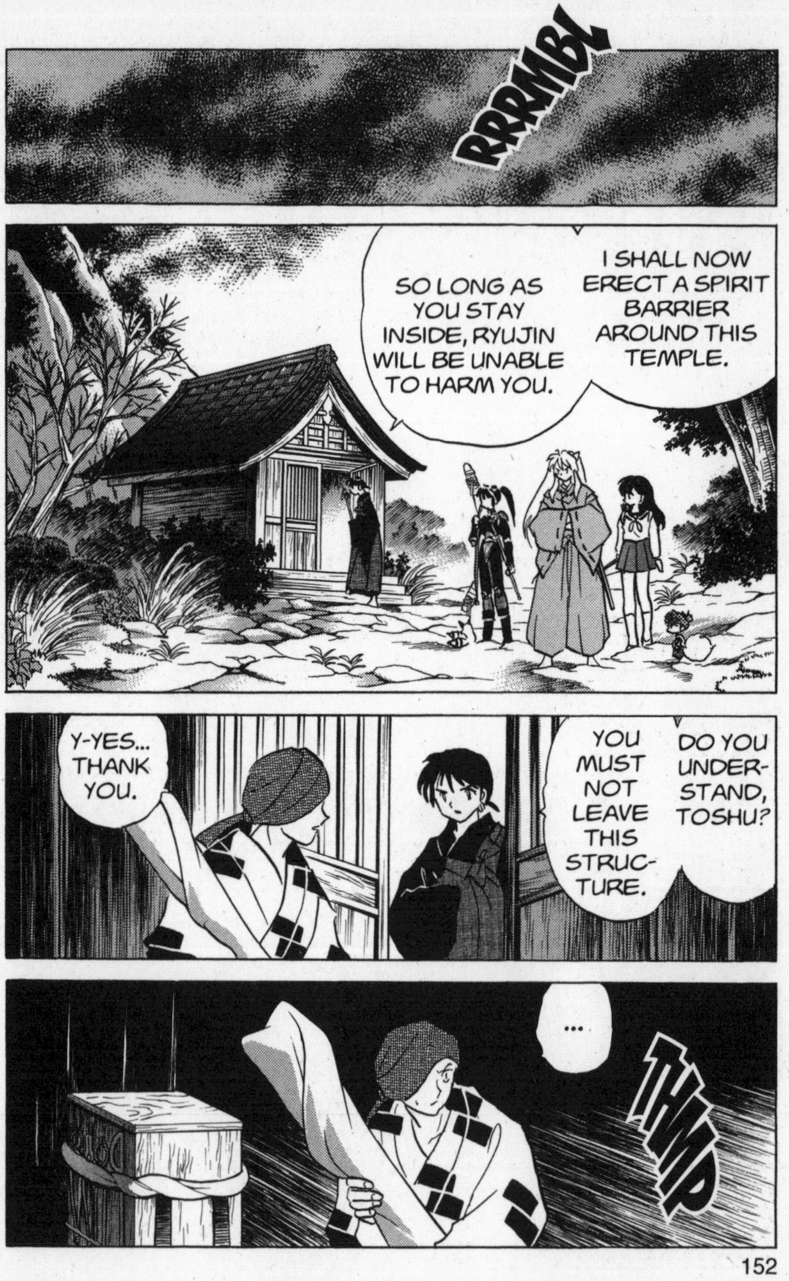
RRRMBL
I SHALL NOW ERECT A SPIRIT BARRIER AROUND THIS TEMPLE.
SO LONG AS YOU STAY INSIDE, RYUJIN WILL BE UNABLE TO HARM YOU.
DO YOU UNDER-STAND, TOSHU?
YOU MUST NOT LEAVE THIS STRUC-TURE.
Y-YES... THANK YOU.
...
THMP

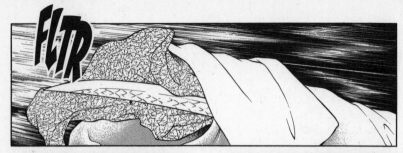

FLTR
BZZZ
DAKKI IS... AGITATED...
ARE YOU SURE ABOUT THIS, LORD INUYASHA?
ABOUT WHAT, OLD MAN?
THE DEMON-BLADE DAKKI IS RIGHT IN FRONT OF YOU!

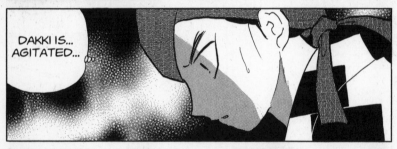

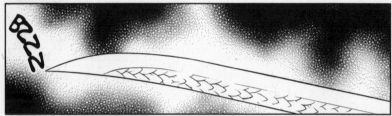

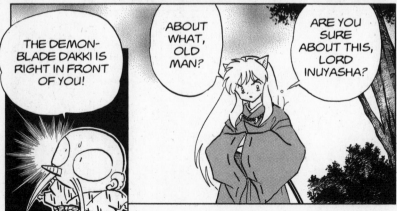

WEREN'T YOU PLANNING TO DEFEAT DAKKI IN ORDER TO STRENGTHEN TETSUSAIGA?
SO GO FOR IT!
ARE YOU SAYING I SHOULD JUST GRAB THE BLADE FROM THAT SWORDSMITH?
OF COURSE YOU SHOULD!
DO I LOOK LIKE A THIEF TO YOU?!
OH DEAR ...
MYOGA'S AS SHAMELESS AS EVER...
IN TRUTH... I MUST AGREE WITH LORD MYOGA ON THIS ONE.
WHAT?!

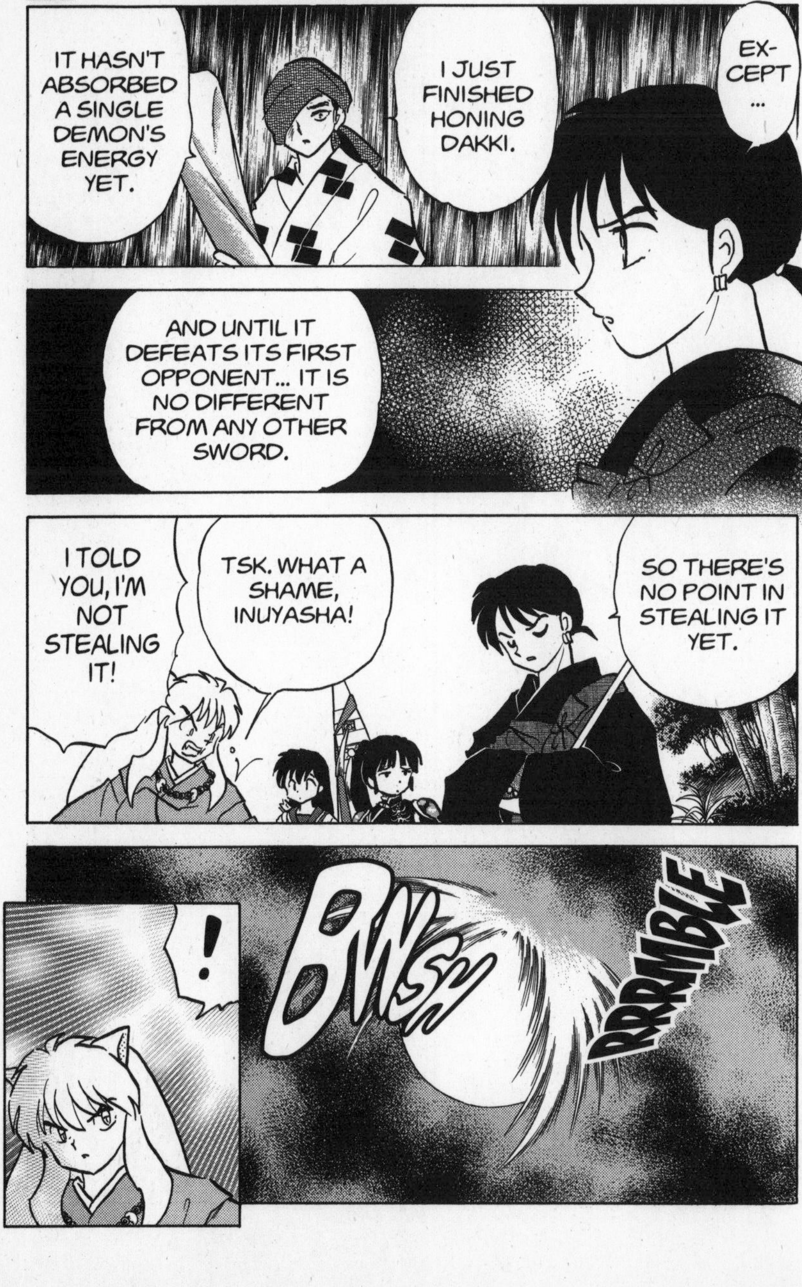
EX-CEPT ...
I JUST FINISHED HONING DAKKI.
IT HASN'T ABSORBED A SINGLE DEMON'S ENERGY YET.
AND UNTIL IT DEFEATS ITS FIRST OPPONENT... IT IS NO DIFFERENT FROM ANY OTHER SWORD.
SO THERE'S NO POINT IN STEALING IT YET.
TSK. WHAT A SHAME, INUYASHA!
I TOLD YOU, I'M NOT STEALING IT!
RRRMBLE
BWSH
!

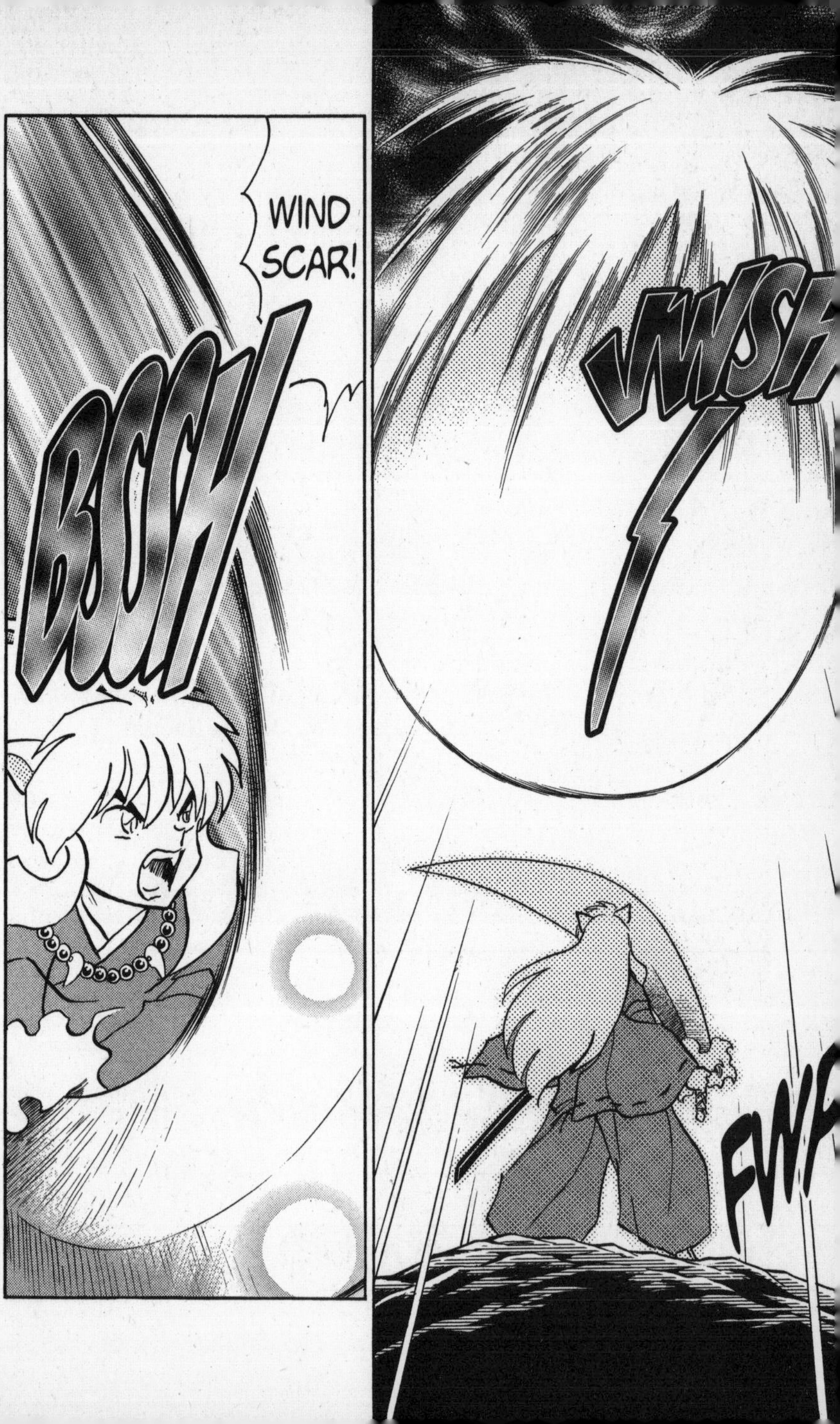
WIND SCAR!

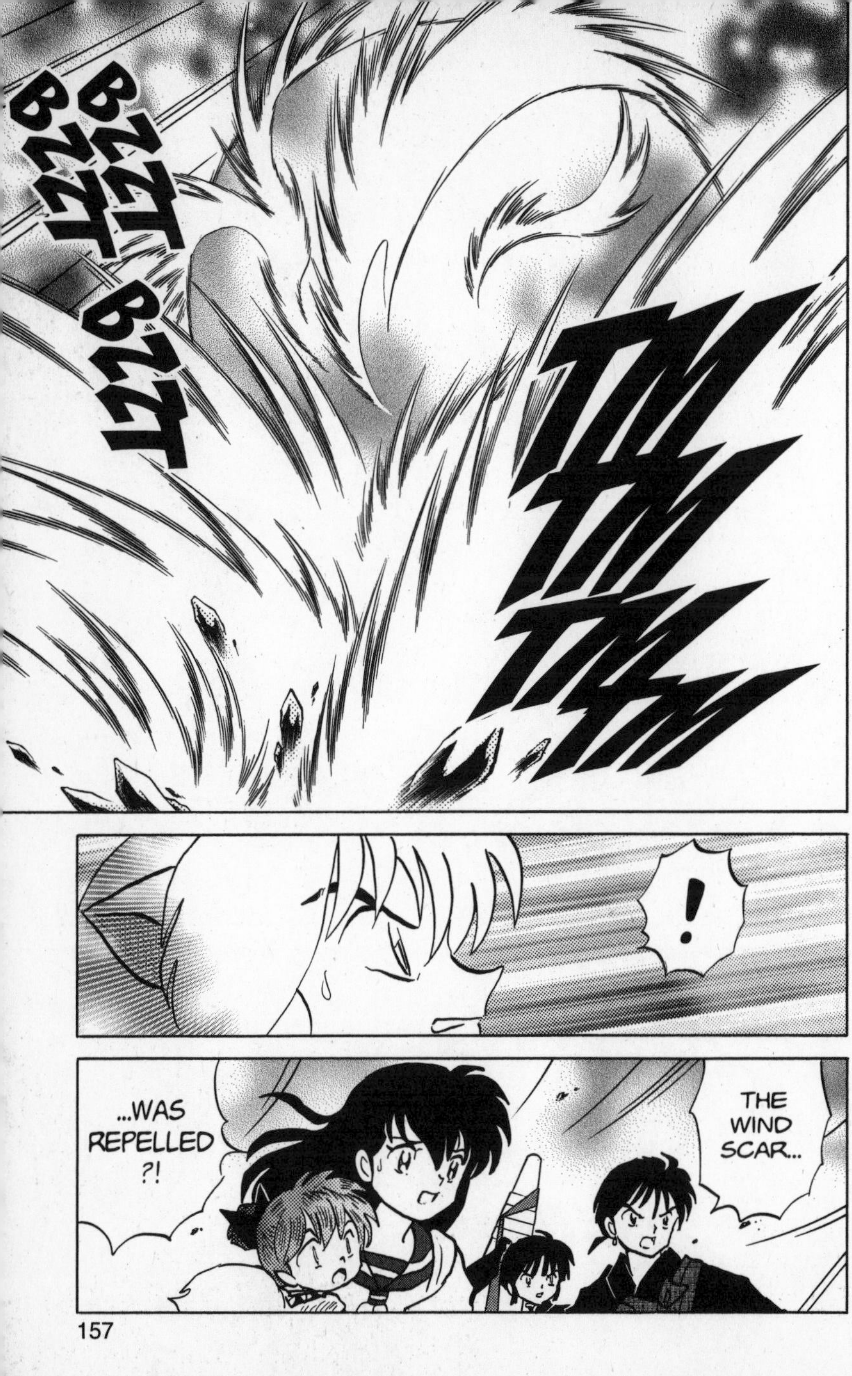
BZZT BZZT
BZZT BZZT
!
THE WIND SCAR...
...WAS REPELLED ?!

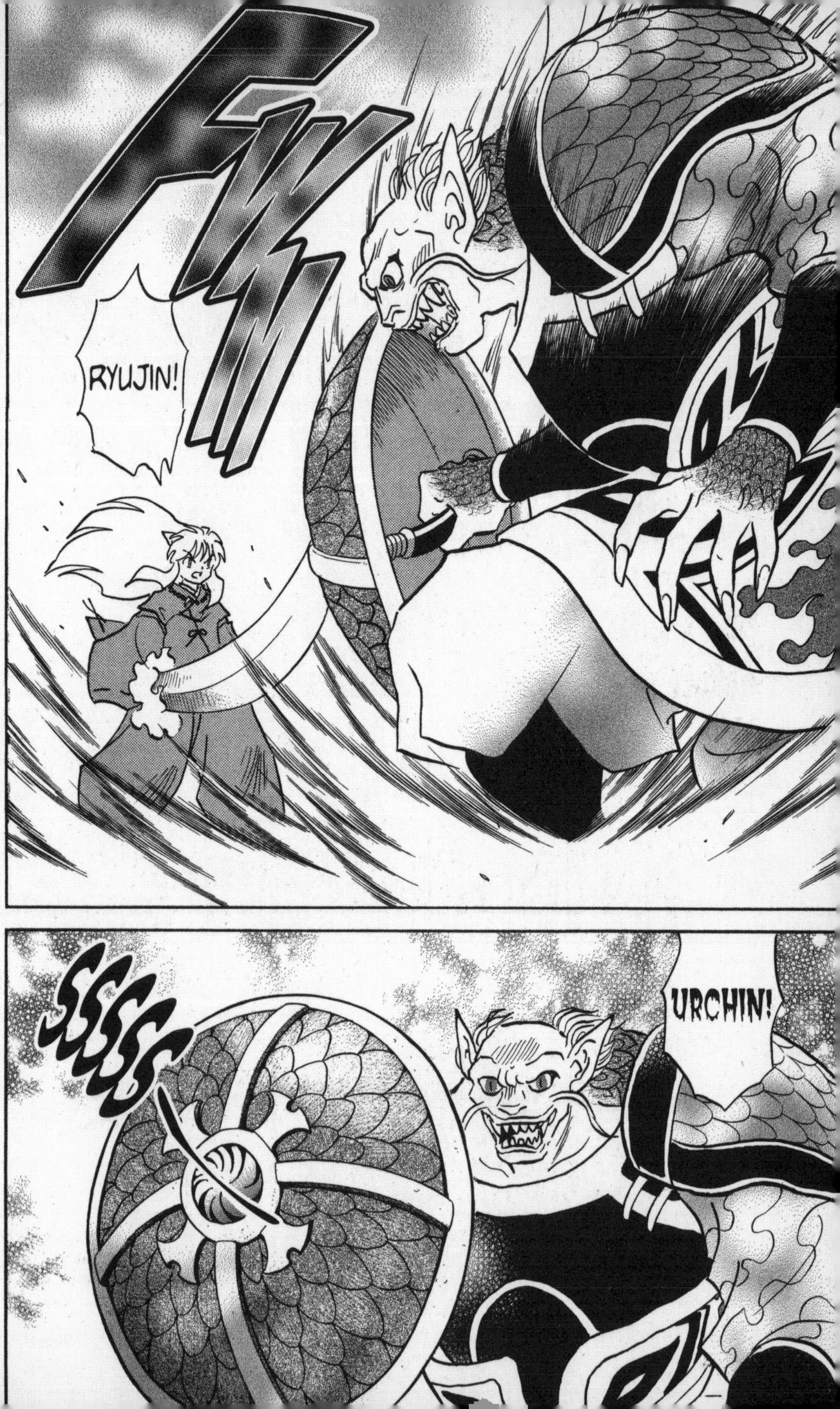
FWM
RYUJIN!
URCHIN!
SSSSS

THAT'S HOW HE DEFLECTED THE WIND SCAR!

A SHIELD ?!

YOU'RE HARBORING TOSHU, AREN'T YOU?!

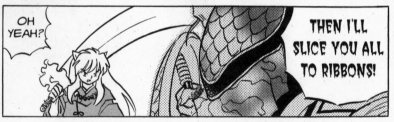

OH YEAH?

THEN I'LL SLICE YOU ALL TO RIBBONS!

SO TRY IT!

VWSH

I LIKE RIBBONS.

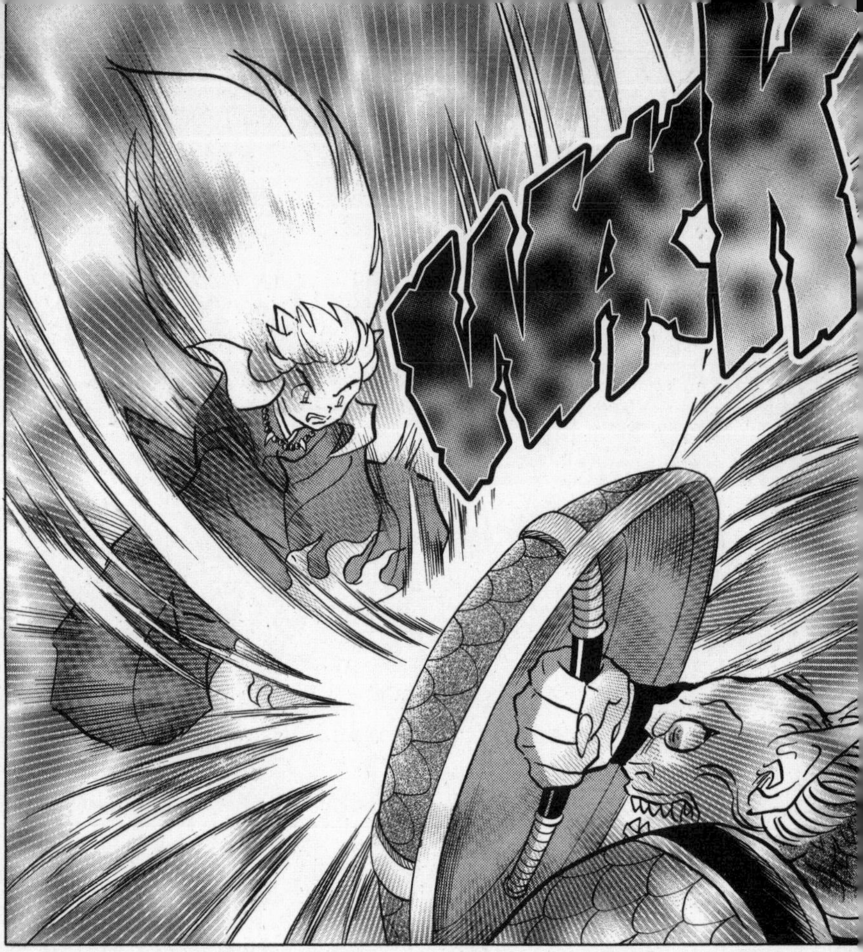

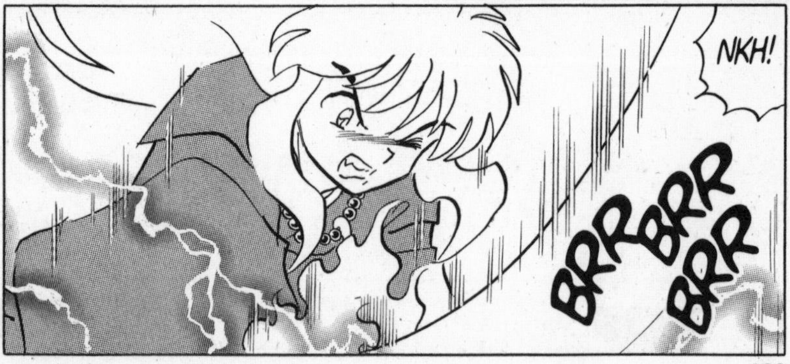
NKH!
BRRBRR
BRR
BRR

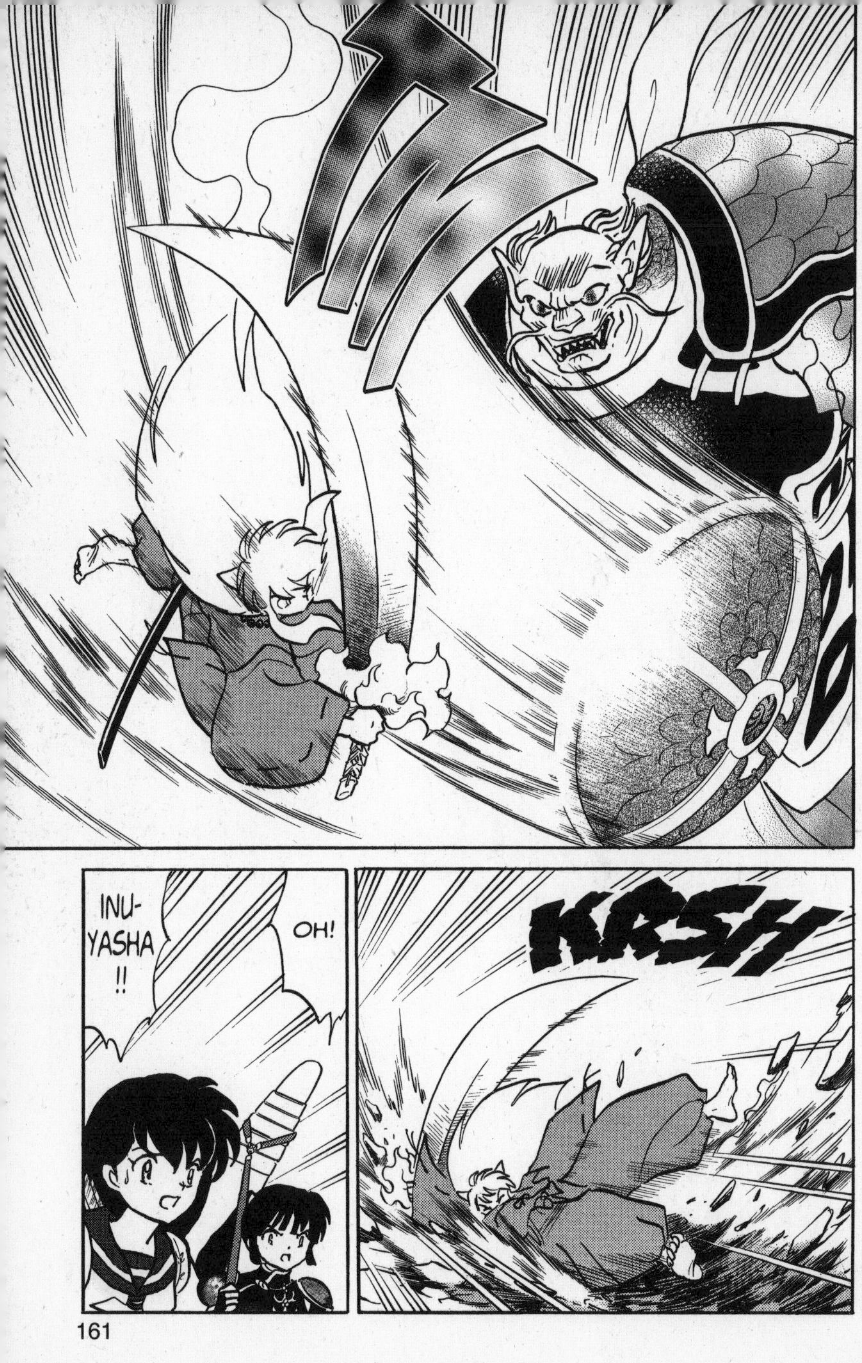
KRSH
OH!
INU-YASHA!!

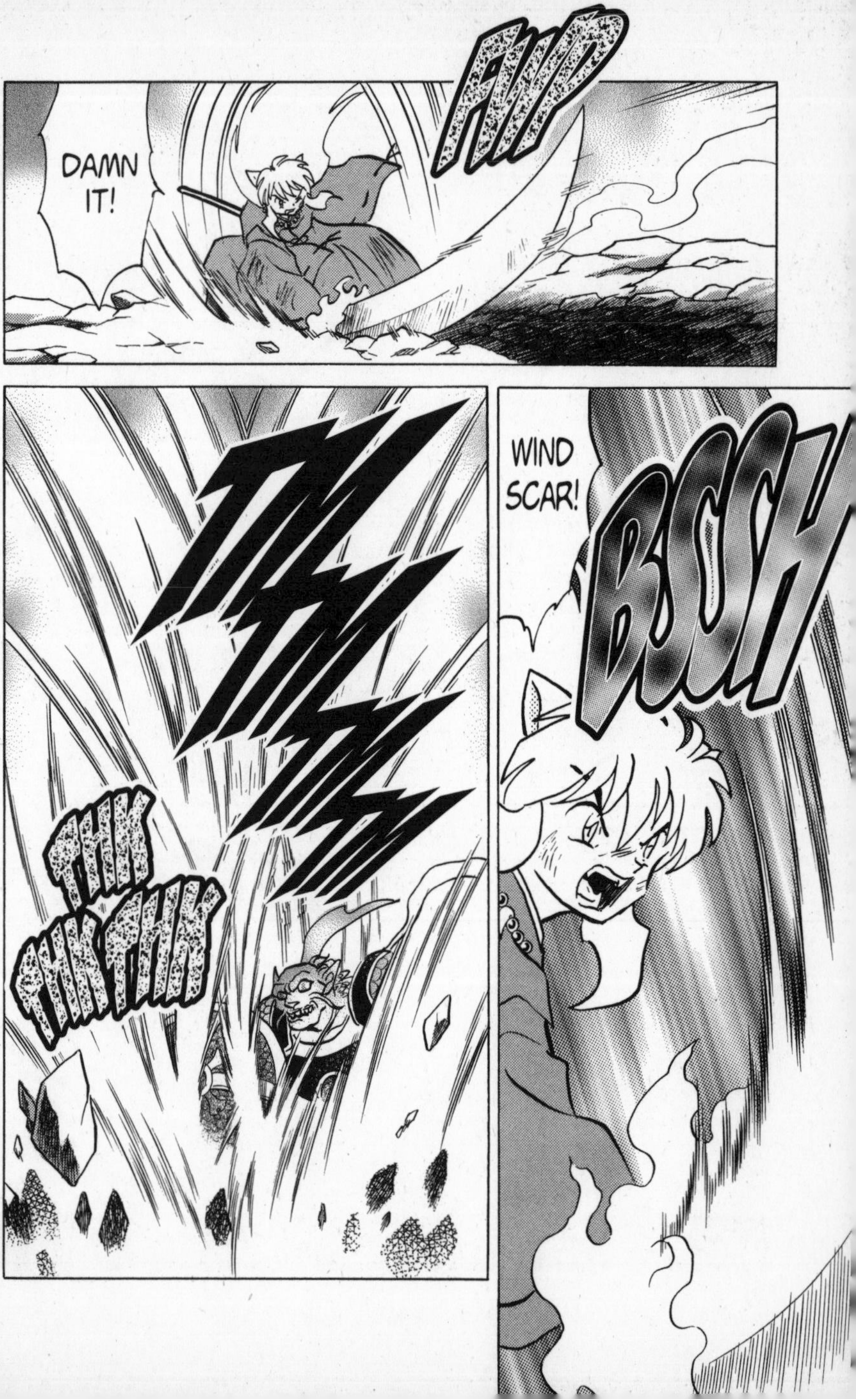
FWP
DAMN IT!
WIND SCAR!
BSCH
THK
THK THK

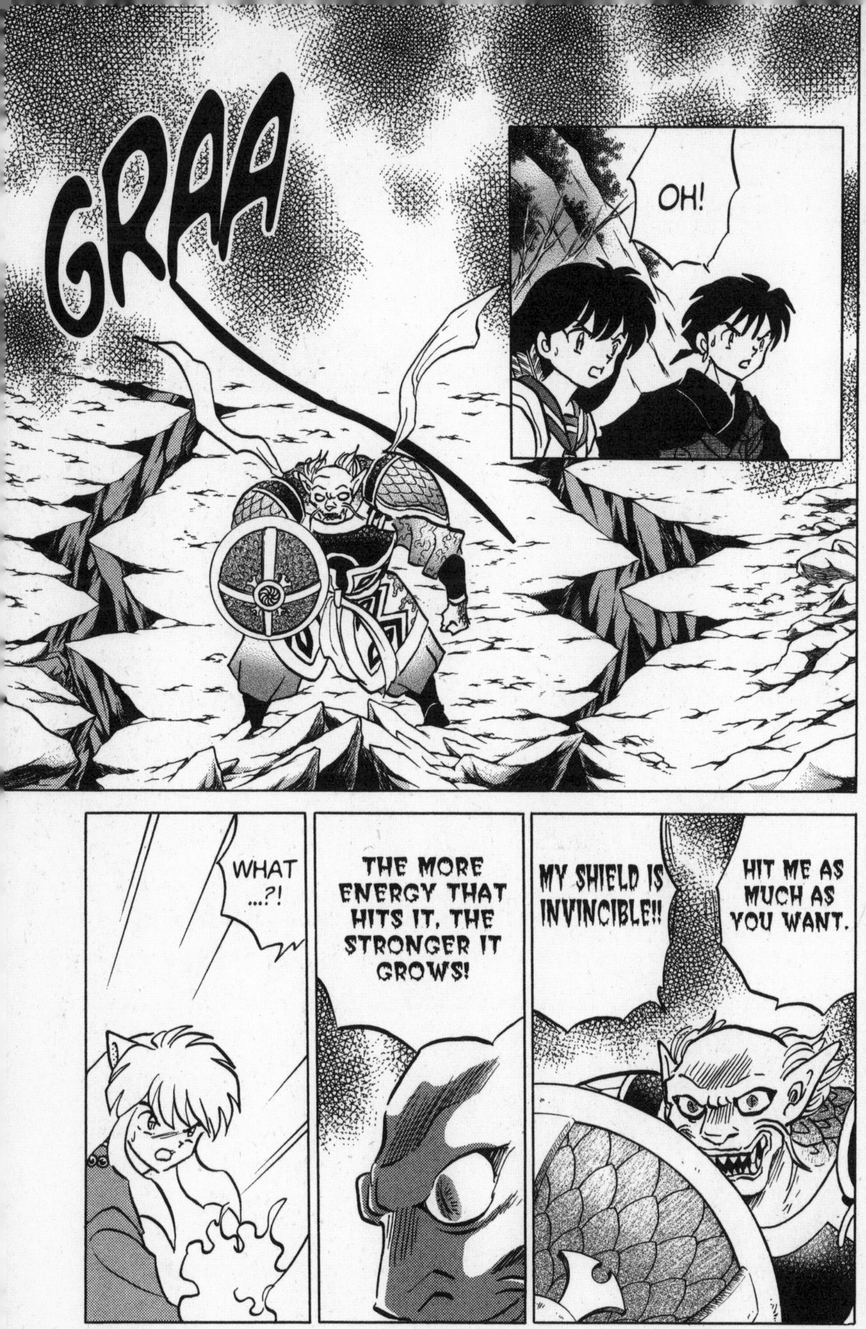
OH!
GRAA
HIT ME AS MUCH AS YOU WANT.
MY SHIELD IS INVINCIBLE!!
THE MORE ENERGY THAT HITS IT, THE STRONGER IT GROWS!
WHAT ...?!

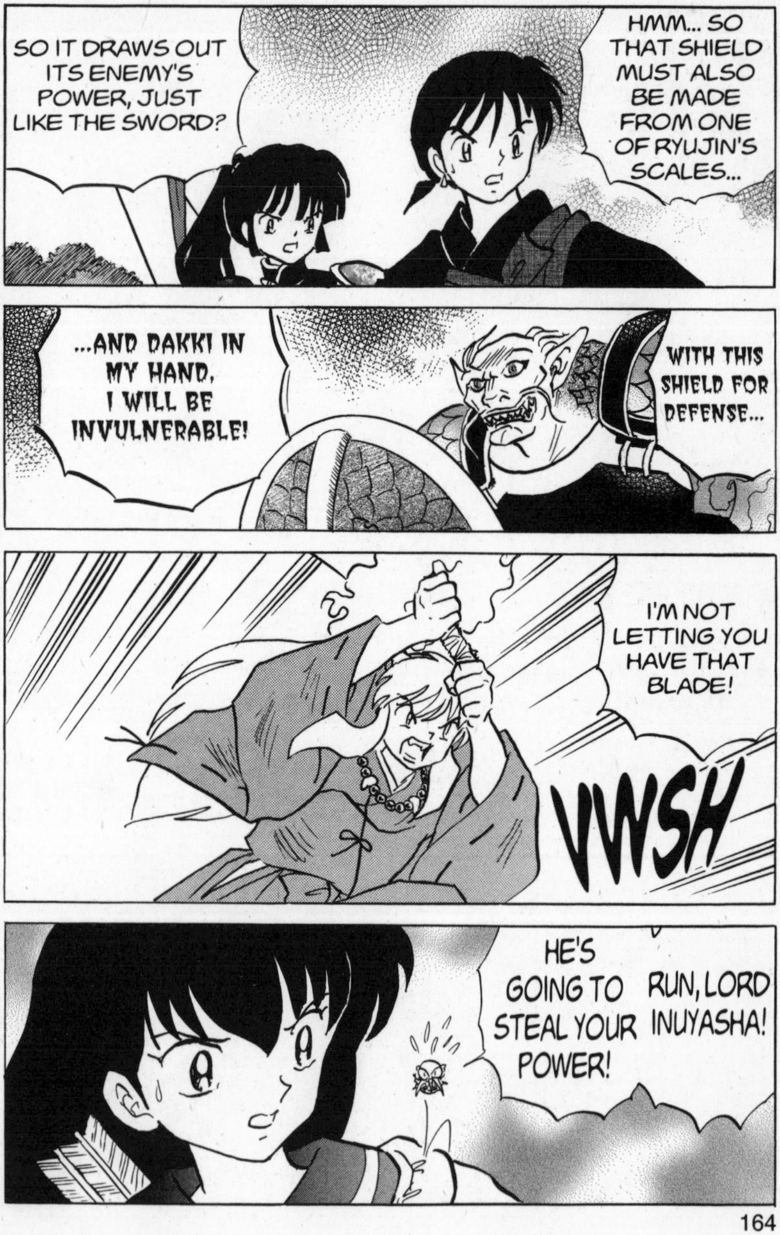
HMM... SO THAT SHIELD MUST ALSO BE MADE FROM ONE OF RYUJIN'S SCALES...
SO IT DRAWS OUT ITS ENEMY'S POWER, JUST LIKE THE SWORD?
WITH THIS SHIELD FOR DEFENSE...
...AND DAKKI IN MY HAND, I WILL BE INVULNERABLE!
I'M NOT LETTING YOU HAVE THAT BLADE!
VWSH
RUN, LORD INUYASHA!
HE'S GOING TO STEAL YOUR POWER!

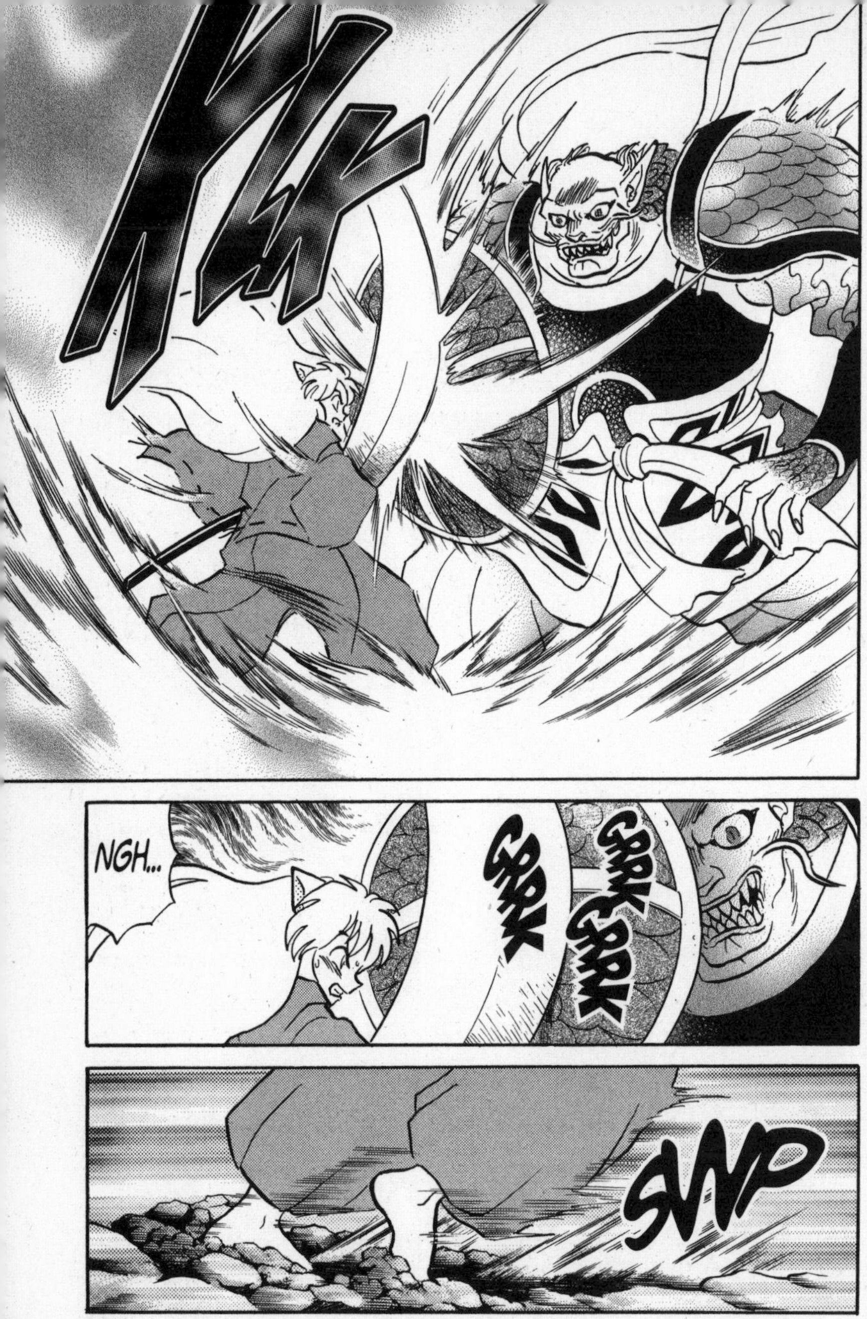
GRRK
GRRK
GRRK
GRRK
NGH...

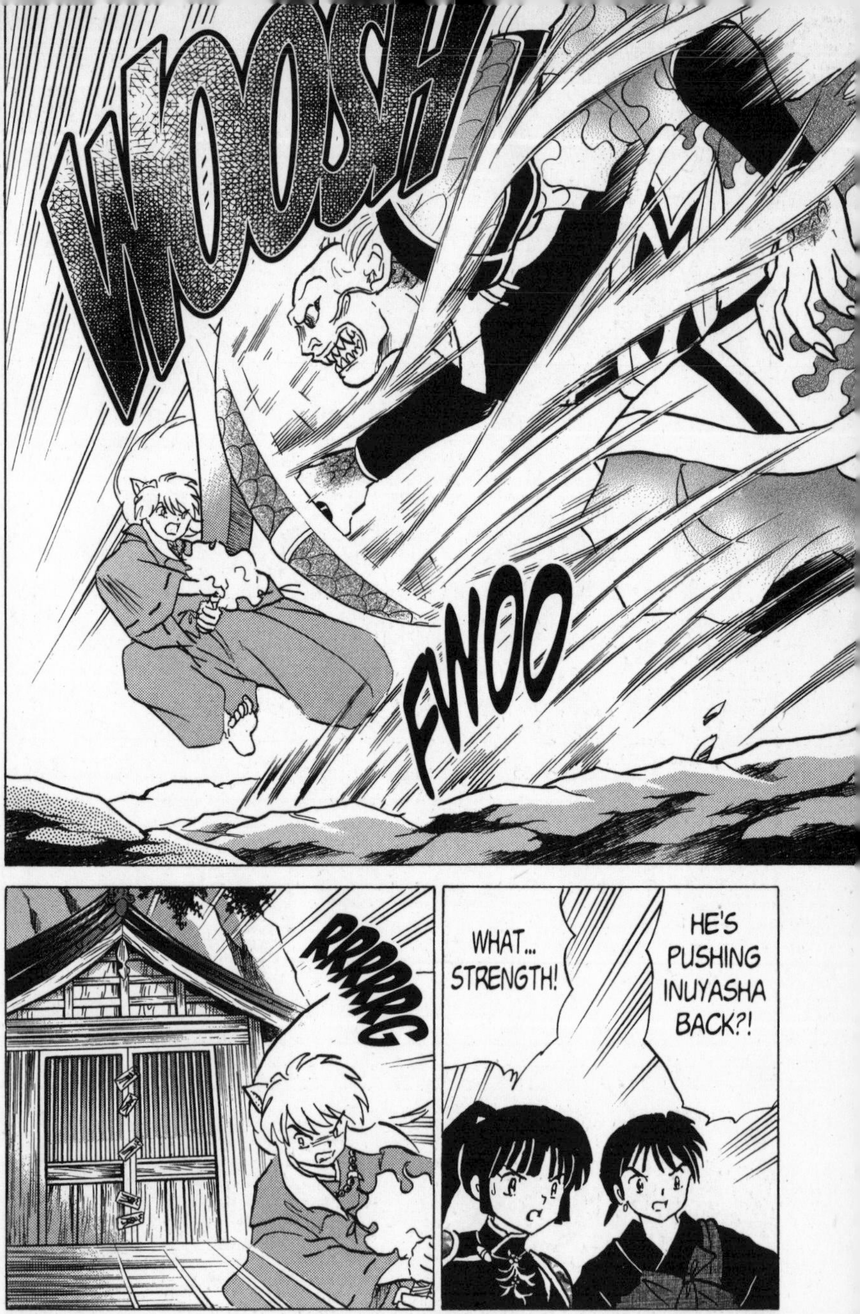
WOOSH
FWOO
HE'S PUSHING INUYASHA BACK?!
WHAT... STRENGTH!
RRRRRG

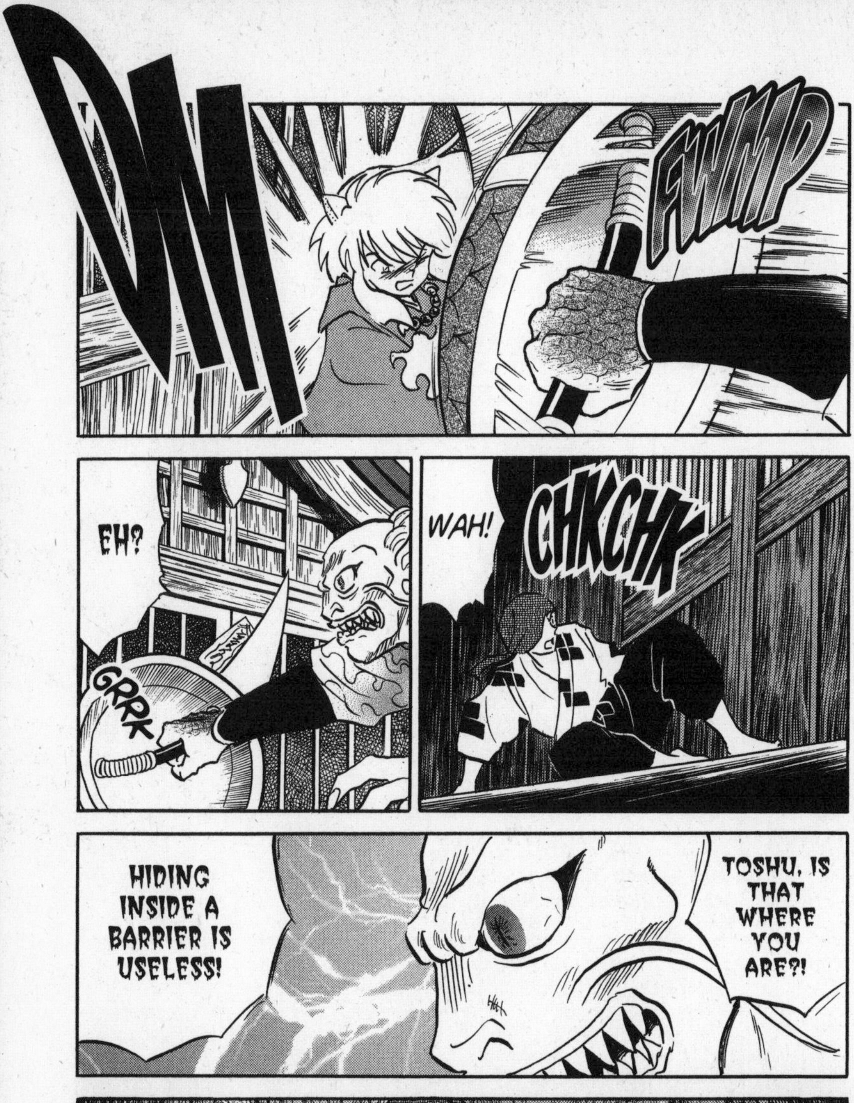
FWMP
DM
CHKCHK
WAH!
EH?
GRRK
TOSHU, IS THAT WHERE YOU ARE?!
HIDING INSIDE A BARRIER IS USELESS!
CHKH CHKH CHKH

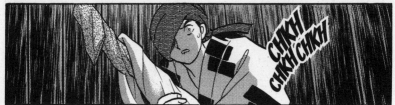

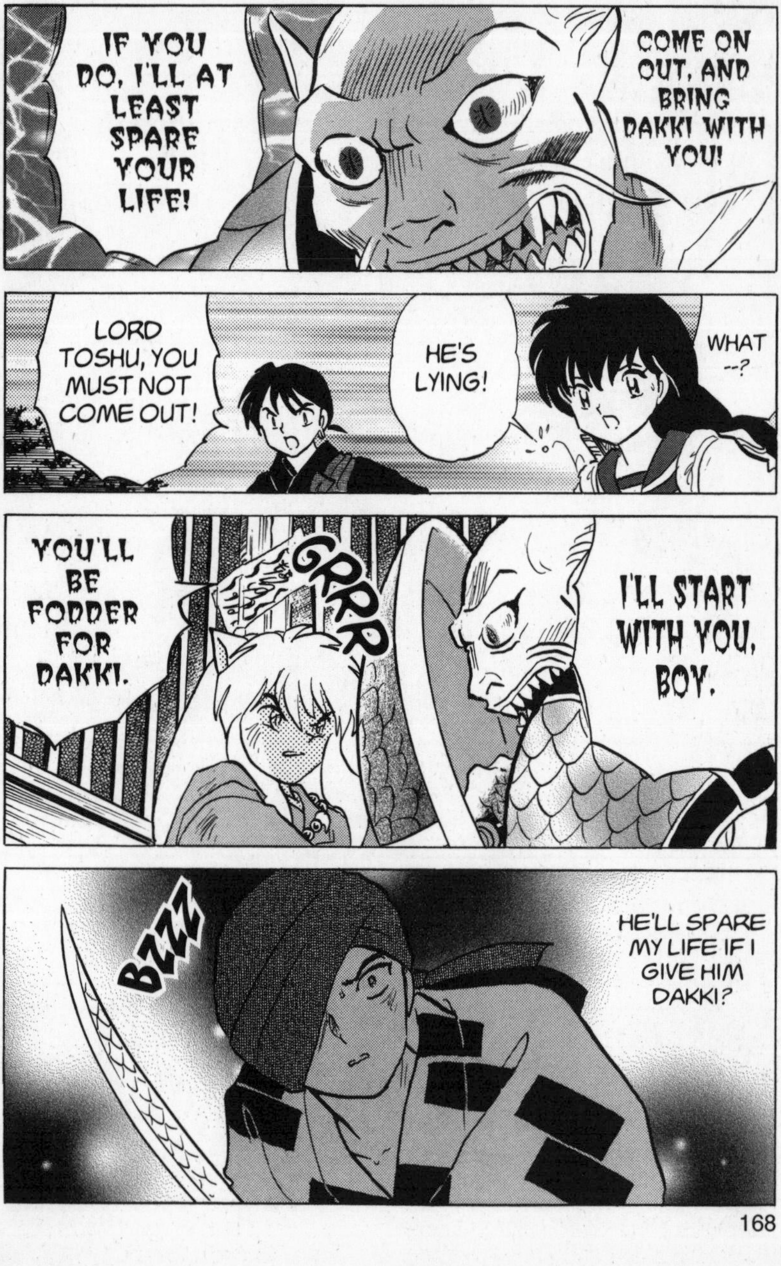
COME ON OUT, AND BRING DAKKI WITH YOU!
IF YOU DO, I'LL AT LEAST SPARE YOUR LIFE!
WHAT --?
HE'S LYING!
LORD TOSHU, YOU MUST NOT COME OUT!
I'LL START WITH YOU, BOY.
GRRR
YOU'LL BE FODDER FOR DAKKI.
HE'LL SPARE MY LIFE IF I GIVE HIM DAKKI?
BZZZ

SCROLL 10

THE WIELDER OF DAKKI

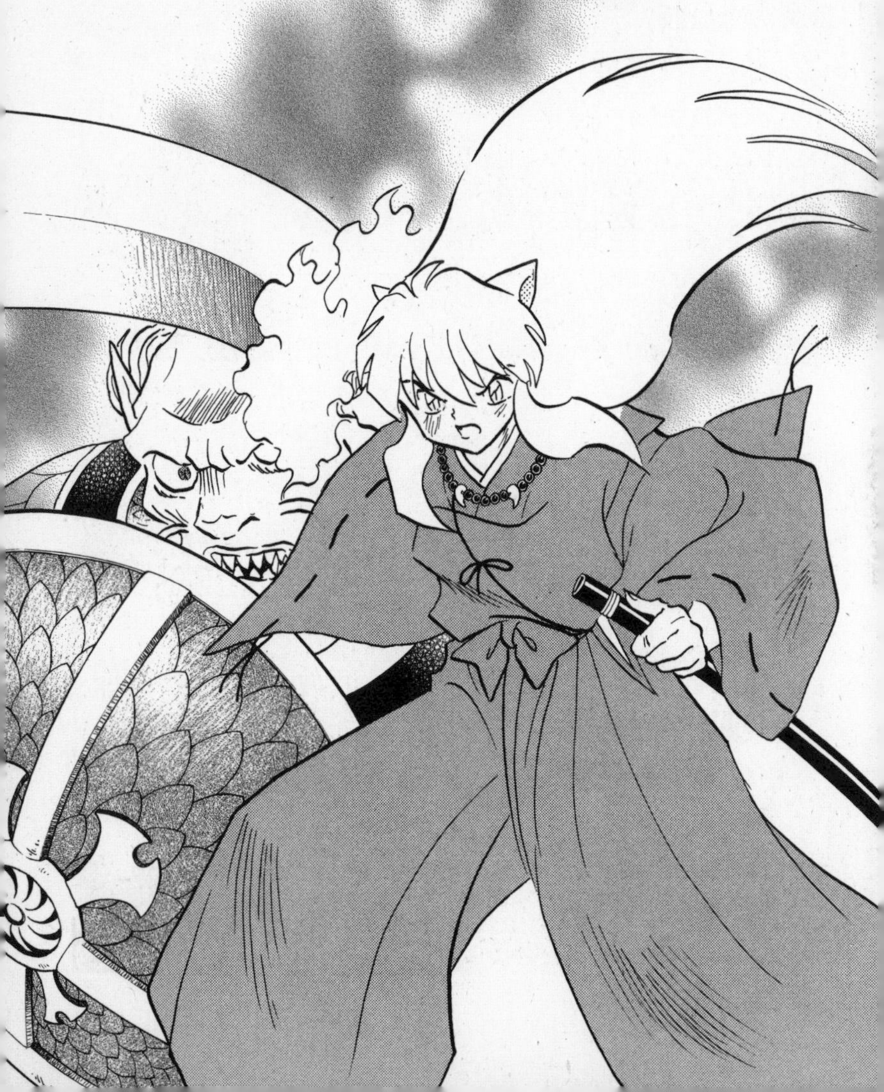

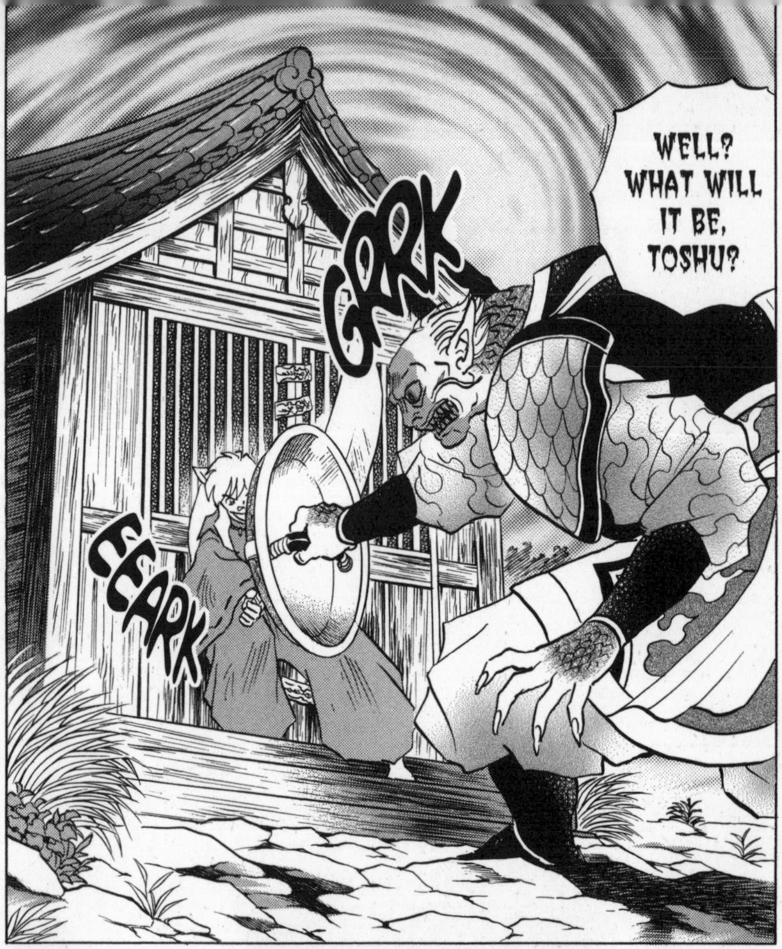
WELL? WHAT WILL IT BE, TOSHU?
GORK
EEARK
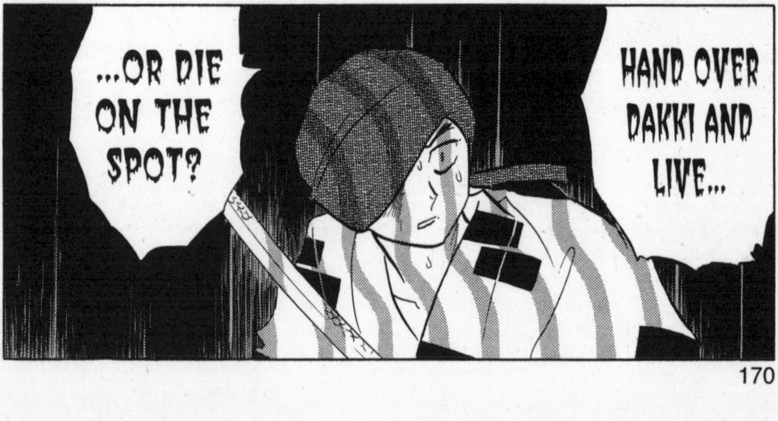
HAND OVER DAKKI AND LIVE...
...OR DIE ON THE SPOT?

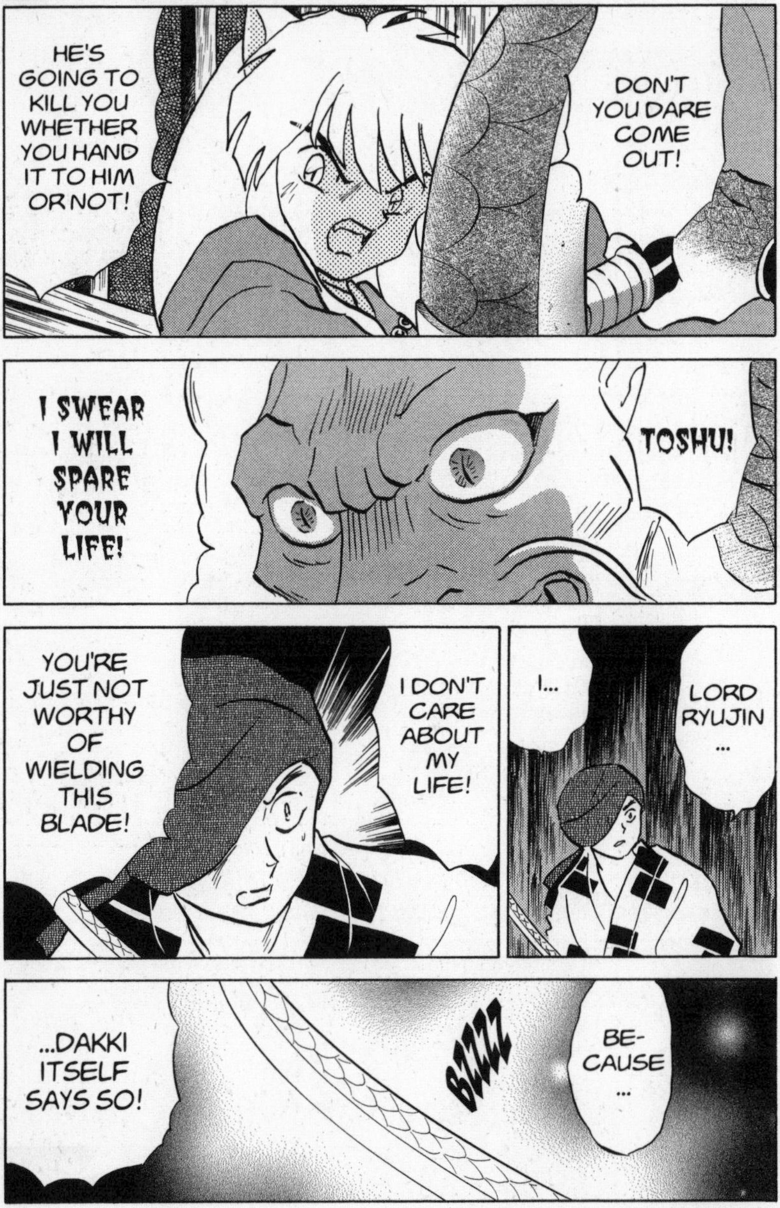
DON'T YOU DARE COME OUT!
HE'S GOING TO KILL YOU WHETHER YOU HAND IT TO HIM OR NOT!
TOSHU!
I SWEAR I WILL SPARE YOUR LIFE!
LORD RYUJIN ...
I...
I DON'T CARE ABOUT MY LIFE!
YOU'RE JUST NOT WORTHY OF WIELDING THIS BLADE!
BE-CAUSE ...
BZZZZ
...DAKKI ITSELF SAYS SO!

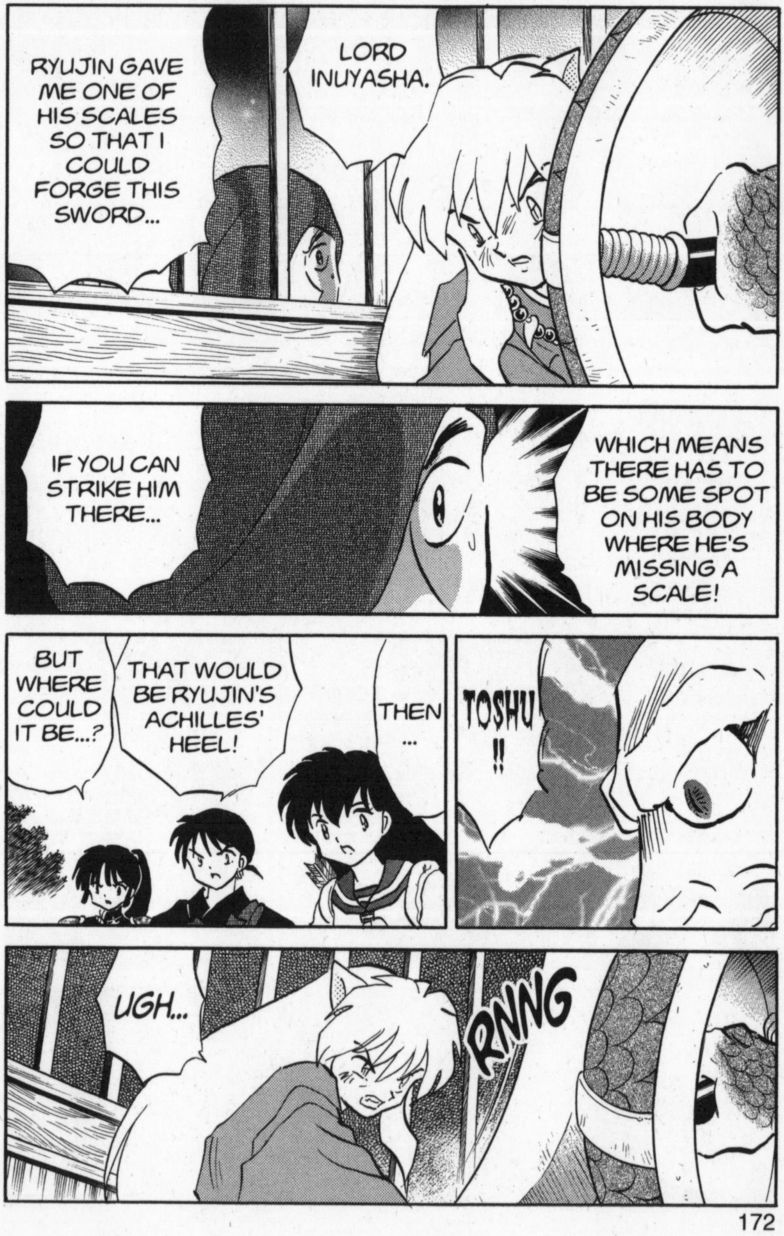
LORD INUYASHA.
RYUJIN GAVE ME ONE OF HIS SCALES SO THAT I COULD FORGE THIS SWORD...
WHICH MEANS THERE HAS TO BE SOME SPOT ON HIS BODY WHERE HE'S MISSING A SCALE!
IF YOU CAN STRIKE HIM THERE...
TOSHU!!
THEN...
THAT WOULD BE RYUJIN'S ACHILLES' HEEL!
BUT WHERE COULD IT BE...?
RNNG
UGH...

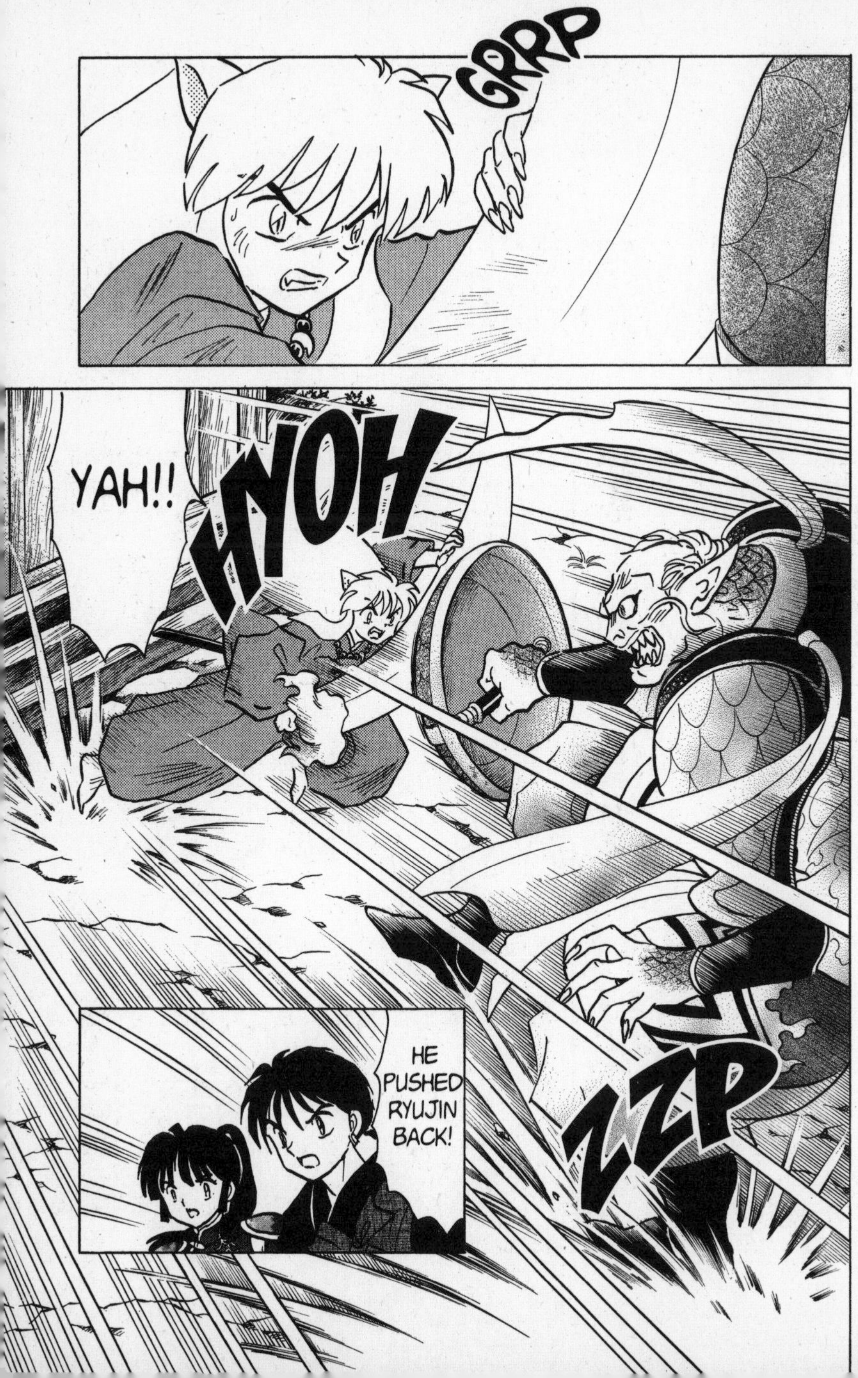
GRRP
HYOH
YAH!!
ZZZP
HE PUSHED RYUJIN BACK!

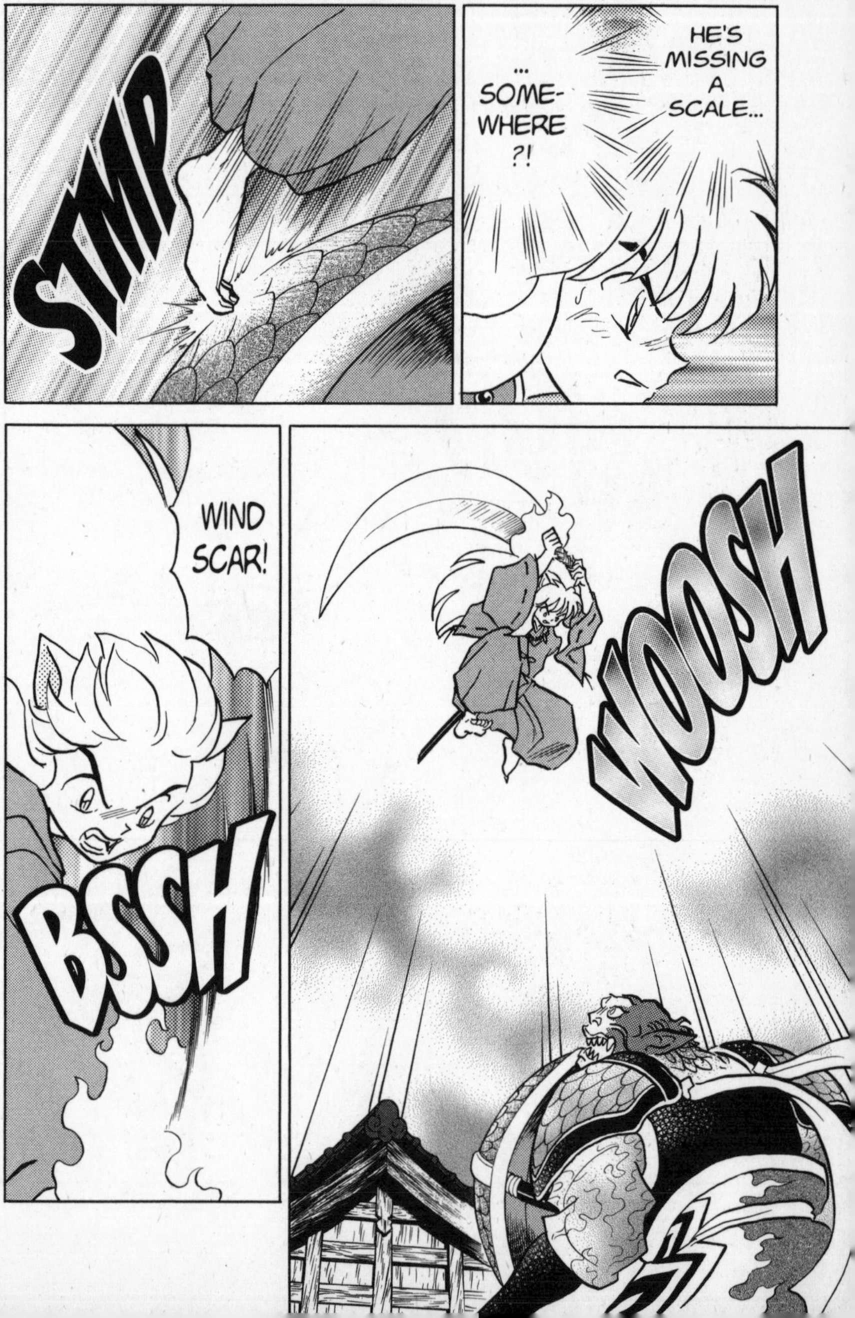
HE'S MISSING A SCALE...
... SOME-WHERE ?!
STMP
WOOSH
WIND SCAR!
BSSH

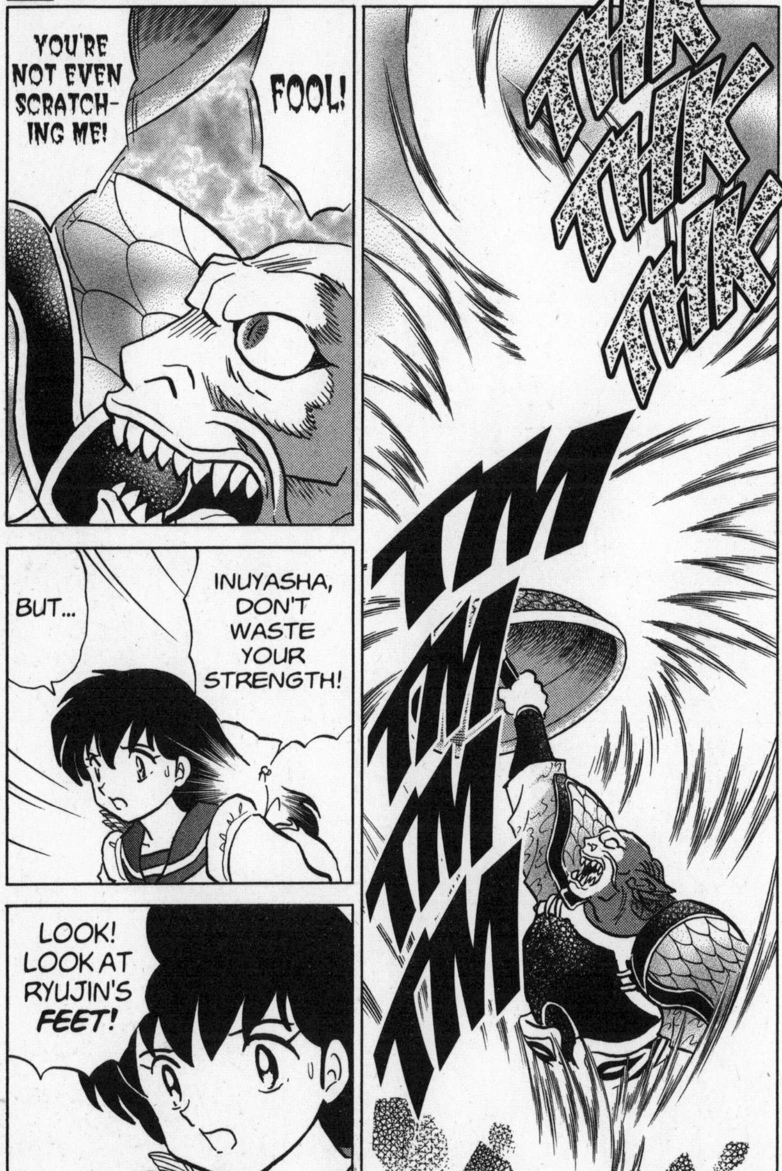
THK THK THK
TM TM TM TM TM
FOOL!
YOU'RE NOT EVEN SCRATCHING ME!
INUYASHA, DON'T WASTE YOUR STRENGTH!
BUT...
LOOK! LOOK AT RYUJIN'S *FEET*!

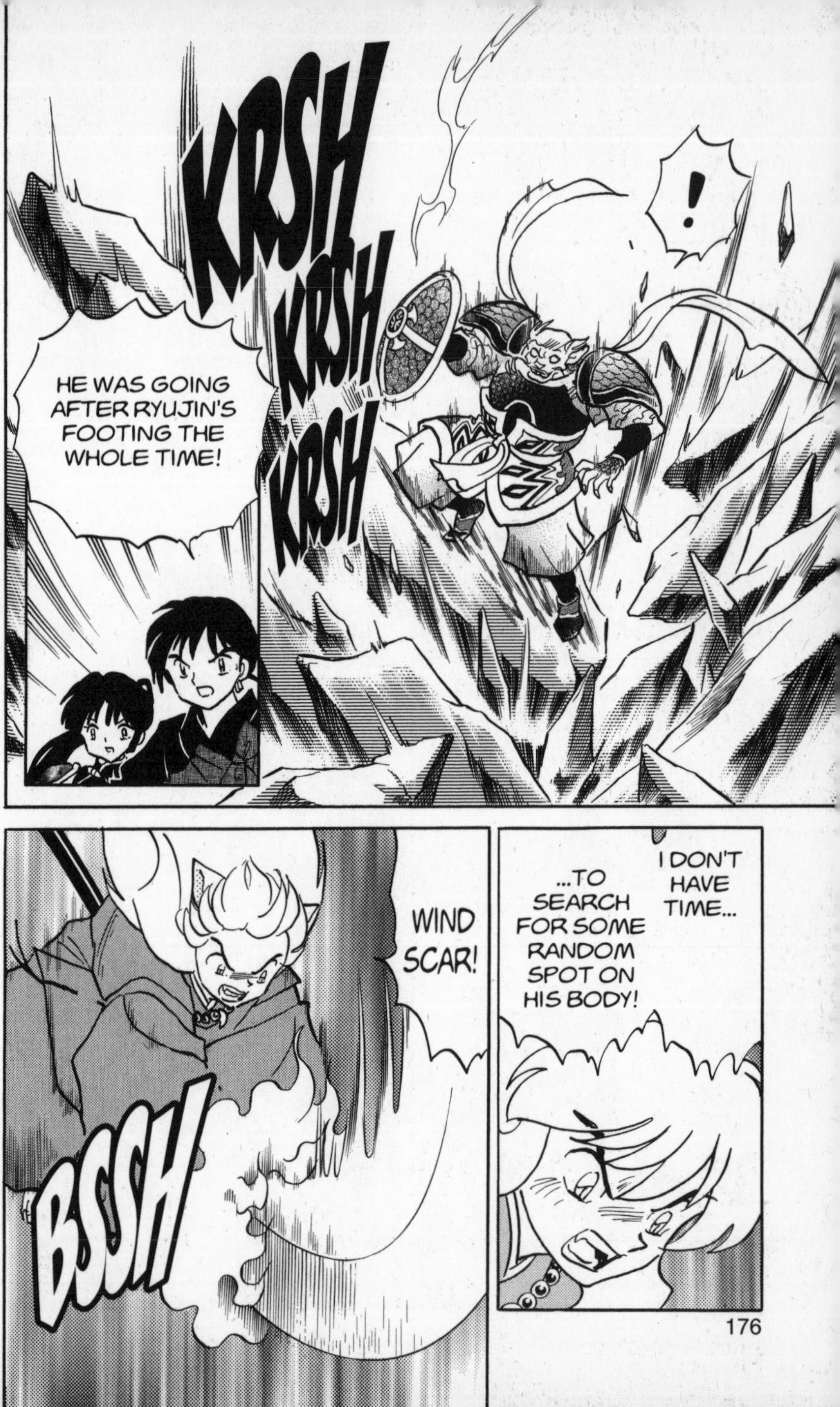

!
KRSH KRSH KRSH
HE WAS GOING AFTER RYUJIN'S FOOTING THE WHOLE TIME!
I DON'T HAVE TIME...
...TO SEARCH FOR SOME RANDOM SPOT ON HIS BODY!
WIND SCAR!
BSSH

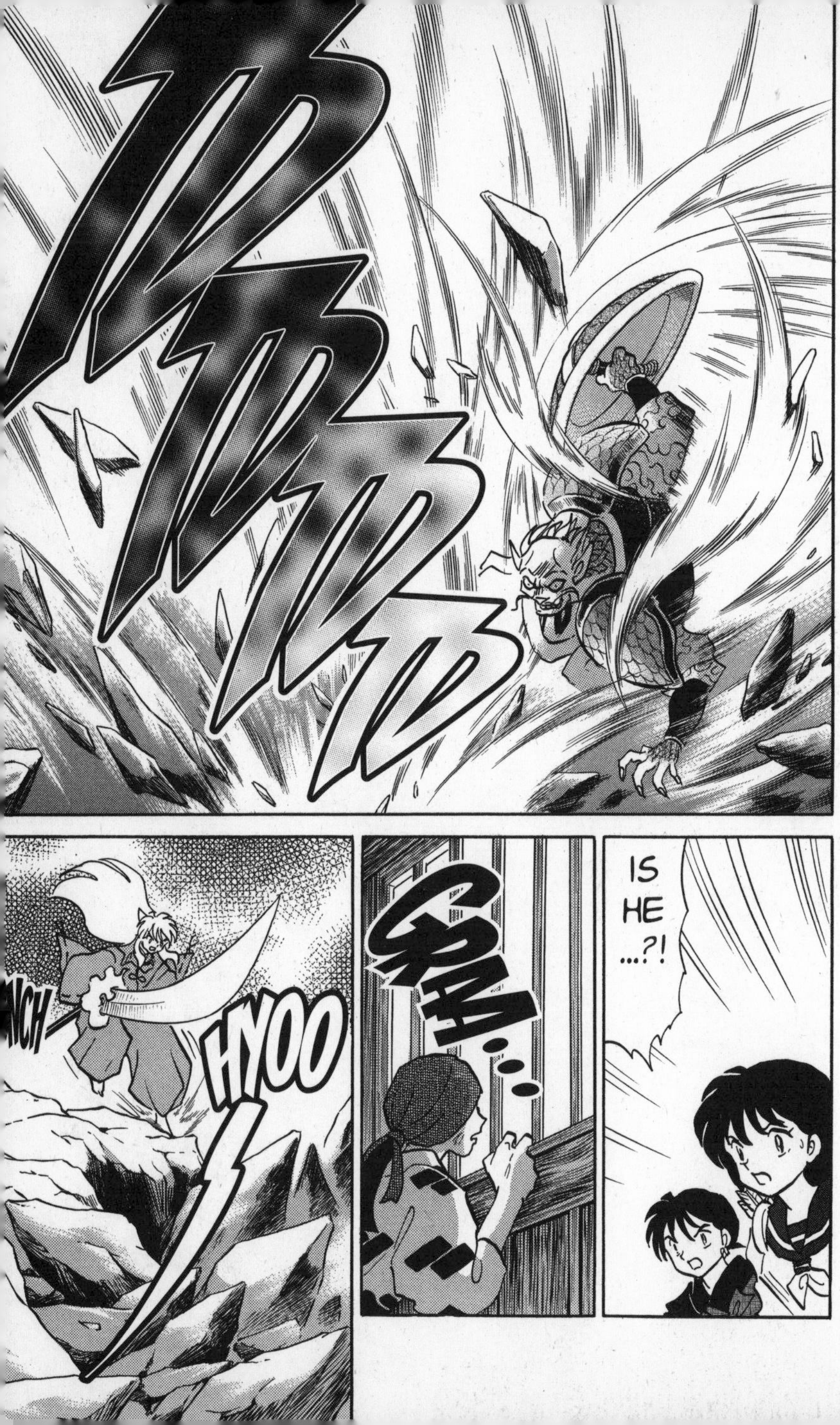
IS HE ...?!
HYOO

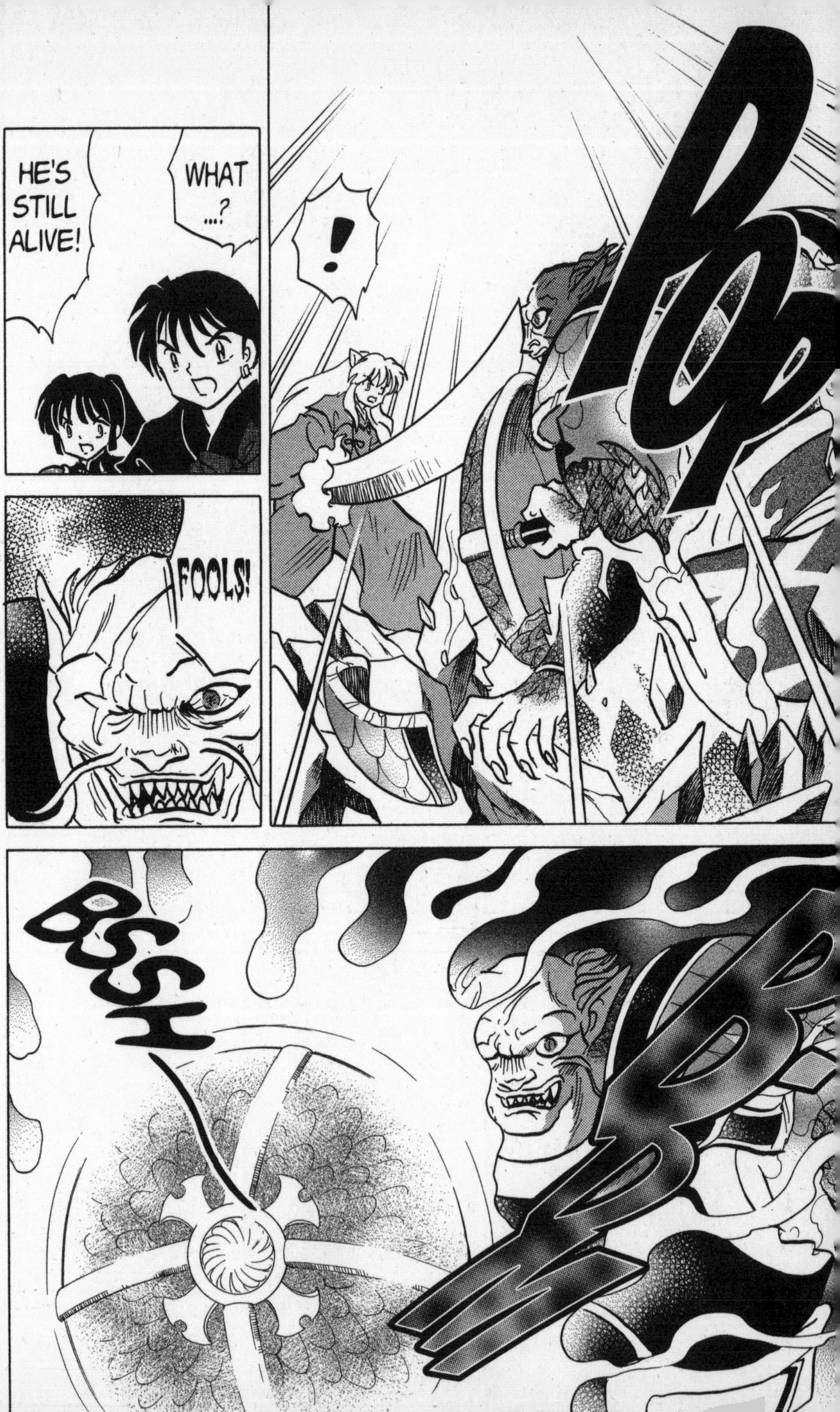
!
WHAT ...?
HE'S STILL ALIVE!
FOOLS!
BSSH

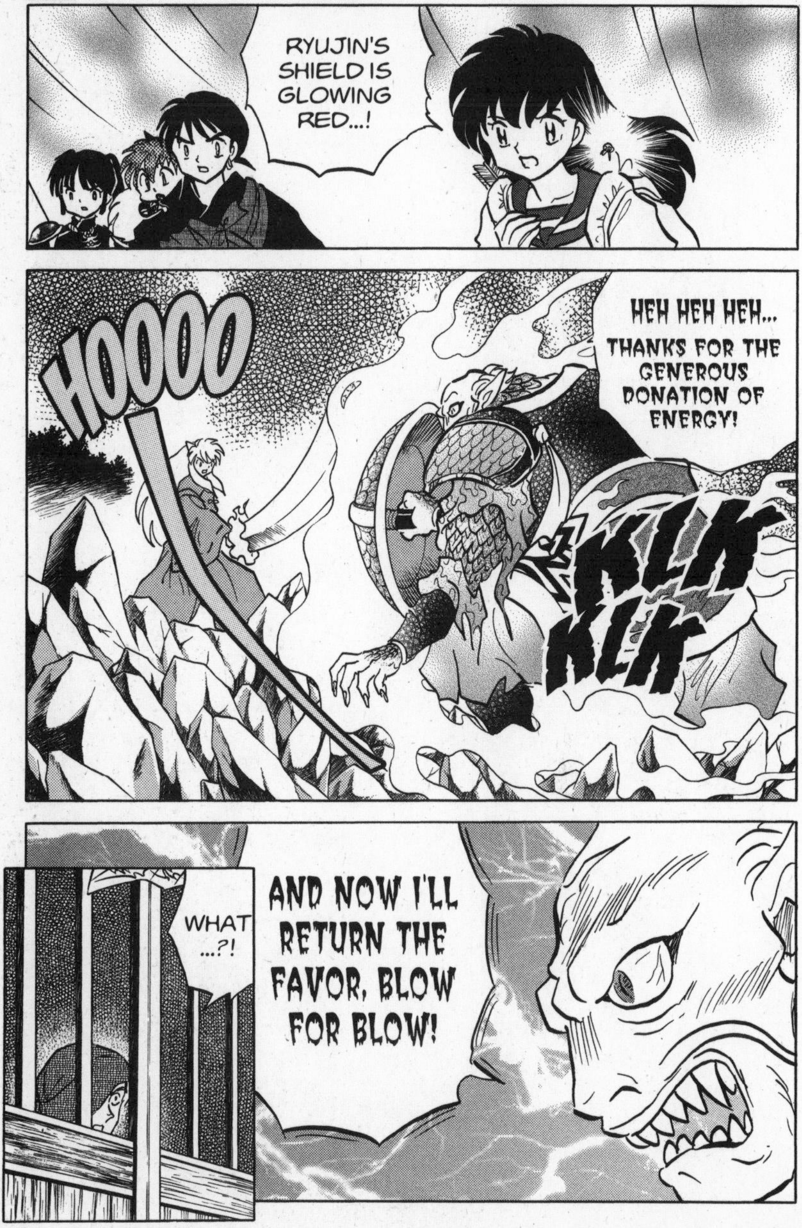
RYUJIN'S SHIELD IS GLOWING RED...!
HEH HEH HEH... THANKS FOR THE GENEROUS DONATION OF ENERGY!
HOOOO
KLIK KLIK
AND NOW I'LL RETURN THE FAVOR, BLOW FOR BLOW!
WHAT ...?!

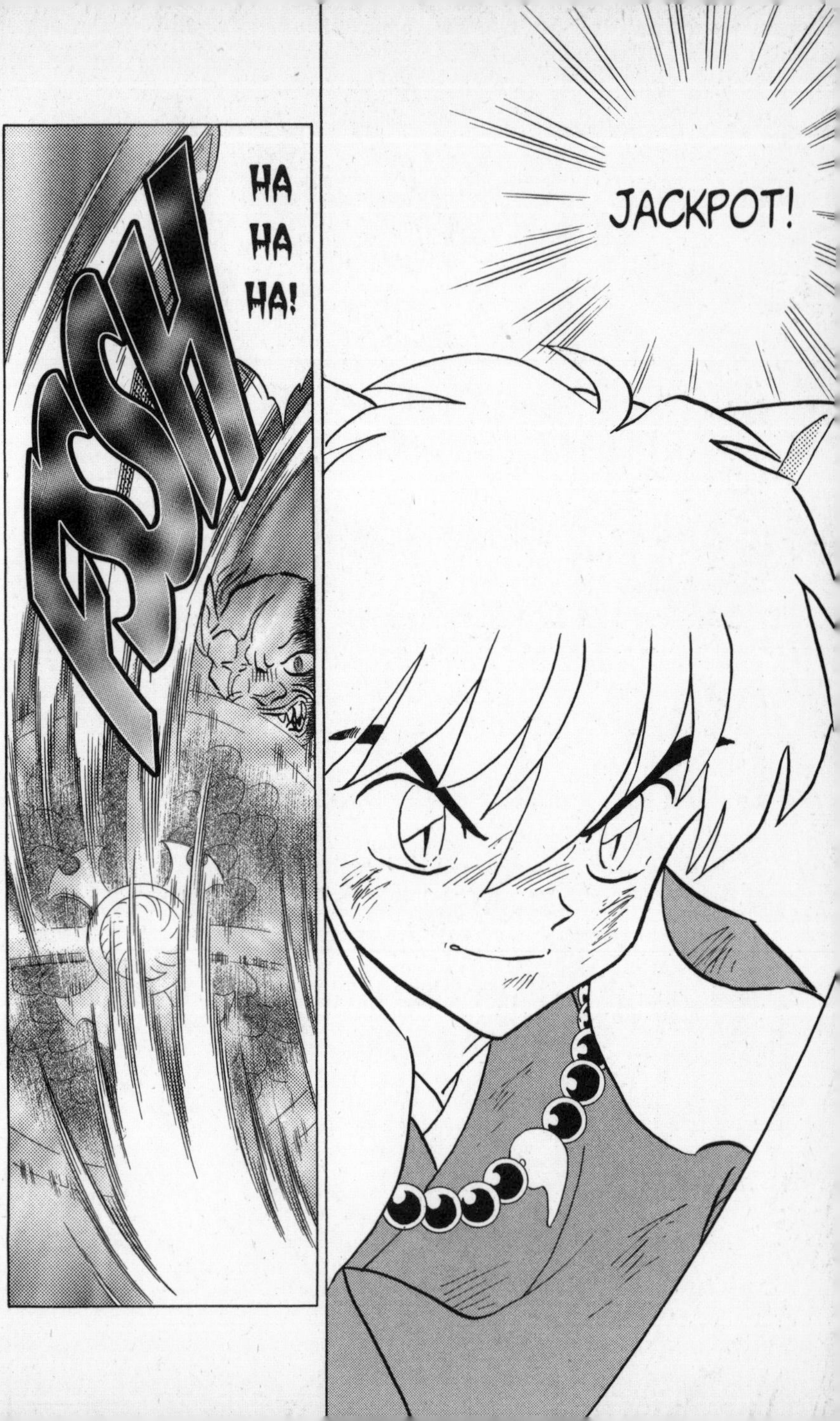
JACKPOT!
HA HA HA!
FSSH

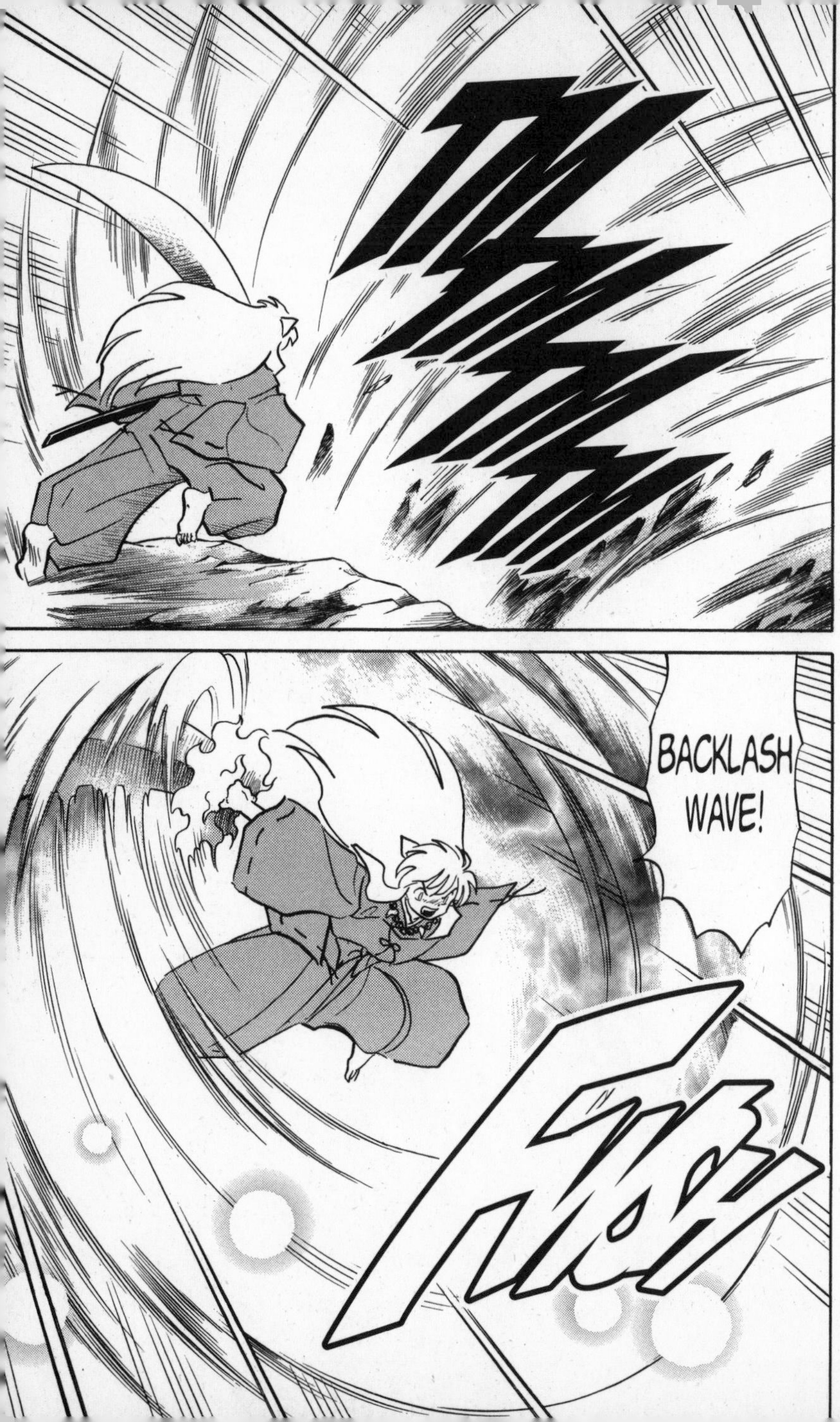
BACKLASH WAVE!

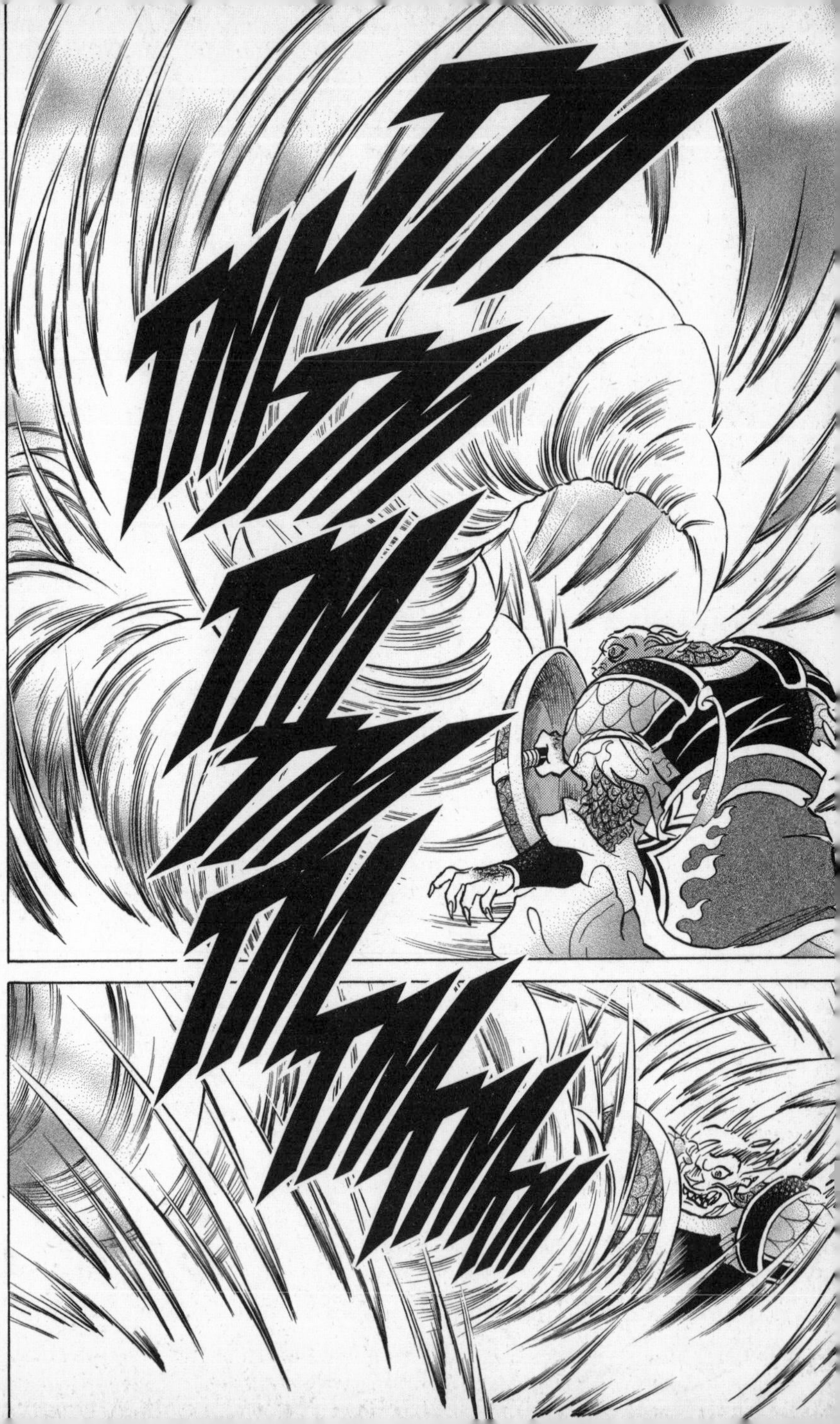

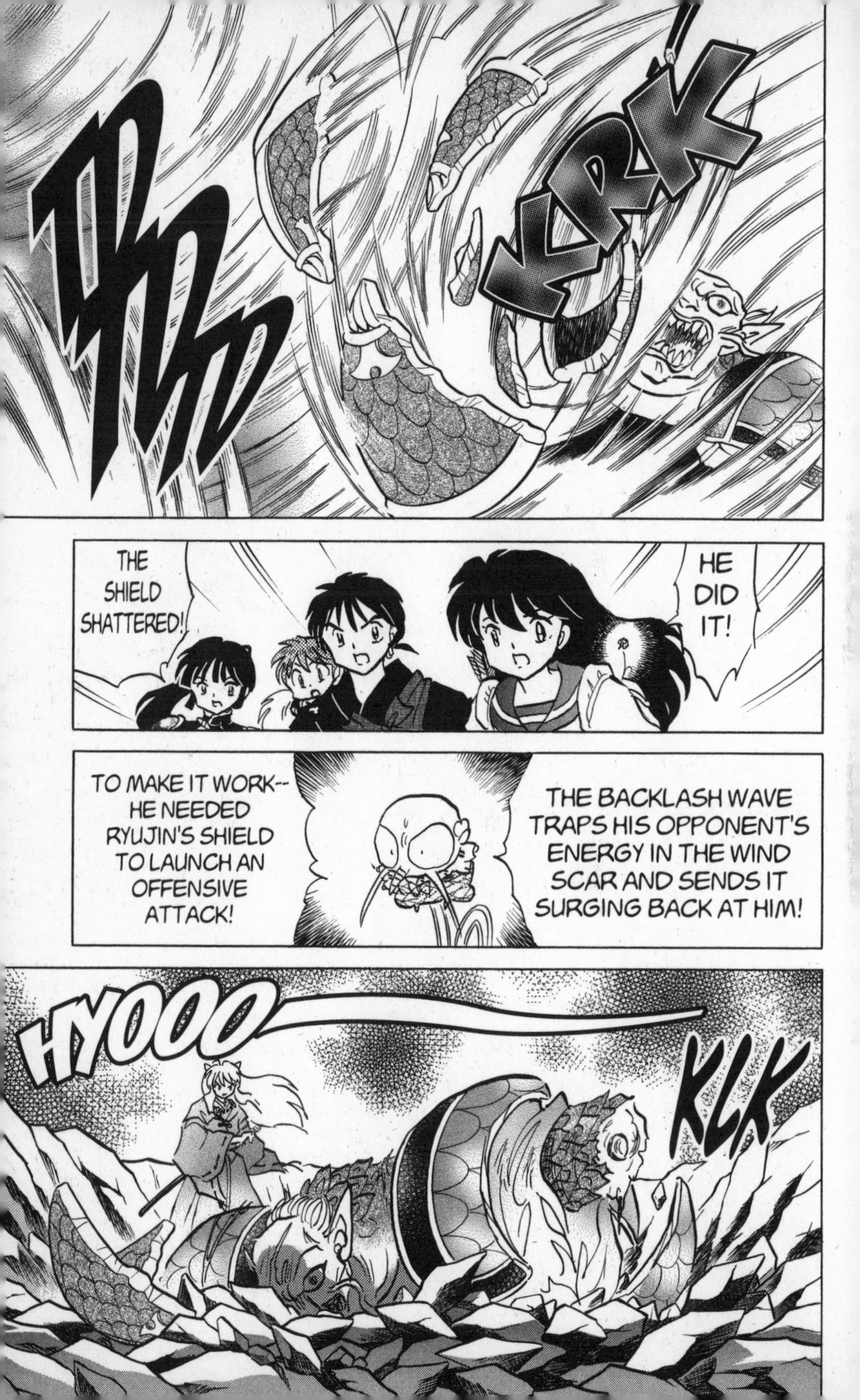
KRK
TRZZ
HE DID IT!
THE SHIELD SHATTERED!
THE BACKLASH WAVE TRAPS HIS OPPONENT'S ENERGY IN THE WIND SCAR AND SENDS IT SURGING BACK AT HIM!
TO MAKE IT WORK-- HE NEEDED RYUJIN'S SHIELD TO LAUNCH AN OFFENSIVE ATTACK!
KLK
HYOOO

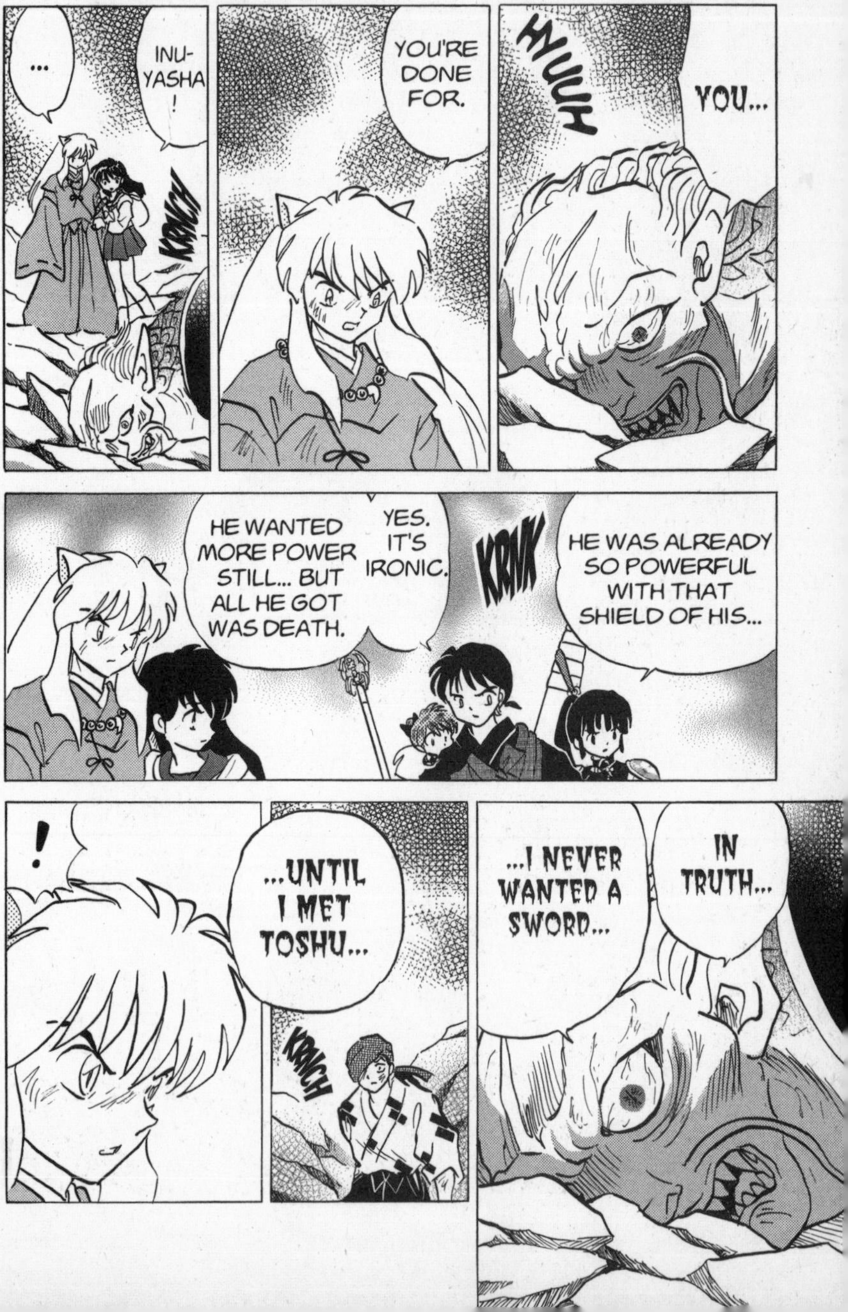
HYUUH
YOU...
YOU'RE DONE FOR.
INU-YASHA!
KRNCH
...
HE WAS ALREADY SO POWERFUL WITH THAT SHIELD OF HIS...
KRNK
YES. IT'S IRONIC.
HE WANTED MORE POWER STILL... BUT ALL HE GOT WAS DEATH.
IN TRUTH...
...I NEVER WANTED A SWORD...
...UNTIL I MET TOSHU...
KRNCH
!

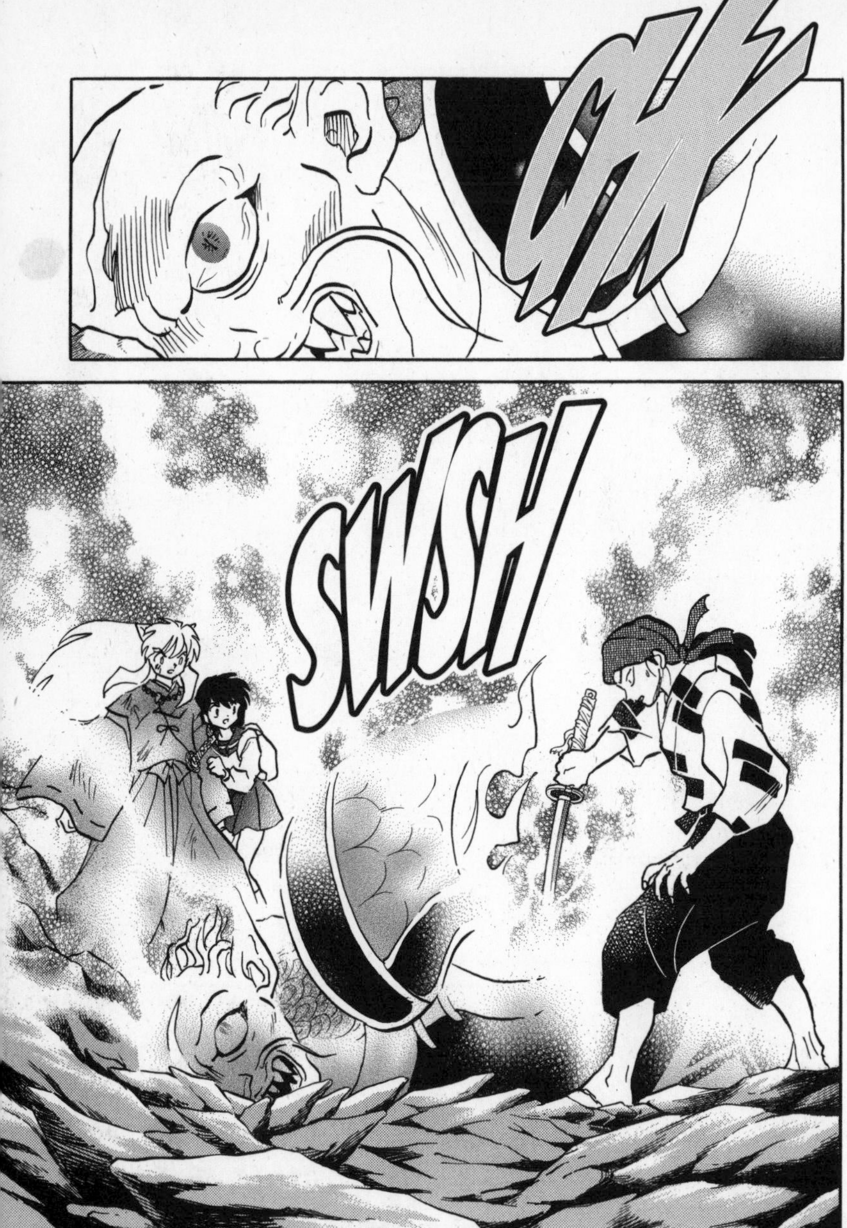
GAK
SWISH

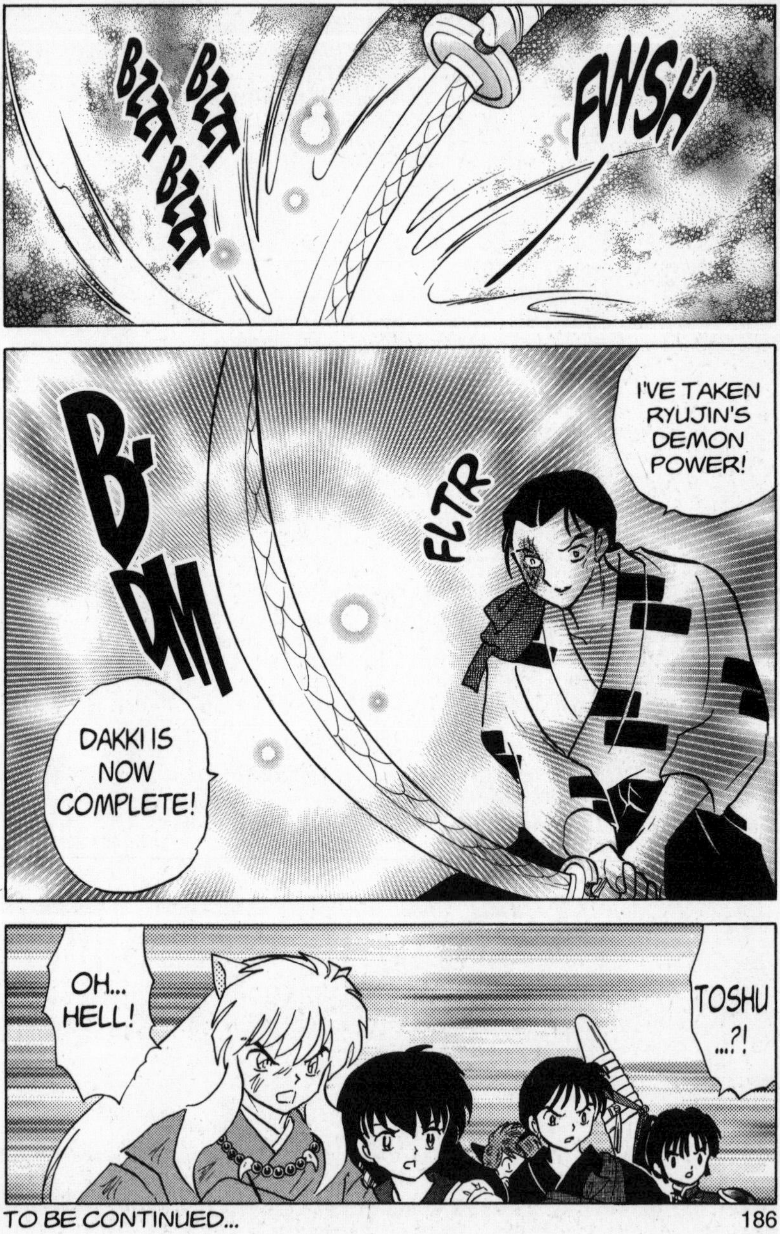
FWSH
BZZT BZZT
BZZT
I'VE TAKEN RYUJIN'S DEMON POWER!
FLTR
B'DM
DAKKI IS NOW COMPLETE!
TOSHU ...?!
OH... HELL!

TO BE CONTINUED...

INU YASHA

Half Human, Half Demon—All Action!

INUYASHA

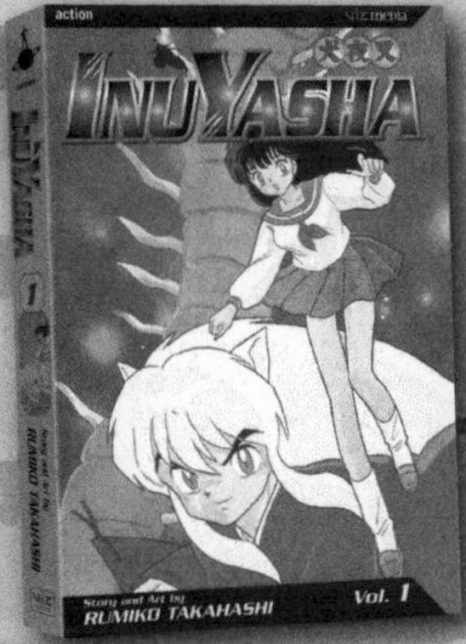

action
VIZ media
INUYASHA
犬夜叉
Story and Art by
RUMIKO TAKAHASHI
Vol. 1

Read the action from the start with the original manga series

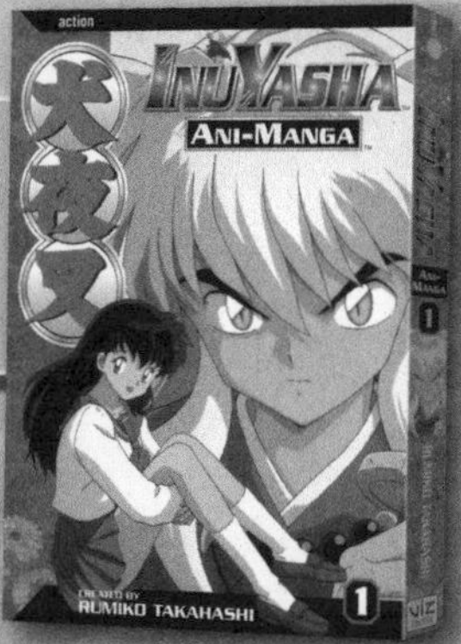

action
INUYASHA
ANI-MANGA
犬夜叉
CREATED BY
RUMIKO TAKAHASHI
1

Full color adaptation of the popular TV series

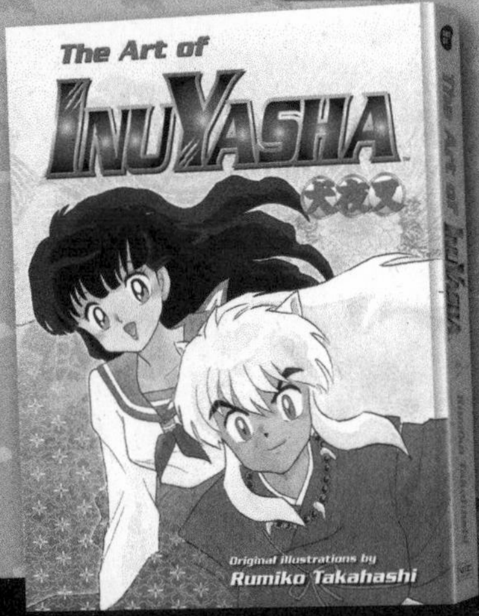

The Art of
INUYASHA
犬夜叉
Original illustrations by
Rumiko Takahashi

Art book with cel art, paintings, character profiles and more

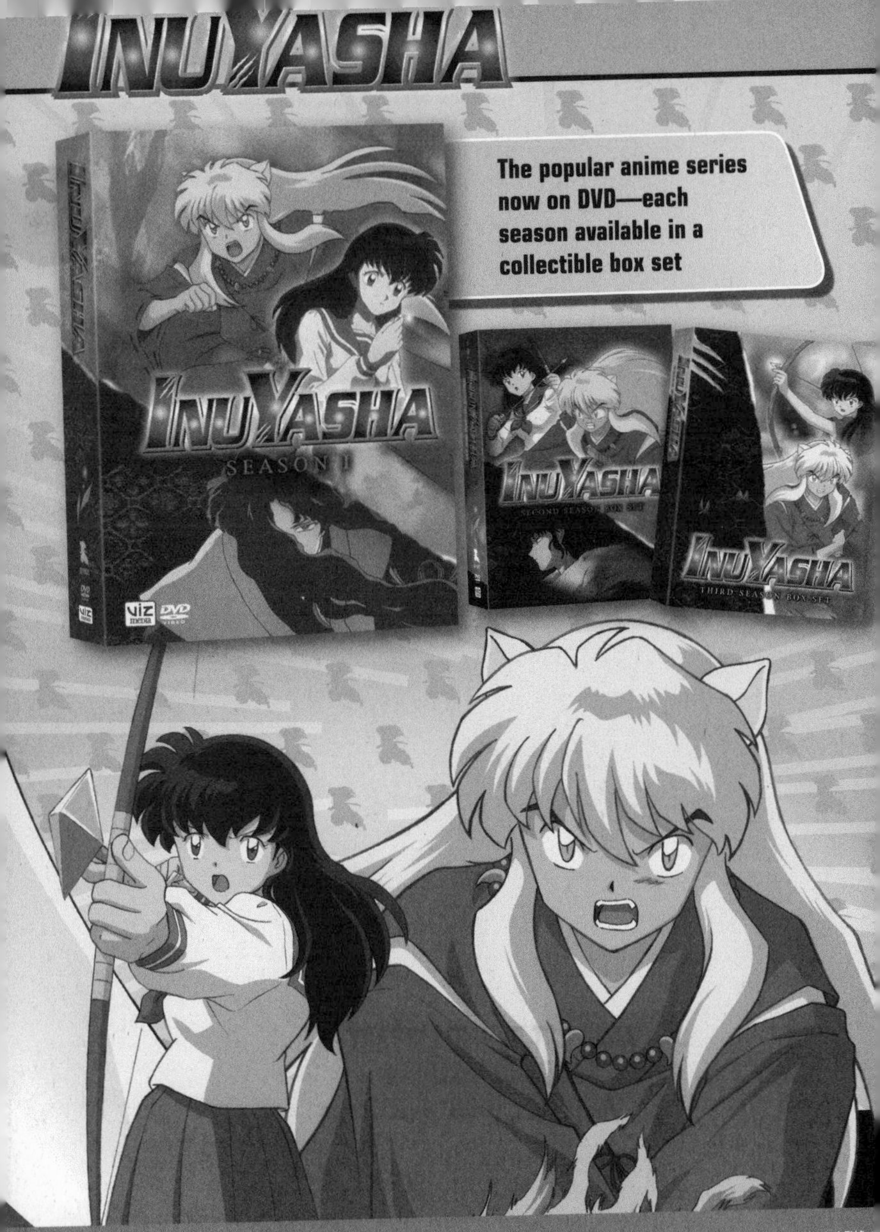
INUYASHA
The popular anime series now on DVD—each season available in a collectible box set
INUYASHA
SEASON 1
INUYASHA
INUYASHA
THIRD SEASON BOX SET

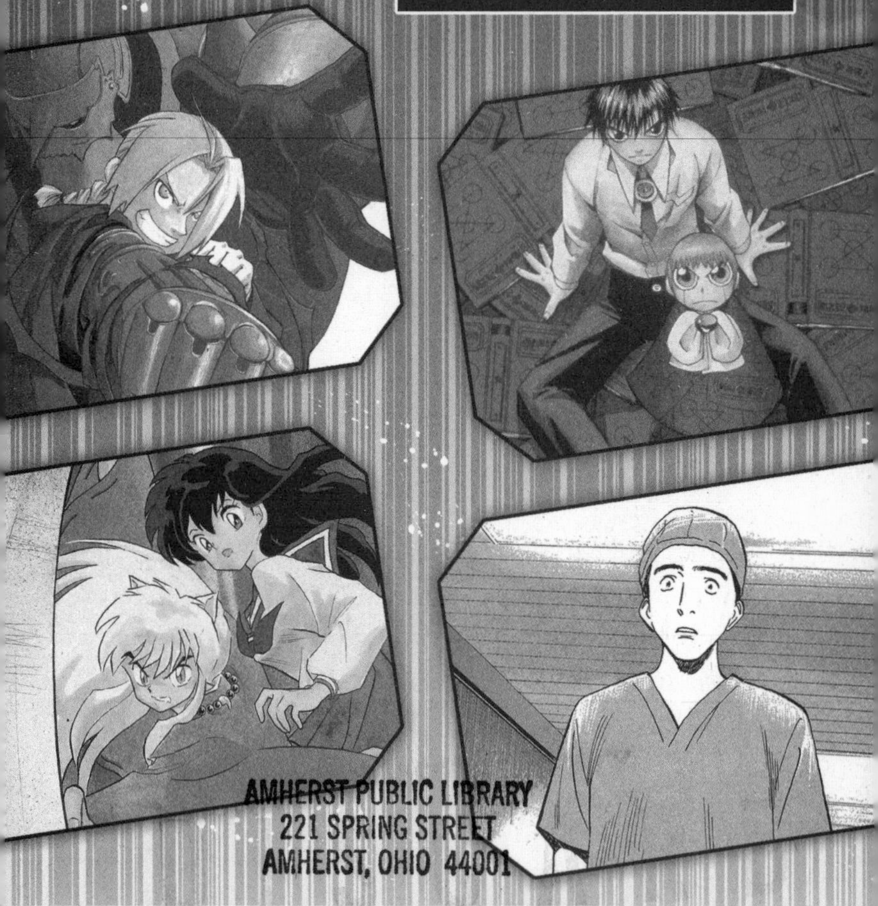